RESEARCH IN THE HISTORY OF ECONOMIC THOUGHT AND METHODOLOGY

RESEARCH IN THE HISTORY OF ECONOMIC THOUGHT AND METHODOLOGY

Founding Editor: Warren J. Samuels (1933–2011)

Series Editors: Luca Fiorito, Scott Scheall, and Carlos Eduardo Suprinyak

Recent Volumes:

EDITORIAL BOARD

RESEARCH IN THE HISTORY OF ECONOMIC THOUGHT
AND METHODOLOGY   VOLUME 41C

RESEARCH IN THE HISTORY OF ECONOMIC THOUGHT AND METHODOLOGY: INCLUDING A SYMPOSIUM ON JOHN KENNETH GALBRAITH: ECONOMIC STRUCTURES AND POLICIES FOR THE TWENTY-FIRST CENTURY

EDITED BY

LUCA FIORITO
University of Palermo, Italy

SCOTT SCHEALL
Arizona State University, USA

AND

CARLOS EDUARDO SUPRINYAK
American University of Paris, France

United Kingdom – North America – Japan
India – Malaysia – China

Emerald Publishing Limited
Emerald Publishing, Floor 5, Northspring, 21-23 Wellington Street, Leeds LS1 4DL.

First edition 2024

Editorial matter and selection © 2024 Luca Fiorito, Scott Scheall and Carlos Eduardo Suprinyak.
Published under exclusive licence.
Individual chapters © 2024 Emerald Publishing Limited.

British Library Cataloguing in Publication Data
A catalogue record for this book is available from the British Library

ISBN: 978-1-80455-931-4 (Print)
ISBN: 978-1-80455-930-7 (Online)
ISBN: 978-1-80455-932-1 (Epub)

ISSN: 0743-4154 (Series)

Printed and bound by CPI Group (UK) Ltd, Croydon, CR0 4YY

INVESTOR IN PEOPLE

CONTENTS

**PART II
ESSAYS**

ABOUT THE EDITORS

Luca Fiorito received his PhD in Economics from the New School for Social Research in New York and is currently Professor at the University of Palermo. His main area of interest is the history of American economic thought in the Progressive Era and the interwar years. He has published many works on the contributions of the institutionalists and on the relationship between Economics and Eugenics.

Scott Scheall is Assistant Professor in the Faculty of Social Science in Arizona State University's College of Integrative Sciences and Arts. He has published extensively on topics related to the History and Philosophy of the Austrian School of Economics. Scott is the Author of *F. A. Hayek and the Epistemology of Politics: The Curious Task of Economics* (Routledge, 2020) and *Dialogues Concerning Natural Politics: A Modern Philosophical Dialogue About Policymaker Ignorance* (Substack, 2023).

Carlos Eduardo Suprinyak is Associate Professor of Economics at the American University of Paris. He specializes in the history of Political Economy, exploring the intersections between Economics and Politics in different historical contexts, from early modern England to Cold War Latin America. Besides numerous papers in peer-reviewed journals, he is also Co-editor of *The Political Economy of Latin American Independence* (Routledge, 2017) and *Political Economy and International Order in Interwar Europe* (Palgrave, 2020).

LIST OF CONTRIBUTORS

Irène Berthonnet	Université Paris Cité, Le Laboratoire Dynamiques Sociales et Recomposition des Espaces, Paris, France
Alexandre Chirat	University Paris-Nanterre, Nanterre, France
Basile Clerc	University Paris-Nanterre, Nanterre, France
Adem Yavuz Elveren	American University in Bulgaria, Blagoevgrad, Bulgaria
Luca Fiorito	University of Palermo, Palermo, Italy
Richard P. F. Holt	Southern Oregon University, Ashland, OR, USA
William McColloch	Keene State College, Keene, NH, USA
Steven Pressman	New School for Social Research, New York, NY, USA, and Monmouth University, West Long Branch, NJ, USA
Scott Scheall	Arizona State University Polytechnic Campus, Mesa, AZ, USA
Eric Scorsone	Michigan State University, East Lansing, MI, USA
Carlos Eduardo Suprinyak	American University of Paris, Paris, France
Matías Vernengo	Bucknell University, Lewisburg, PA, USA

VOLUME INTRODUCTION

Volume 41C of *Research in the History of Economic Thought and Methodology* features a symposium on the work of John Kenneth Galbraith, guest edited by Richard P. F. Holt. The symposium includes contributions from Steven Pressman, Alexander Chirat, Eric Scorsone, and Adem Yavuz Elveren, as well as a recently discovered archival piece, originally written by Galbraith in 1979, and edited for the symposium by Holt, Chirat, and Basile Clerc.

The volume also includes new research essays by William McColloch and Matías Vernengo on the history of regulation, and Irène Berthonnet on Maurice Allais's role in the development of the concept of Pareto efficiency.

The Editors of *Research in the History of Economic Thought and Methodology*
Luca Fiorito
Scott Scheall
Carlos Eduardo Suprinyak

PART I

A SYMPOSIUM ON JOHN KENNETH GALBRAITH: ECONOMIC STRUCTURES AND POLICIES FOR THE TWENTY-FIRST CENTURY

Edited by Richard P. F. Holt

CHAPTER 1

INTRODUCTION

Richard P. F. Holt

When Galbraith passed away on April 29, 2006, prominent figures worldwide remembered him as a social critic and one of the great public intellectuals of the 20th century. He profoundly influenced politics and literature as a best-selling author, a confidant of presidents, a public servant, and a political activist for liberal causes. Yet, he received little acclamation from the economics profession. Notwithstanding their respect for Galbraith, most in the profession had reservations about the quality and strength of his scholarly writings. Paul Samuelson remarked casually, "Galbraith, like Thorstein Veblen, will be remembered and read when most of us Nobel Laureates will be buried in footnotes down in dusty library stacks" (Stanfield, 2001, p. 7). Milton Friedman said he represented "old wine in a new bottle" (*Time*, February 16, 1968). Neil Jacoby, Dean of the University of California at Los Angeles' Graduate School of Business Administration, commented, "Mr. Galbraith is a very talented journalist and a very bad economist. I wouldn't have him on my faculty" (*Time*, February 16, 1968).

Galbraith's supporters claim such comments represent a methodological bias in the profession. Following classical economists, Galbraith focused on the evolution of economics over time. Moreover, like John Stuart Mill, he separated theory from policy (Mill, 1848). The neoclassical approach makes no distinction. You start with theory, define a measurable goal, and implement policies to achieve it. Instead of looking at the complexities of the real world, you let theory define public policy. By considering history, politics, and institutions, Galbraith saw larger changes than most economists. For example, he recognized the significance of the United States economy evolving from entrepreneurial to corporate capitalism in the 19th Century. By the mid-20th century, the economic problem had been redefined from scarcity of material goods to social and quality of life deficiencies. The shift came about through industrialization and the government's

Research in the History of Economic Thought and Methodology: Including a Symposium on John Kenneth Galbraith: Economic Structures and Policies for the Twenty-First Century
Research in the History of Economic Thought and Methodology, Volume 41C, 3–16
Copyright © 2024 by Emerald Publishing Limited
All rights of reproduction in any form reserved
ISSN: 0743-4154/doi:10.1108/S0743-41542024000041C001

role in the economy. He saw the best policies (like Roosevelt's New Deal) as those responding and guiding the economic system or "nudging" it. Related to this, mainstream economics ignored power:

> Years ago, I concluded that economics divorced from the concept of power was extensively irrelevant. One can understand modern economic behavior only as one sees it not alone as a pursuit of wealth but also a pursuit of power. Also one can understand the limits of economic power only as one sees its dialectic – the tendency I've discussed in past times for one exercise of power to be countered and neutralized by another exercise of power. The employer and the trade union. The corporation and the consumer movement. Polluters and environmentalists. One has a very incomplete view of modern corporation, in particular, if one thinks of it purely as a money-making enterprise. A complete or a more nearly complete view of corporate motivation requires also that there be a theory of power. (Stanfield & Stanfield, 2004, p. 119)

He also criticized neoclassical economics for being unable to shake its "ideological belief." It was stuck in a Robinson Crusoe pre-industrial world of 1719, where entrepreneurs and autonomous consumers made all the decisions in a market economy. Galbraith found the "conventional wisdom" absurd. Instead, he saw corporations in the 1950s expanding their influence with economies of scale, mass production, efforts to control consumer sovereignty, and lobbying the government:

> The initiative in deciding what is to be produced comes not from the sovereign consumer who, through the market, issues the instructions that bend the productive mechanism to his ultimate will. Instead, it comes from the great producing organization which reaches forward to control the markets it is presumed to serve and, beyond, to bend the customer to its needs ... The imperatives of technology and organization, not the images of ideology, determine the shape of economic society ... the trend of public policy has been highly favorable to its needs. If this is accidental, it reflects from the point of view of the mature corporation, one of the happiest conjunctions of circumstance in history. (Galbraith, 1967, pp. 7 & 327)

HETERODOX ECONOMICS

Galbraith is unique in that he is a heterodox economist, not just among traditional economists but also among heterodox economists as well. By emphasizing the success of capitalism, it put him at odds with the critics. For Galbraith, the success of capitalism in the postwar era cannot be attributed just to markets. Economic power of large corporations and government intervention, also played a significant role. In the first chapter of *American Capitalism* (1952a), "The Insecurity of Illusion," Galbraith argued the neoclassical story with its consumer sovereignty and small firms was mainly fiction. He insisted that an "emancipation of belief" was called for. Economists had to get beyond its "illusion" and look at the real world. Given the magnitude of corporate size and concentration, it cannot survive just by producing goods for basic needs. It must create a desire for an every-increasing quantity of goods. Galbraith saw consumers having limited power since corporations influence the type of goods produced and the range. In addition, he defined consumer freedom as more than the number of goods one can choose. Expanding choices meaningfully requires increasing the number of *relevant choices* a consumer has. If one has 30 different candy bars to choose from where their difference is minimal, this does not significantly increase a person's freedom. However, if one has a choice between candy bars and fruit, that is, a meaningful choice. Following this example, to enlarge consumer freedom in a meaningful way, requires expanding choices for Galbraith from private to public goods. The individual is better off with the option of both public and private goods that provide access to social power, education, and social security.

Galbraith saw large corporations as a double-edged sword. In *The New Industrial State* (1967), he argued that the development of large firms, with government support, allowed for significant resources for major technological breakthroughs and economies of scale. For Galbraith, it is an endogenous force. Given the cost of technological development, firms must have some guarantee of a return on their investments; this requires some control of markets, which comes about through firm size and oligopolistic power to markup their prices. Size and the ability to plan for long-term growth allow large corporations to "transcend the market" and achieve levels of productivity and power beyond the reach of the entrepreneurial firm. A downside to corporate hegemony is a "social imbalance" between private and public goods. Following John Stuart Mill and Keynes, Galbraith saw capitalism reaching a mature state allowing it to produce enough private goods for society's material well-being. It could then shift production to social and merit goods to improve the overall quality of life, and deal with the inherent inequalities generated by capitalism. Instead, corporate capitalism created a modernized consumption model that turned "wants" into "needs." Galbraith looked at material "needs" as being relatively limited but material "wants" as insatiable (Galbraith, 1958). With the help of advertisement, the focus of modern corporations moved from industrial production to market manipulation.

Another issue was price setting and its distribution effects. Galbraith saw the oligopolistic sector of the economy as price makers, not price takers, where prices are set as a markup over costs. Since markups affect the overall general price level of the economy, Galbraith saw cases where the government should establish price controls, particularly with corporate inflation. Unlike neoclassical economics, he saw the causes of inflation evolving. In the 1950s and 1960s, he focused on conflict inflation between groups like unions and managers. In the 1970s and 1980s, he looked at import and supply-side causes. His criticism of the neoclassical explanation of inflation was their "religious" commitment to their theory instead of looking at political and social factors. For example, in the late 1950s, William Phillips published a paper that empirically linked inflation and employment. In 1967, Milton Friedman questioned the Phillips curve by using theory. The problem, Friedman declared, is that theory can't explain the link. Since theory dominates, then the Phillips curve must be a short-term aberration. In the 1970s, as the United States experienced stagflation, Friedman claimed victory. Galbraith was not so sure. What overcame the Phillips curve was not its incompatibility with theory as much as conflict between labor and managers, the Vietnam war, and the Organization Petroleum Exporting Countries (OPEC) supply-side shocks – all institutional and political factors. These other factors, more than demand-pull or price expectations, were the causes of the dissolution of the Phillips curve.

Overall, Galbraith saw inflation as a political issue rather than an economic theory problem.

Galbraith also took on consumer sovereignty. According to neoclassical theory, the consumer has the power. Galbraith questioned this assumption for various reasons; a significant one is corporate advertisement. Suppose corporations can affect consumer demand through advertising, then one cannot say the market is allocating resources in the most efficient way to meet individual preferences, but the preferences of the corporation. Advertisement for Galbraith was more than just explaining the comparative advantage of one product over another. Using Veblen's "conspicuous consumption" (1899), he saw significant economic consequences caused by commercial advertisement. In the 1950s, General Motors (GM), the largest corporation in America at that time, led an aggressive advertisement campaign that "bigger is better" (Halberstam, 1994). This meant building cars with more horsepower with high-compression engines that used higher octane gas. The car became something more than just for transportation but a social status symbol. The marketing department's goal at GM was to convince consumers of the connection between social mobility and consumer goods. If you are part of the working class, you own a Buick. To be part of the white-collar workforce, you own a Cadillac. The difference between a Buick and Cadillac was size, power, and amenities.

Another example is housing. Homes with two bedrooms, one bath, a living room, and a kitchen were considered too small and lacked the right amenities for the new "American Dream" (Halberstam, 1994). With affluence, many consumption goods became what economist Robert Frank called positional goods, "the tendency will be to steer expenditures in favor of consumption categories that signal high ability ... items such as cars, clothing and jewelry" (Frank, 2007, p. 72). Galbraith observed that competitive consumption diverts resources from what will genuinely make people's lives better, like public investments in social and environmental capital. Galbraith was also concerned with corporate influence with government policies. Corporations want the government to carry out monetary and fiscal policies compatible with their own economic planning. Galbraith saw economic policy in Washington as an extension of corporate planning. The only way to combat this power and influence was through other public voices demanding corporate and government accountability, campaign finance reform, environmental legislation, and consumer protection as counterbalancing forces. Though, as Steve Pressman's chapter explains, his views about countervailing power evolved, Galbraith saw it as a way to neutralize corporate power in an industrial democratic society.

An additional issue for Galbraith with corporate power is its inability to address major social issues in the United States. After the war, rising incomes plus the availability of consumer credit provided consumers with new opportunities to increase their consumption. Yet, for all its economic growth and new wealth, America could not solve fundamental social problems like poverty or racism. In 1960, President John F. Kennedy claimed that continued economic growth would act like a "rising tide that lifts all boats." From the end of World War II to the mid-1970s, Kennedy was right. There was a positive trickle-down. Expansion in the educational, workplace safety, and economic opportunities changed the well-being for millions of Americans. Government programs like Social Security allowed older people to live independently longer. The GI bill, and the Federal Housing Administration allowed more social and economic mobility.

Discrimination still restricted the mobility of Blacks, women, and other minority groups, but overall, economic progress was made. That started to change in the late 1970s with a significant increase in inequality between income groups that created a negative trickle-down effect (Greenwood & Holt, 2010). Neoliberal theory rationalizes inequality as necessary for growth and is offset by a positive trickle-down benefitting all income groups. However, benefits from growth failed to reach most of the population in the 1970s. Increased inequality and stagnant wages exacerbated conspicuous consumption with positional goods, which can be private or public. Income inequality generates a differentiation not just with private goods but also public goods between segments of the population. Wealthy neighborhoods can afford high-quality public goods like excellent schools and safe streets. Impoverished and Black communities have poorer and fewer public goods because of wealth disparities. This creates a two-tier system where neighborhoods with better public goods saw the prices of homes reach levels beyond the means of working class families. Increased inequality was not caused by a lack of economic growth or technology. Galbraith points out there is more "stuff" today for each individual in the United States than 50 years ago. Yet, many cannot afford health care, housing, or high-quality education. Economic growth cannot provide solutions to our social problems alone. Galbraith thought it artificial to equate social welfare with material welfare. But that's precisely what we did in the postwar era. Focusing primarily on private production cannot by itself increase wellbeing. Galbraith explained the consequences of unrelenting production of private over public goods:

> Central is that as the modern economy has developed and expanded, ever more responsibilities have been imposed on the state. There are, first, the services that the private economy does not, by its nature, render and that, with economic advance, create an increasing and increasingly embarrassing discrepancy between the private and public living standards. Expensively produced television programs are shown to children who attend bad public schools. Houses in the better sections of the city are elegant and clean, while the streets and sidewalks in front are filthy. Books are widely and diversely available in the bookstores but not in the public libraries. (Galbraith, 1996, p. 18)

Galbraith claimed it didn't have to be this way. The challenge was not scarcity, but changing society's economic priorities in an affluent and industrialized society. The shift was necessary to achieve a good society (Galbraith, 1996).

THE GALBRAITHIAN METHOD

Galbraith has always had the Scotch luck of being at the right place at the right time. When he left Berkeley and went to Harvard in 1934, he found himself in a heated debate about the modern structure and organization of firms. An essential question was on the pricing behavior of imperfectly competitive firms. It led to

Galbraith's first single-authored paper, "Monopoly and Price Rigidities" (1936). The neoclassical approach focuses on competition and the gains from competition. Galbraith developed two distinct critiques of the competitive model. First, he explained the logical flaws of the perfectly competitive model. Second, he pointed out that neoclassical analysis ignores the benefits of imperfect market structures.

The first argument started with Piero Sraffa (1926) with the neoclassical supply curve for the industry. According to standard neoclassical analysis, the supply curve of every firm is independent of the supply curve of other firms in the industry. An industry supply curve is derived by adding up the individual supply curves of firms. Sraffa argued that a firm's production conditions affect all other firms' production function. When one firm expands production, it will increase demand for raw materials for all firms in the industry, so the price of raw materials will increase. With higher material costs, all firms make less profit. As a result, they will want to produce fewer goods at each price. Because of such interdependences, Sraffa argued that drawing independent supply curves for each firm in the industry was invalid. Galbraith (1948) saw the importance of Sraffa's article:

> The first influential new step in the field of ideas was the publication in 1926 by Piero Sraffa of his now famous article, "The laws of returns under perfect competitive conditions" … if large scale and accompanying requirements in capital and organization brought substantial economies, the small newcomer was faced with an organic handicap. Nevertheless, these barriers, though widely recognized, were conventionally assumed to be of secondary effect. They were frictions that muddled and at times diverted but did not check the great underlying current which was toward a competitive equilibrium. Given that equilibrium, there was a presumption, again subject to many dissenting voices, that economic resources would be employed with maximum efficiency and the product so distributed as to maximize satisfactions. Sraffa attacked the assumption that the "frictions" were in fact a secondary and fugitive phenomenon. He argued they were stable and indeed cumulative and yielded a solution consistent not with a competitive, but a monopolistic equilibrium. He argued that monopoly, not free competition, was the more appropriate assumption in market theory.

Sraffa's article also influenced Joan Robinson. She evaluated Marshall's assumptions of perfect competition in her 1933 book on imperfect competition and came up with more generalized assumptions of market behavior that showed perfect competition as a special case "of what in general is a monopolistic situation" (Robinson, 1933). Working independently, Edward H. Chamberlin published a volume on imperfect competition the previous year (1932). Chamberlin argued that the classical view of two market structures with perfect competition at one end and monopoly at the other with nothing in between didn't capture reality. Chamberlin saw market structures as a continuum rather than a polarization of two opposites – pure competition and monopoly. Besides the work of Robinson and Chamberlin, Galbraith was influenced by Adolf Berle' and Gardiner Means' *The Modern Corporation and Private Property* (1933). The authors argued the traditional view of competitive-price firms is a myth in an advanced industrial society. The reality is a large concentration of firms with a new technostructure where power has shifted from shareholders to managers. They saw minimal benefit from government corporate trust-busting, for it would kill the goose that laid the golden eggs of economic growth. Galbraith now saw corporations not as autonomous firms but *as organizations with an internal governance influenced by market structures.* Robinson, Chamberlin, Adolph Berle, and Gardiner Means played an important role in redefining the nature of market structures, which greatly influenced Galbraith in the 1930s. He summarized their effect:

> The new market categories, plus the evidence of Berle and Means and the scholar's own eyes as to their need, set the stage for the revived interest in monopoly and its allied issues. One must also emphasize the esprit Chamberlin's and Robinson's works gave to field students. Even though they substituted a new set of frustrations for the old ones, the new ones were welcome. It has been suggested that the most revolutionary feature of the monopolistic competition theories [was] the unprecedented pace at which they conquered their audience ... Their most effective critic, Professor Schumpeter, centered attacks not on the validity of their analysis per se [in themselves] but more generally on the notion that it much affected the assessment of capitalist reality. Rarely in economics have ideas had such an enthusiastic and uncritical welcome. (Galbraith, 1948)

To answer the second point of the benefits of imperfect competition, he turned to Berle and Means (1967). He argued size has advantages "as a means of facilitating technological change by emancipating it from the uncertainties of the market" (Dunn & Pressman, 2005, p. 171). Following Schumpeter (1942), Galbraith saw technological change as a principal characteristic of the industrial world and a primary challenge facing all firms. Technology requires more capital and a specialized workforce and requires planning. Moreover, as production becomes more complex due to technical changes, one person can no longer be familiar with all aspects of production and sales. Group decisions rather than individual decisions become predominant in large firms that create the technostructure of the corporation. Size comes with numerous advantages. It allows firms to control the market, suppliers, influence consumers, and pressure the government. All this generates larger profits for the firm. Smaller firms, with little or no economic profits, lack the resources to invest in new technology, innovate, expand their markets, and influence the government.

The most significant influence on Galbraith in the 1930s was the publication of Keynes' *The General Theory* in 1936. Galbraith claimed it hit him like a "tidal force" (Parker, 2005, p. 119). Keynes saw classical macroeconomics caught up in a theoretical world far from reality. As Keynes stated, "Trying to solve unemployment with a theory which is based on the assumption that there is not unemployment is not going to solve the problem" (Keynes quoted in Parker, 2005, p. 122). Keynes did not see monetary policies as being able to do the heavy lifting to achieve aggregate levels for full employment. The Great Depression showed Keynes that changing interest rates would not affect investments by itself, but changes in aggregate income over time would. If the private sector could not achieve aggregate income levels needed for full employment, then the government had to step in. In addition, Keynes had no interest in the Marxist view of government ownership of the means of production. Instead, he looked at the role of the government to stabilize markets for the private sector to allowed it to thrive and reach full employment. If the market economy could not help itself, then the visible hand of the government had to step in to save capitalism from itself. A precept well learned by Galbraith.

In the 1940s, there would be two other major influences on Galbraith's approach to economic problems. The first was becoming Roosevelt's "price czar" during World War II. Galbraith found himself in 1942 as head of price controls at the Office of Price Administration (OPA). Here he learned first-hand about the rough and ideological world of Washington politics. Faced with political opponents that wanted to shut down the OPA, Galbraith kept general prices, growth, and employment stable in the United States. Inflation stayed around 2 percent; unemployment was practically zero, and the US' production rates rose 250 percent (Parker, 2005, p. 151). Even with these successes, political ideology dominated. He was accused by business leaders and conservative politicians of "showing communistic tendencies," among other political sins. Galbraith was finally fired from his post (Parker, 2005, p. 152). A political lesson he never forgot. The second major influence on Galbraith in the 1940s came from an unusual benefactor: Henry Robinson Luce, the iconic American publisher. Galbraith said of his influence:

> [...] Harry Luce's instruction in writing was a lifetime gift. And there was another professional benefit. The early *Fortune*, more than any other journal anywhere in the industrial world, saw the modern large corporation as a primary economic and social force. My years there as writer and editor provided a diversity and intimacy of exposure to its structure, operating goals and economic, social and political influence that could not have been had in any other way. (Galbraith, 1981, p. 268)

From his academic experience at Harvard with John Black, working in the bureaucracies of Washington during the New Deal and World War II, and learning how to become a journalist from Henry Luce, Galbraith established the tools, skills, and confidence to navigate between the worlds of academics, politics, and journalism. All of which culminated into a unique style and method of analysis later known as the "Galbraithian method."

GALBRAITH AND COMPLEXITY ECONOMICS

With *American Capitalism* (1952a) and *The Affluent Society* (1958), Galbraith took dissenting shots across the mainstream bow. Galbraith criticized orthodox microeconomics with its Max-U models and competitive firms working under the constraint of prices. His dislike of traditional macroeconomics increased over time, particularly with its development of rational expectations and Dynamic Stochastic General Equilibrium (DSGE) models in the 1970s. He saw the profession's macroeconomic models as theoretically abstruse and empirically hollow, which he criticized in his novel, *A Tenured Professor* (1990). Similar to the cutting-edge work being done with complexity economics today, Galbraith found it incredulous that one could seriously develop a micro foundation for macroeconomics without considering the feedback of the macro system on the behavior of individual firms and consumers with no room for heterogeneous firms and consumers (Holt, Rosser, & Colander, 2011). In many ways, he anticipated the cutting-edge work being done today in ecological economics and evolutionary game theory, where institutions are integrated into economic analysis with behavioral economics (Fehr & Schmidt, 1999). To use contemporary terminology, Galbraith saw the economy as a complex system that is endogenously organized where the macro system feedbacks on micro agents and groups. He used a transdisciplinary approach that led to new ideas and insights that allowed him to explore interactions that traditional economics ignored. He recognized the endogenous feedback loops within economic systems all in the context of institutional and historical changes.

It was also with *American Capitalism* (1952a) and *The Affluent Society* (1958) that Galbraith started to part ways from the liberal branch of mainstream economics. In his remarks remembering Galbraith after his death, Robert Solow stated they shared a common belief:

> the dogma that a decentralized market economy is a very delicate, fragile piece of economic machinery. There is only one way to preserve it, and that is to leave it alone. If you tinker with it, especially if the state tries to modify the outcome into something more acceptable on equity grounds, unintended bad things will happen ... Our essential point of agreement was that if this was the state of professional opinion, then professional opinion was wrong. (Solow, 2006)

What Solow leaves out is the difference Galbraith had with the neoclassical Keynesians. As Stanfield and Stanfield correctly point out, "Galbraith concluded that liberal opinion needed a more plausible, more realistic model of the economy's functioning" (2001, p. 69). If one goes through Galbraith's notes in preparation for writing the *New Industrial State* (1967), one can see the struggle he went through to come up with a new approach. Though he believed that the liberal wing of the economics profession was trying to develop policies that would make a social difference, he did not like the methodological approach of neoclassical liberals. Galbraith focused instead on a more descriptive method that studied the "matrix of change which has brought modern industrial society into being" (Galbraith, n.d., p. 1). This could only be understood if one looked at the economy as a complex interactive and adaptive system affected by politics and institutions and its evolution. Galbraith acknowledged that what he was trying to do was ambitious. He recognized the difficulty of providing a "formal method" rooted in the "complexity of modern social organization" (Galbraith, n.d., p. 1). But he felt the need to push the "problem of presentation" forward and insisted, "... to wait for matters to become simpler does not commend itself" (Galbraith, n.d., p. 1). Galbraith suggested that social organizations and structures, not individuals acting by themselves, are essential for understanding the evolution of an economy, particularly in an industrial state. Organizations create networks, structures, and power, which affect individuals and economic outcomes. A great admirer of Herbert Simon, Galbraith would agree with Simon's definition of how a modern economy is a complex one:

> Roughly by a complex system, I mean one made up of a large number of parts that interact in a non-simply way. In such systems, the whole is more than the sum of the parts, not in an ultimate metaphysical sense but in the important pragmatic sense that, given the properties of the parts

and the laws of their interaction, it is not a trivial matter to infer that properties of the whole. In the face of complexity, an in-principle reductionist may be, at the same time, a pragmatic holist. (Simon, 1962, p. 267)

Such a definition puts into perspective Galbraith's efforts to understand the nature of economic systems and the role large corporations, institutions, government, and consumers play in it. Galbraith was an institutionalist and, following Herbert Simon, a complexity economist who saw economics as evolving with uncertainty. He saw the development of the industrial state through "the massive application of technology to modem economic processes" (Galbraith, n.d., p. 1). The change from entrepreneurial to corporate capitalism came about through the use of massive technological changes such as railroads, electricity, and the combustion of fossil fuels, which gave corporations large profits and political power. Given that he was an evolutionary economist, he saw that transformation continuing into the future with new corporate structures and power. Galbraith hoped counterbalance forces would develop against that power. As corporate and technostructure evolved, so did the need for counterbalancing forces. As Steve Pressman points out in his chapter, Galbraith's earlier view about counterbalance forces was too optimistic. Over the postwar years, he changed his views of the type of counterbalance forces needed to check corporate power. First, in the 1950s, it was the power of unions. In the 1960s, he shifted to consumer groups, suppliers, and an "enlightened" technostructure to transform corporate power. In the 1970s, he turned to government laws and agencies like the Environmental Protection Agency.

Starting in the 1980s, the technostructure changed. With unions losing power, globalization, and equity firms pushing corporate mergers a new technostructure developed with large financial rewards tied to increasing the value of company's stock, lowering wages, and increasing outsourcing and automation. There was no meaningful counterbalancing force to respond to the technological and financial changes. In the 1960s, you had consumer protection groups like Ralph Nader's efforts to combat corporation neglect. In the 1970s, you had the government responding with new agencies like Occupational Safety and Health Administration and the Environmental Protection Agency – all were countervailing forces, to check industrial and corporate power. Today, such countervailing powers are much weaker if there at all.

FUTURE DIRECTION OF GALBRAITH'S WORK

The chapters in this volume take Galbraith's work and look at the future. Alexandre Chirat and Eric Scorsone in their chapters extend Galbraith's work of the evolution of firms and economic systems by looking at how digital technology has impacted consumer sovereignty, the relationship between corporate ownership and control, and the creation of counterbalancing forces. Chirat suggests that Galbraith's "Dependence Effect," where the production process creates wants and then satisfies them, is still relevant today with online advertisement. Galbraith asked in the 1950s whether production that requires advertisement improves the overall standard of living. Chirat raises the same question in the era he calls "platform capitalism." He points out that corporate digital platforms have brought back Galbraith's "the revised sequence," where social media can easily generate misinformation and consumer fraud. Chirat rightly states there are few counterbalance forces to challenge "platform capitalism" and the power it has over users and consumers. He proposes that platform capitalism is a "mature form" of Galbraith's "new industrial state" but even more powerful and controlling over consumers and users. Eric Scorsone continues Chirat's theme by looking at Galbraith's social balance theory. As we move from industrial to digital platform capitalism, how does this impact the social balance between private and public goods and the type of public goods we need? Again, the key is the need for a countervailing power.

In the 1950s and 1960s large industrial corporations promised a better future with good jobs, higher wages, and increased well-being. Big Tech giants today make the same promises. Caught in a digital utopia, corporate giants insist that productivity growth, workers, and consumers' well-being would improve with continued automation and new technological breakthroughs. Yet productivity numbers and quality of life indicators do not support such claims. "Platform capitalism" has given corporations tremendous power to control and manipulate information, control what products are made, and how technology will be used in society today. Countervailing powers are urgently needed. This requires consumers taking steps to have more control of how platform capitalism works and for whose interest through public advocacy groups and government policy.

Galbraith saw corporation ideology during the industrial state for what it was – another promise from the Industrial Revolution of the 19th century of continuing growth and shared prosperity. That promise could only be realized, by forcing corporations to share their power and affluence. The same ideological force is in play today with Big Tech firms. It's important to remember that Galbraith saw the industrial society as something that evolves and countervailing forces need to change with it:

> […] the industrial society is in a process of continuous and organic change, that public policy must accommodate to such change, and that by such public action performance can, in fact, be improved. The relevant historical change to which there must now be accommodation is in the nature of the industrial market. The market, with its maturing of industrial society and associated political institutions, loses and loses radically its authority as a regulatory force. Partly this is inherent in industrial development – in the institutions that modern large-scale production, technology, and planning required. Partly it is an expression of the democratic ethos, and paradoxically, this is often much applauded by scholars of liberal views who are also. And inconsistently, defenders of the market. (Galbraith, 1978, pp. 7–9)

That change and evolution have continued into the 21st century as we shift from an industrial to a digital age. With the shift, new countervailing forces are required. In a market and democratic society that means more consumer groups confronting the tech giants and the government through regulation and incentives to redirect technology that benefits workers and consumers. Galbraith's overall message of the technostructure and its evolution seems all the more relevant today with worldwide corporate giants like Apple, Google, Microsoft, and

Facebook. Given how new technology dominates work, our private lives, and society reinforces, Galbraith's claim that corporate influence would grow and its scope widen over our lives. Chirat's and Scorsone's chapters provide us with some major insights in how to deal with this digital power.

Adem Yavuz Elveren looks at the development of corporate power in a different light by looking at the impact of corporations and technological change today has on the military–industrial complex (MIC). Such a complex creates a network between business, government, and the military. Like the tech giants, the MIC tries to influence public opinion and government support for increased military spending. Galbraith asked the same question about MIC as he did with private corporate growth and advertisement and its impact on social well-being (1967). Similar to the private sector, he saw the importance of countervailing power with the MIC. The MIC can lead to unnecessary defense spending, distort the US foreign policy interests, and shift the development of technology away from what would improve well-being. Again, you need consumer and citizen groups to create counterbalancing forces. The last chapter in the volume is a piece written by Galbraith himself that has not been published before on inflation. The question Galbraith asked is similar to the one that Keynes imposed on himself (Keynes, 1936, p. 9): Can capitalism achieve price stability without an unacceptable unemployment level? Galbraith questioned the wisdom of neoclassical monetary and fiscal policies that inflict pain through a "planned recession." It is planned in that neoclassical economists have a religious faith that their models of long-run equilibrium with its assumption of full employment and stable prices will automatically stabilize the economy. Besides questioning whether full employment and stable prices will occur using neoclassical assumption, Galbraith insists that such pain is not necessary. Galbraith's solution is to socially internalize the conflict caused by inflation with fair income policies that will provide maximum production with full employment and stable prices.

All the chapters in this book suggest that many of our current economic and social problems are rooted in the power of corporations, especially today in the tech industry. Instead of adding to our well-being, they are limiting it with a new technostructure that controls the type of technology we develop and for what purpose. New economic incentives have been put into place where the technostructure tries to maximize shareholders values and market shares. There is a new danger with digital corporate power in that it is developing new technology to replace workers through automation and collect data for surveillance and intrusive advertisement. The authors of this volume tell us we can respond to this digital pernicious power through new countervailing capabilities similar to those Galbraith mentioned: unions, consumer groups, government regulation, and democratic citizens insisting on changes of social norms where technological advancement works to make a better and more equitable world.

REFERENCES

Adams, W. (1953). Competition, monopoly and countervailing power. *Quarterly Journal of Economics*, *67*, 469–492.
Berle, A. (1953). American capitalism. *Review of Economics and Statistics, 35*, 81–84.

Berle, A., & Means, G. (1933). *The modern corporation and private property.* New York, NY: Macmillan.

Chamberlin, E. (1932). *The theory of monopolistic competition.* Cambridge, MA: Harvard University Press.

Dunn, S., & Pressman, S. (2005). The economic contributions of John Kenneth Galbraith. *Review of Political Economy, 17,* 161–209.

Fehr, E., & Schmidt, K. M. (1999). A theory of fairness, competition and cooperation. *Quarterly Journal of Economics, 114,* 817–868.

Frank, R. H. (2007). *Falling behind: How rising inequality harms the middle class* (p. 72). Berkeley, CA: University of California.

Friedman, M. (1970). The social responsibility of business is to increase its profits. *New York Times,* September 13.

Galbraith, J. K. (1936). Monopoly power and price rigidities. *Quarterly Journal of Economics, 50*(3), 456–475.

Galbraith, J. K. (1949). Monopoly and the concentration of economic power. In H. E. Ellis (Ed.), *A survey of contemporary economics* (pp. 99–128). New York, NY: Blakiston Company.

Galbraith, J. K. (1952a). *American capitalism.* Boston, MA: Houghton Mifflin.

Galbraith, J. K. (1952b). *A theory of price control.* Cambridge, MA: Harvard University Press.

Galbraith, J. K. (1954). *The great crash 1929.* Boston, MA: Houghton Mifflin.

Galbraith, J. K. (1958). *The affluent society.* Boston, MA: Houghton Mifflin.

Galbraith, J. K. (1967). *The new industrial state.* New York, NY. New American Library, 1968.

Galbraith, J. K. (1970). *The liberal hour.* New York, NY: New American Library.

Galbraith, J. K. (1973). *Economics and the public purpose.* New York, NY: New American Library.

Galbraith, J. K. (1975). *Money: Whence it came, where it went.* Boston, MA: Houghton Mifflin.

Galbraith, J. K. (1978). On post Keynesian economics. *Journal of Post Keynesian Economics, 1*(1).

Galbraith, J. K. (1990). *A short history of financial euphoria.* New York, NY: Penguin Books.

Galbraith, J. K. (1996). *The good society: The humane agenda.* Boston, MA: Houghton Mifflin.

Galbraith, J. K. (n.d.). The industrial system. In Box 193 of the inventory of personal papers of John Kenneth Galbraith at the John F. Kennedy Presidential Library and Museum (pp. 1–4).

Galbraith, J. K., & Black, J. D. (1938). The maintenance of agricultural production during the depression: The explanation reviewed. *Journal of Political Economy, 46*(3), 305–323.

Greenwood, D. T., & Holt, R. P. F. (2010). *Local economic development in the 21st century: Quality of life and sustainability.* London: Routledge.

Halberstam, D. (1994). *The fifties.* New York, NY: Open Road.

Hansen, A. (1939). Economic progress and declining population growth. *American Economic Review, 29,* 1–15.

Holt, R. P. F., Rosser, J. B., Jr, & Colander, D. (2011). The complexity era of economics. *Review of Political Economy, 23*(3), 359–371.

Keynes, J. M. (1936). *The general theory of employment, interest and money.* London: Macmillan.

Mill, J. S. (1848). *Principles of political economy.* London: Longmans, Green.

Parker, R. (2005). *John Kenneth Galbraith: His life, his politics, his economics.* New York, NY: Farrar, Straus & Giroux.

Robinson, J. (1933). *The economics of imperfect competition.* London: Macmillan.

Samuelson, P. A., & Solow, R. M. (1960). Analytical aspects of anti-inflation policy. *American Economic Review Papers and Proceedings, 50*(2), 177–194.

Schumpeter, J. (1942). *Capitalism, socialism and democracy.* New York, NY: Harper & Brothers.

Simon, H. A. (1962). New developments in the theory of the firm. *The American Economic Review, 52*(2).

Solow, R. (2006, October). Remembering John Kenneth Galbraith. After dinner speech at a conference commemorating John Kenneth Galbraith, Kennedy School.

Sraffa, P. (1926). The laws of returns under competitive conditions. *The Economic Journal, XXXVI*(144), 535–550.

Stanfield, J. R. (2001). The useful economist. In M. Keaney (Ed.), *Economic with a public purpose* (p. 7). London: Routledge Press.

Stanfield, J. R., & Stanfield, J. B. (Eds.). (2004). *Interviews with John Kenneth Galbraith* (p. 119). Jackson, MS: University Press of Mississippi.

Stigler, G. (1954). The economist plays with blocs. *American Economic Review, 44*, 7–14.

Time Magazine. (1968). The Great Mogul. *Time Magazine*, February 16.

Veblen, T. (1899). *A theory of the leisure class*. New York, NY: Macmillan.

Veblen, T. (1921). *The engineers and the price system*. New York, NY: B.W. Huebsch.

CHAPTER 2

GALBRAITH AND ECONOMIC POWER

Steven Pressman

ABSTRACT

Economists usually shy away from talking about power. They assume an economy comprised of many small and medium-sized firms, each competing for consumer dollars. This circumvents the problem of economic power. John Kenneth Galbraith, however, refused to ignore power. It stood at the center of his economics, and he saw it as a key reason the US economy thrived in the years following World War II (WWII). This chapter examines Galbraith's changing views regarding economic power. American Capitalism explains how countervailing power, or power on the other side of the market, solves the problem of economic power. In The New Industrial State, scientists and educated managers within the firm (the technostructure) mitigate the negative consequences of economic power wielded by large firms. The Affluent Society and Economics and the Public Purpose look to the government as the main check on corporate power. It does this through labor legislation or programs such as the New Deal and Fair Deal. This chapter then evaluates the different solutions Galbraith proffered to the problem of economic power. It contends that Galbraith got three things right when analyzing economic power. First, we no longer live in a world of scarcity due to oligopolistic firms. Second, capitalism was different in the post-WWII era because the US economy thrived and gains were shared widely. Third, Galbraith understood that power was unequally distributed – both between the public and private sectors and within the private sector itself. On the other

Research in the History of Economic Thought and Methodology: Including a Symposium on John Kenneth Galbraith: Economic Structures and Policies for the Twenty-First Century
Research in the History of Economic Thought and Methodology, Volume 41C, 17–33
Copyright © 2024 by Emerald Publishing Limited
All rights of reproduction in any form reserved
ISSN: 0743-4154/doi:10.1108/S0743-41542024000041C002

hand, Galbraith was overly optimistic in believing the market economy or the public sector could counter corporate power.

Keywords: Countervailing power; technostructure; market power; government regulation of business; capitalism; scarcity

INTRODUCTION

Power has traditionally been a concern of philosophers, political scientists, and sociologists. Economists, with few exceptions, have ignored it. Adam Smith (1776) lamented the economic power wielded by monopolies and groups of merchants conspiring to raise prices. Karl Marx (1976, 1978, 1981) drew out the consequences of unequal economic power. Most other economists assumed an economy comprised of many small and medium-sized firms, each competing for consumer dollars. This assumption circumvented the problem of economic power.

John Kenneth Galbraith refused to ignore power. It stood at the center of his economics. In several books, he analyzed the power wielded by large firms and its consequences. This chapter examines Galbraith's changing views regarding economic power. The next section explains how countervailing power solves the problem of economic power and discusses several critiques of this doctrine. After *American Capitalism* (1952a), Galbraith abandoned this term but not his belief in the need to counter the power of large firms. In *The New Industrial State* (1967), scientists and educated managers within the firm (the technostructure) perform this function. The section "Technostructure" examines the technostructure and its ability to constrain the power of large corporations. *The Affluent Society* (1967) and *Economics and the Public Purpose* (1973) look to the government as the main check on corporate power. The section on "The Rise and Fall of Government Power" presents this view and evaluates this solution to the problem of corporate power. The section "The Power of Galbraith" concludes.

But first, a short historical excursion. Galbraith did his most important work during the third quarter of the 20th century. It was a time of rapid economic growth in the United States, with widely shared benefits. Galbraith sought to understand why economic success occurred at a time of rising corporate power, an anomaly from the perspective of economic theory. In doing so, he turned the views of Joseph Schumpeter on its head.

Capitalism, Socialism and Democracy (Schumpeter, 1942) asked a big question – could capitalism survive? Schumpeter answered "no" – *not* because of capitalism's failures but because of its success in raising living standards. As incomes grew and firms became larger, bureaucrats rather than capitalist entrepreneurs came to run large firms. Rather than taking risks, seeking faster growth, and maximizing profits, managerial bureaucrats prefer steady but slow growth, thereby destroying the dynamic nature of capitalism. In addition, higher incomes make it possible to support a group of middle-class intellectuals, who, by their nature, will criticize capitalism and push for measures to control rising inequality. The result will be rising taxes that reduce incentives for risk taking and innovation.

In contrast to Schumpeter, Galbraith thought capitalism would thrive due to the rise of large firms that produce goods more efficiently, thereby raising living standards throughout the nation. These large firms also possessed considerable economic power. The issue for Galbraith was whether this power was a problem and what (if anything) to do about it, so that nations could enjoy the benefits of affluence brought about by monopolistic firms. Early in his career, Galbraith thought that corporate power would be constrained by other forms of power that evolved in the market economy (countervailing power and the power of the technostructure). Later, he looked for government action to counter the power of large firms. The following sections lay out and critique this evolving analysis of how to restrain economic power under capitalism.

COUNTERVAILING POWER

As World War II (WWII) began, Harvard economist Alvin Hansen raised concerns that the world economy would return to a state of economic depression once the war ended. Without military spending to ensure sufficient demand, firms would hesitate to invest, leading to stagnation and high unemployment. The result would be "sick recoveries which die in their infancy and depressions which feed on themselves" (Hansen, 1939, p. 4) or secular stagnation (Summers, 2016) in today's jargon. Nonetheless, the US economy performed remarkably well following the war. Yes, there was a recession in 1946 when the war ended, but vigorous economic growth soon returned. From the perspective of today, the 1950s and 1960s stand out as the best years of US economic growth – a "golden age of capitalism" (Eichengreen, 1995; Marglin & Schor, 1992). This required an explanation. *American Capitalism* (Galbraith, 1952a) took up the challenge. It held that the efficiency of large firms was responsible for the superior performance of the US economy, a view contrary to nearly 200 years of economic analysis.

Since Adam Smith (1776), most every economist put their faith in competition as the key to an efficient economic system that would improve the living standard of most people. Yet, mergers and acquisitions continually reduced competition and increased firm size, thus enhancing corporate power. This provided a challenge to economic theory, one that was evaded by pointing out that there were few actual monopolies. In the 1930s, Edward Chamberlin (1932) and Joan Robinson (1933) argued that many industries were neither monopolies nor competitive but operated like monopolies. Oligopolistic firms reduced output and hiring. They charged higher prices to consumers because competition no longer disciplined them. Their high profits went to their rich owners. Workers and consumers suffered. Inequality rose.

With rising economic concentration during WWII and the post-war years, liberals proposed that antitrust laws be enforced more rigorously and strengthened. Galbraith (1952a, p. 55) thought this solution impractical because it meant that American capitalism, with a small handful of firms dominating many industries, was largely illegal, and because breaking up large corporations would reduce living standards. Fearing that large corporations were exploiting people, radical economists pushed for greater regulation of large business firms.

Galbraith (1952a, p. 56) felt this was more intervention in the US economy than liberals were ready to accept, making this proposal a non-starter politically. *American Capitalism* provided a way around this dispute. It argued for abandoning antitrust efforts and focusing on the development of countervailing power within the private sector of the economy.

Still, the question remained – why did the US economy perform so well after WWII when oligopolies wielded such great power? *American Capitalism* provided an answer with three components. First, Galbraith (1952a, chapter 7) thought that technical change was *only* possible with large firms that could plan, manage demand, and invest huge sums of money with the hope of a large payoff far in the future. Technical change is what led to efficiency gains in production. It also lowered costs and countered the tendency for oligopolies to raise prices. The result was higher living standards despite the lack of traditional forms of competition. It also meant that managers usurped control of the corporation from owners, who now just passively received dividends (see Berle & Means, 1933). Second, John Maynard Keynes (1936) had developed policies to deal with the problem of inadequate demand and high unemployment (Galbraith, 1952a, chapter 6). If unemployment was high because oligopolies reduced output, the government needed to invest in schools, hospitals, and infrastructure, so that employment was plentiful. This would also counter any downward pressure on wages from high unemployment that stemmed from reduced output or from greater productivity due to the use of new technology. Third, and most important for Galbraith, was the changing nature of competition. Chapter 9 of *American Capitalism,* "The Theory of Countervailing Power," contends that competition no longer comes from other firms within the same industry, producing the same goods. Instead, competition comes from other markets. The rise of countervailing power in these markets restrains the forces that otherwise would reduce wages and increase prices; it keeps large firms from exploiting workers and consumers. Manufacturers must deal with suppliers, as well as retailers. If a manufacturer acquires market power, suppliers have incentives to develop economic power to defend themselves from exploitation and to partake in the gains of monopoly rents. Likewise, labor unions become forces of countervailing power within the firm (Galbraith, 1952a, p. 133). Going further, Galbraith (1952a, p. 117) sees retailers developing countervailing power on behalf of consumers. One can think of Amazon as a contemporary real-world example of this. Finally, even consumers can organize to develop countervailing power. Galbraith (1952a, pp. 126–127) points out that this occurred in Scandinavia, and even in the US with the formation of farmer cooperatives (such as the Grange League Federation of the early 20th century) to purchase supplies and equipment.

Where countervailing power doesn't arise on its own, the state has a role to play (Galbraith, 1952a, chapter 10). It must support the right of labor to organize and aid segments of the economy seeking to develop countervailing power, such as large retail chain stores. In this way, widespread countervailing power would enable everyone to share in the monopoly rents created by oligopolies. If workers gained, if consumers gained, and if firms up and down the supply chain received some monopoly profits, prosperity would prevail throughout the nation.

This rosy view of post-war American capitalism encountered a good deal of criticism. Walter Adams (1953) noted that oligopolies engage in little research and development, the main driving force of technological change. Rather, it is small and medium-sized businesses that are the dynamic forces of innovation. Considerable empirical analysis supports this view (Acz & Audretsch, 1990; Audretsch, Lehmann, & Keilbach, 2006). Adams (1953) and George Stigler (1954, p. 13) noted that countervailing power was far from universal. They both identified the housing sector and farmers as lacking such power, and there were virtually no consumer co-operatives in the United States. Moreover, according to Stigler, bilateral oligopoly redistributes monopoly gains unevenly. If auto dealers reduced the economic power of manufacturers to hike prices, this doesn't help consumers seeking to buy a new car. Instead, car dealers pocket some of the monopoly gains previously made by the manufacturer. Finally, Stigler (1954) and Berle (1953) disputed Galbraith's claim that the state would help disadvantaged groups develop countervailing power. This is a political objection more than an economic objection, and something that we will return to discuss later.

Another problem, raised by Galbraith (1952a, p. 128) himself, is that retail firms would not exercise countervailing power in the interest of consumers during times of high demand and inflationary pressures. This problem is considerably greater than Galbraith himself seemed to recognize. With low unemployment, assured by the success of Keynesian demand policies (something Galbraith assumed in *American Capitalism*), it is not clear how and why countervailing power would operate *at any time*. In a 1960 essay, "Inflation: What it Takes," Galbraith (1970, pp. 59–70) seems to admit this. He contends that inflation arises from the ability of large corporations and unions to control prices due to the lack of price competition. The obvious solution to this problem, some form of wage and price controls, is just the sort of radical policy that Galbraith rejected as politically untenable in *American Capitalism*, although it is worth pointing out that Galbraith had advocated government controls on prices in *A Theory of Price Control* (Galbraith, 1952b), published in the same year as *American Capitalism*.

THE TECHNOSTRUCTURE

While Galbraith abandoned the term "countervailing power" after *American Capitalism*, he never abandoned the idea that lies behind this notion. He still sought to understand how corporations improved economic performance and how their economic power could be countered or constrained so that capitalist economies reap the benefits of large firm size (Parker, 2005, p. 244). In principle, restraint could come either from the public sector or the private sector of the economy. *The New Industrial State* focused on restraints imposed from within the private sector or countervailing power that arises from within the firm itself. Its answer was something Galbraith (1967, chapter 6) called "the technostructure." This idea harkens back to Thorstein Veblen's (1921) engineers, who were enemies of the price system and capitalist predators, and the champions of quality and efficiency. Galbraith's (1967, chapter 8) technostructure was broader than Veblen's class of engineers; it included scientists, marketing and sales experts, managers, as well as all educated employees involved in decision-making processes for the firm. For Galbraith, large firms needed a large technostructure because they needed people with technical knowledge and considerable expertise regarding production, demand, quality, and labor relations. This group of employees countered the power of large corporations.

The New Industrial State argues that power in capitalist economies had shifted from capital, or firm owners, to specialized manpower. By the mid-20th century, power within the firm sat with the technostructure. The rise of the technostructure was due to technology, which required planning to reduce risks, and the ability to wait several years before making profits on an investment. This idea, as we have seen, was present in *American Capitalism*. *The New Industrial State* (Galbraith, 1967, chapter 2) expands on it, explaining how and why technology increases the time between the start and end of a task and also requires specialized knowledge, organization, and planning. The technostructure provides expertise, and it guides the planning efforts of the firm. Such planning is necessary because the market is unstable and unreliable, and because without planning there would be little research and development.

This change has significant economic consequences. With the rise of the technostructure, firms no longer maximize profits (Galbraith, 1967, chapter 10), a point also stressed by post-Keynesian economists (such as Alfred Eichner, 1967). Instead, they seek to maximize the success of the organization. They do this by protecting their investments through planning in order to overcome the uncertainty of markets (Galbraith, 1967, chapter 15) and by ensuring some minimum growth and some minimum level of profits to give the technostructure autonomy (Galbraith, 1967, chapter 17). Moreover, Galbraith (1967, chapter 10) contends that even the top executives of the firm don't want all members of the firm to maximize its profits. If scientists and engineers followed the example set by the economic maximization model, and the maximizing behavior of senior managers, they would sell information to competitors, or go work for competitors, which would hurt the firm and lead to chaos in the economy.

As the technostructure arises and gains power within the firm, antitrust laws become obsolete. Large corporations don't want to exploit other firms as much as they want to engage in planning (Galbraith, 1967, chapter 17). And labor does better working for a large corporation than working for a small firm (Galbraith, 1967, chapter 23) because the firm is not interested in maximizing profits and because the higher prices charged by oligopolists lead to higher wages for labor.

While *The New Industrial State* was positively received in general, critics raised many objections. Several repeated criticisms of *American Capitalism*, maintaining that Galbraith exaggerated the efficiency gains from large firms as well as the economic power they possessed. Others objected to some new ideas in *The New Industrial State* on economic power and the technostructure. David Reisman (1980) noted that Galbraith had no answer to the problem of large firms manipulating consumers, except for general education to make consumers aware of demand creation and the need to resist it. But for Reisman, this is not sufficient. Without emancipating beliefs, something Galbraith (1973, chapter 22) himself later advocated, it is hard to see how consumers can keep from being manipulated and exploited by oligopolies. Myron Sharpe (1973) contended, contra Galbraith, that power in the corporation was still held by senior executives, who hired members of the technostructure, set their pay and benefits, set goals for the firm (and its various parts), and were able to get the results they desired. In support of this position, we can add a contemporary observation. Again, Amazon provides us with a good example. While it has led to lower prices for consumers, it also seeks to maximize profits and is notorious for exploiting workers (Bloodworth, 2018; Geissler, 2018) as well as suppliers.

As with *American Capitalism*, some of the more telling critiques of *The New Industrial State* came from Galbraith himself. Despite championing the technostructure, Galbraith seemed uneasy about its rising power and how it used that power to influence national values through advertising for particular goods and propaganda for private goods in general (Galbraith, 1967, p. 218). Similar to the criticism later made by Reisman, Galbraith (1967, chapter 30) expressed doubt about whether the technostructure would accommodate itself to the social goals of the firm and raised concerns about the loss of aesthetic values in favor of the values of industry. He also bemoaned the useless products given primacy through advertising. This sentiment is perhaps best captured in the famous quote from *The Affluent Society* (published nine years before *The New Industrial State*) about social imbalance (see next section). Given all this, it is not clear how the technostructure could solve the problem of rising power in oligopolistic capitalism.

But perhaps the biggest problem with *The New Industrial State* is that it became obsolete soon after publication, in large part for the reason pointed out by Sharpe. Galbraith (1967, chapter 10) assumed the technostructure would keep CEOs and shareholders under control, as was the case in the decades after WWII. But corporate power revived in the 1970s and the 1980s. In the world of economic ideas, two works were instrumental in this change. Milton Friedman (1970), in a *New York Times* Magazine article, and Michael Jensen and William Meckling (1976) in one of the most influential economic papers ever written, argued that corporations had only one constituency – their shareholders – and that its sole goal was to maximize shareholder value.

In the real world, corporations seemed to follow this advice (or find this path on their own). They became nastier, giving greater rewards to senior executives and shareholders, while giving relatively less to average workers. They outsourced production to low-wage countries, outsourced tasks (like cleaning company offices) to firms in competitive industries (Weil, 2014), and outsourced tasks to single individuals, giving rise to the gig economy. Workers were exploited, and competitive firms were squeezed, in order to increase the profits made by large oligopolies. We can see this change clearly in firm-level data on markups, or the percentage firms charge above cost. While markups remained constant between 1950 and 1980, they rose from 18% above cost in 1980 to 67% above cost in 2015 (De Loecker & Eeckhout, 2017; also see Hall, 2018). We can also see this change in the rise of hostile takeovers in the 1980s, which are nothing more than battles for corporate control (Shleifer & Vishny, 1990), and which mainly redistribute value to shareholders from other firm stakeholders (Shleifer & Summers, 1988).

Other economic data also document a resurgence of shareholder capitalism. Starting around the 1980s, the ratio of CEO pay to average pay in the firm
soared, and senior executives received more stock options so that their interests
and the interests of shareholders would coincide (Mishel & Wolfe, 2019). The top
0.5%, those making more than $2 million a year, received a much larger share
of national income, leaving relatively less for everyone else (Piketty, 2014). And
finally, wages stagnated. From the end of WWII to at least 1973, wage growth and
worker productivity growth moved in tandem. It is somewhat unclear what happened between 1973 and 1980. There was some, but not great, divergence. Since
the 1980s, however, the trend is perfectly clear – worker productivity continued
to increase, but wages (and benefits) flattened. For several decades after WWII,
wages rose with greater worker productivity. Since around 1980, additional
worker productivity increased firm profits, and the incomes of senior executives,
but it did not benefit average employees (Mishel & Bivens, 2021, p. 13).

The technostructure may have wanted steady growth. However, firms followed
Friedman, Jensen, and Meckling; they wanted to maximize returns and paid higher
wages to employees who furthered these ends. The result was a technostructure
bought out with a share of monopoly rents – especially when a large fraction of
the value of their savings (in the form of bonuses and stock options) as well as their
company retirement benefits depended on the share prices of the firm that employed
them. The technostructure thus came to identify with the firm and accepted its
values because they were well paid, even though they didn't fully accept the values
of predator capitalism. They also identified with human capital development, a
doctrine Galbraith (1958, chapter 18) set forth even before the pioneering work
of Gary Becker and Theodore Schultz in the early 1960s that earned them both a
Nobel Prize in Economics (Dunn & Pressman, 2005, p. 189). The technostructure
worked hard to develop its human capital, and thus increase its pay, something that
firms promoted and supported. This, too, encouraged the technostructure to identify with the values promoted by oligopolies. In the end, the technostructure came
to believe that their own rewards were merited based upon their own abilities and
hard work. They sold out in addition to being bought out.

THE RISE AND FALL OF GOVERNMENT POWER

American Capitalism held that labor unions and other firms in the supply chain
would check the market power of large firms. *The New Industrial State* saw
internal forces within the firm restraining the power of oligopolies – the technostructure. In both books, Galbraith thought that the government should help
constrain corporate power, but he also thought that little help was necessary
because the forces constraining oligopolistic power arose naturally. At the same
time, Galbraith recognized that the private sector had difficulty restraining existing corporate power, and he expressed concerns about the technostructure. A new
approach was needed.

The Affluent Society (Galbraith, 1958) laid the groundwork for this new
approach by undermining a main tenet of neoclassical economics – the notion of

scarcity. Its main argument is that we were living in a post-scarcity world. Growth was no longer crucial, as it had been in the 18th and 19th centuries. With scarcity and subsistence wages no longer critical issues, governments could assume responsibility for creating something like countervailing power. This approach took center stage in *Economics and the Public Purpose*, as well as in Galbraith's later works. For example, *The Good Society* (Galbraith, 1996) contends that once basic needs are met, people would focus on the quality of their life or living in a society that provided personal liberty, the right to vote, and the ability to live a rewarding life. A good life also requires some economic security against misfortunes such as becoming unemployed, poor, ill, or too old to work. Liberal government policies were required to achieve this end.

The good news, Galbraith contends, is that in an affluent society, as we consume more and more goods produced by the private sector, we receive less and less satisfaction from each additional good. The fact that advertising is necessary to create private demand shows that the need for many goods is not great and does not arise from within (as standard economic theory holds). This creates two problems. First, rising debt (Galbraith, 1958, chapter 13). Greater debt keeps the economy growing, but there are limits to this. At some point, debt will become too large for consumers to handle. Payment periods can be extended only so long, credit standards can be relaxed only so much, and there are limits to how much debt households can accumulate before it becomes a burden and the debt cannot be repaid. Yet, without this debt, continued economic growth is not possible. It is unfortunate that Galbraith did not pursue this line of inquiry further in his later work, as rising household debt has become a major economic problem (see Pressman & Scott, 2009). Second, the social balance gets disrupted. Years of favoring private production and neglecting the provision of public goods has created a situation of private affluence and public squalor. A much-quoted passage describes this contrast:

> The family which takes its mauve and cerise, air-conditioned, power-steered and power-braked automobile out for a tour passes through cities that are badly paved, made hideous by litter, blighted buildings, billboards, and posts for wires that should long since have been put underground. ... They picnic on exquisitely packaged food from a portable icebox by a polluted stream and go on to spend the night at a park which is a menace to public health and morals. Just before dozing off on an air mattress, beneath a nylon tent, amid the stench of decaying refuse, they may reflect vaguely on the curious unevenness of their blessings. (Galbraith, 1958, 98f.)

The Affluent Society advocates redressing this imbalance by having the government provide more public goods. Of necessity, this means higher taxes. Funds must be diverted from private hands, where they will purchase less-needed commodities, to the public treasury, where they will be used to provide for public needs.

Undoubtedly, *The Affluent Society* was Galbraith's best-received book. *The Guardian* placed put it at #24 on its list of the greatest non-fiction books of all time.[1] However, some commentators raised pointed criticisms of the book. One problem is that economic growth is a positive sum game. With slow growth or no growth, gains by someone require redistribution, which is a zero-sum game. Some benefit but at the expense of others. Slower growth also creates problems because people care about their relative position, something that Galbraith underestimates. As Robert Frank (2011) points out, relative position is important for survival; it increases one's chances to mate and have offspring. Likewise, it impacts decisions such as the size of a car one should buy. While Veblen (1899) emphasized conspicuous consumption as leading to a desire to show that I have more than others, Frank emphasizes that in a car crash, if you drive a bigger car, you are more likely to avoid serious injury and death. This sparks an arms race in car size that no one can win and that makes no one better off; in a world that is rapidly warming, everyone actually becomes worse off.

Another problem is that when Galbraith wrote *The Affluent Society*, the United States was *not* an affluent society for a large part of the population. Poverty was not marginal in the late 1950s, as Galbraith implied. To the contrary, it was invisible, as Michael Harrington (1962) contended, and it affected a large segment of the US population, as we learned when Mollie Orshansky (1965) developed the official US poverty measure and estimated that 22% of Americans were poor in 1959.

Economics and the Public Purpose comes back to the issue of government policy and economic power. It makes a case for government action to remedy the problem of economic power in the private sector. Galbraith (1973) contends that the US economy had become bifurcated. Large firms, part of the "planning system," had acquired enormous economic power. The technostructure still runs these firms and continues to focus on growth rather than profit maximization, according to Galbraith (1973, chapters 9 and 11). They control prices and have substantial resources that enable them to manipulate public opinion. The marketing and advertising undertaken by large firms equates happiness with goods produced by the private sector of the economy. Advertising can also be used to urge the public that environmental damage is imaginary, benign, or being eliminated (Galbraith, [1973] 1975, p. 136).

In contrast, small firms are subject to classical competition or the dictates of the market. They have little economic power and little ability to sway public opinion or the political process. They are at a competitive disadvantage relative to the planning system (Galbraith, 1973, chapters 6–8). The result is unequal economic development – the planning system produces too many goods and the market system produces an inadequate supply of goods. This leads to a new role for government – redressing the imbalance between the oligopolistic and competitive economic sectors. When important economic and social issues are viewed as a conflict between two competing segments of the nation, the state acquires an additional function. It must side with people lacking economic power, and it needs to counter the power of large corporations to promote their goods. Complementing his case in *The Affluent Society* that we need more public goods and fewer private goods, Galbraith wants fewer goods from the planning system and more from the market system. For this to happen, however, Galbraith (1973, chapter 22) recognizes, popular beliefs concerning US capitalism must be emancipated from the convenient social virtues promulgated by the planning sector.

Economics and the Public Purpose was Galbraith's most radical book. It argued for greater government involvement in the economy; it also supported socialism (1973, chapter 27). Reaction to this book was more critical than Galbraith's other major works. One likely reason for this was its dour tone; it was less humorous and less optimistic than the 1950 and 1960 books that made Galbraith famous. Murray Weidenbaum (1973), President Reagan's first Council of Economic Advisors (CEA) chair and a strong advocate of deregulation, accused Galbraith of being inconsistent because he wanted to strengthen the market system and at the same time that he pushed socialism. Charles Hession (1973) thought that Galbraith was not clear about how beliefs could be emancipated or how Congress could be persuaded to pass legislation redressing the power imbalance between small firms and the planning system. Going further, it is worth noting how difficult it is to change people's beliefs, especially when it comes to political issues (Nyhan & Reifler, 2010). But the bigger problem, as alluded to in the previous section, is that Galbraith's brand of liberalism was on the wane in the 1970s. During the last quarter of the 21st century, it went into full retreat, as American capitalism changed in important ways.

Leading liberal Democrats (such as Hubert Humphrey, Ted Kennedy, and Walter Mondale) sat on the sidelines, as the party nominated Jimmy Carter to be their presidential candidate in 1976. As President, Carter began deregulating industries, such as airlines, trucking, and railroads. Airline deregulation reduced the relative earnings of airline workers by 10% between 1980 and 1990, according to David Card (1996). The largest deregulation involved the financial industry, with the Institutions Deregulation and Monetary Control Act of 1980, which paved the way to the rise of finance and the resurgence of predator, shareholder-value capitalism. These actions led to even more deregulation under President Ronald Reagan as well as tax cuts going mainly to the rich, which choked off money for needed social goods. This had further negative socio-economic consequences. As the quality of education fell, the rich used their tax cuts to send their children to private schools. As the environment deteriorated, the rich moved to the few remaining pristine areas, which were protected from pollution to a large extent, by zoning ordinances. Most everyone else was forced to deal with deteriorating schools, unsafe drinking water, and poor air quality. And with less tax revenue, governments were forced to cut funding for higher education, resulting in tuition prices increasing more than any other good or service over the past 40 years. Students thus graduated with more debt, as well as a greater need to adopt the values of corporate capitalism in order to succeed in the world and repay their college loans.

Major changes also took place at the level of the firm. Without liberal Democrats backing labor in the late 1970s, it was easier for capital to reassert itself. Ronald Reagan's election in 1980, and his 1984 re-election in a landslide, both signaled and brought forth a major change in power relations in the United States. Rather than siding with unions, and helping them develop countervailing power, the US government threw labor under the bus. In August 1981, just seven months in office, President Ronald Reagan fired the air traffic control Professional Air Traffic Controllers Association (PATCO) workers who went on strike, not for better pay but for better working conditions so that it would be safer for people to fly. This sent a strong message to labor that the government was not on their side (McCartin, 2012). It led to further declines in unionization, a rise in right-to-work states and, according to Stanbury and Summers (2020, p. 22) a sharp drop in labor rents as a share of non-financial business value added (also see Mishel & Bivens, 2021).

At the same time, businesses began to organize and work together, through groups such as the Business Roundtable and Chamber of Commerce, to influence politics. Both rising corporate power and profits, and lower corporate income taxes, facilitated this change. Corporate contributions to political campaigns increased just as campaign costs rose due to TV; the number of corporate Political Action Committees (PACs) increased steadily, from under 300 in 1976 to more than 1,200 by the mid-1980s (Hacker & Pierson, 2010, p. 118). In addition, conservatives had been attacking the Fairness Doctrine for limiting free speech since the 1970s. Its elimination in 1987 enabled the rise of right-wing media, including Fox News and radio shock jocks such as Rush Limbaugh, where people could say what they wanted without regard to its veracity and without having to present alternative views on controversial issues (Hemmer, 2016).

All of this seems to indicate that Galbraith underestimated the ability of capital to defend its interests, reassert itself, and take power back from the technostructure. What we saw in the late 20th century was not greater power sharing within the firm. Nor was it greater power sharing due to government efforts at redressing social and economic imbalances. Rather, the result was a greater emphasis by large corporations on the bottom line, an attempt to break unions and prevent unions from arising, an attempt to acquire greater political power, and greater inequality in the United States.

What spurred this conservative backlash? At bottom, failure by the government to counter the power of large corporations stems from the role of money in politics or the power of money. Galbraith seems to have underestimated the ability of money to influence the public and government policy and to keep the policies advanced by Galbraith from getting passed and put into effect. This is surprising given his interests in, and his extensive writing on, money and finance (Galbraith, 1954, 1975, 1990), but it is not so surprising given the relatively small role that money played in politics during the golden years of capitalism. Starting in the 1970s and taking off in the 1980s, money fought unions, and money supported right-wing think tanks and conservative economists pushing the virtues of competition and the market, while claiming that everyone would gain from this. At the same time, business interests funded think tanks and university positions that would present a more libertarian perspective of the economic world (Stahl, 2016).

Money also influenced the political process and the political system. *Dark Money* (Mayer, 2016) details how the Koch brothers and other ultra-wealthy conservatives supported efforts at voter suppression. They also sought to influence judicial appointments so that laws passed to help average American families could be overturned in the courts. They supported organizations and legislation that made it more difficult for unions to organize. They pushed for the privatization of government services, including prisons. Their efforts led to gerrymandering, where politicians choose their voters, rather than voters selecting the people they think will best represent their interests in Congress and who will push for legislation that furthers the interests of their constituents rather than their wealthy donors. The Supreme Court ruled in 2018 (*Rucho et al.* v. *Common Cause et al.*) that nothing in the Constitution prohibited such gerrymandering.

When done at the local level, the party that redistricts gets to control the state government. But it also gets to determine how many Democrats and how many Republicans will likely be elected to the US House of Representatives. This can affect the composition of Congress, whether anything gets done there and what gets done there.

Perhaps most important of all, money provided access to elected representatives (Task Force on Inequality and American Democracy, 2004). Based on their voting behavior, members of Congress represent the views of their high-income constituents more than the views of their median income constituents (Bartels, 2008; Gilens, 2012; Hacker & Pierson, 2010). Money also enabled senior executives of large corporations to escape responsibility and punishment for corporate wrongdoing that they sanctioned (Eisinger, 2017). Finally, money made it possible for people to influence government regulators – even the Internal Revenue Service (IRS) (Johnston, 2005, 2008).

THE POWER OF GALBRAITH

Galbraith (1952a, 26f.) thought that talk of power made economists uncomfortable because they typically spoke about free markets without economic power. Power never made Galbraith uncomfortable. He understood that we live in a world where a small number of firms held considerable economic power. With great optimism, he thought this power could be tamed, leading to continued growth and rising living standards. Toward this end, he set forth three theories explaining how corporate power could be controlled for the greater good. First, *American Capitalism* saw countervailing power arising naturally in the private sector of the economy and responding to the power of large firms. Second, *The New Industrial State* looked to the technostructure within the firm to limit the power of oligopolies. Third, Galbraith thought that equalizing power was a major function of government as early as *American Capitalism* (1952a, chapter 10). It could do this through labor legislation or broad government programs such as the New Deal and Fair Deal. Although abandoning neither the notion that the power of large firms had to be countered, nor the belief that the technostructure within the firm would help accomplish this, Galbraith increasingly looked to the government as the main solution to the problem of unequal power. *The Affluent Society* argued that public goods were needed more than private goods in a post-scarcity world. *Economics and the Public Purpose* made the case for government power to counter the power of big business.

Galbraith got three important things right when analyzing economic power. First, we no longer live in a world of scarcity. This was due, in large part, to oligopolistic firms with substantial economic power. Its major consequence is that developed economies could provide everyone with the basic requirements for a good life. The loss of private goods was no longer a life and death situation. Public goods were now more important for living a better life, and higher taxes were needed to achieve this end. Public policy needed to move nations in this direction.

Second, capitalism was different in the post-WWII era. As the US economy thrived, gains were shared widely. Part of the reason seems to be the rise of high-paying, mid-level positions in the growing oligopolistic economic sector, essentially the rise of a technostructure within firms. The technostructure intruded itself between workers and owners, and its presence seemed to impact the behavior of the firm positively. Although women and minorities didn't share equally in the gains during the middle third of the 20th century, real wages increased with greater worker productivity, rather than remaining at bare subsistence levels – no matter how productive workers became. We see this also in a more equal distribution of income in the post-war decades (see Piketty, 2014), and in a rising US middle class during this time period. The third quarter of the 20th century was, indeed, the golden age of capitalism.

Third, Galbraith came to understand that power was unequally distributed. It was unequally distributed between the public and private sectors and also within the private sector itself. In addition, he understood that an institutional sharing of monopoly rents is necessary if prosperity is to be widely shared and be sustainable. Although hopeful, Galbraith became increasingly skeptical that institutions could arise within the private sector to achieve this end. Over time, he came to recognize that government power was needed in order to counter corporate power. This involved buttressing power where power did not exist in the private sector and wielding the power of big government to counterbalance the power wielded by big business.

On the other hand, Galbraith got a few things wrong regarding economic power. First, he was too optimistic when it came to the ability of either the market economy or the public sector to counter corporate power. He had faith that people were at bottom Galbraithians, who would pull levers in the voting booth for liberal Democrats, and that these Democratic politicians would then pass legislation demanded by their constituents. As we have seen, this has not happened. Instead, capital reasserted its power over the firm and over market relations, starting in the late 1970s. In addition, we have seen that the private sector of the economy cannot restrain its own power. Countervailing power does not develop widely on its own. The technostructure is not up for the job – partly because power resides with the owners of capital and partly because when so much money is involved, the interests of the technostructure tend to line up with the interests of capital rather than with the interests of a good society.

Second, the absence of scarcity didn't result in the demise of traditional economics or a greater focus on public goods or aesthetic values. One likely reason for this is that people care about their relative position (Frank, 2011). While affluence means that the majority of the population is not living at the edge of starvation, most people still live paycheck to paycheck, with their needs growing as living standards increase around them and (as Galbraith correctly saw) advertising pushed private goods and the private sector of the economy. In short, the absence of scarcity does not mean we are all affluent. From the perspective of the 18th and 19th centuries, the worlds of Smith and Marx, yes, we are rich. From the perspective of today, that is, not the case. Greater social balance, through more public goods that are financed by higher taxes, does not address this problem.

The battle over economic power still rages today. Currently, it is being fought over issues like income and wealth distribution, tax policy, corporate governance, and voting rights. On many of these issues, Galbraith had important contributions to make. In the end, however, while he saw the revolt of the rentiers that began in the 1970s, and while he wrote many articles and books opposing this revolt, he did not see a viable way forward that would counter this trend or counter the rising power of capital in the late 20th century. This great concern of Galbraith remains our most pressing economic and social problem today.

NOTE

1. www.theguardian.com/books/2017/dec/31/the-100-best-nonfiction-books-of-all-time-the-full-list and https://sites.prh.com/modern-library-top-100?ref=PRHDCE405873 13D&aid=34011&linkid=PRHDCE40587313D

REFERENCES

Acz, Z., & Audretsch, D. (1990). *Innovation and small firms*. Cambridge, MA: MIT Press.

Adams, W. (1953). Competition, monopoly and countervailing power. *Quarterly Journal of Economics, 67,* 469–492.

Audretsch, D., Lehmann, E., & Keilbach, M. (2006). *Entrepreneurship and economic growth*. New York, NY: Oxford University Press.

Bartels, R. (2008). *Unequal democracy: The political economy of the new gilded age*. Princeton, NJ: Princeton University Press.

Berle, A. (1953). American capitalism. *Review of Economics and Statistics, 35,* 81–84.

Berle, A., & Means, G. (1933). *The modern corporation and private property*. New York, NY: Macmillan.

Bloodworth, J. (2018). *Hired: Six months undercover in low-wage Britain*. London: Atlantic Books.

Card, D. (1996). The effect of unions on the structure of wages: A longitudinal analysis. *Econometrica, 64,* 957–979.

Chamberlin, E. (1932). *The theory of monopolistic competition*. Cambridge, MA: Harvard University Press.

De Loecker, J., & Eeckhout, J. (2017). *The rise of market power and the macroeconomic implications*. National Bureau of Economic Research. Cambridge, MA: Working Paper No. 23687.

Dunn, S., & Pressman, S. (2005). The economic contributions of John Kenneth Galbraith. *Review of Political Economy, 17,* 161–209.

Eichengreen, B. (Ed.). (1995). *Europe's post-war recovery*. Cambridge: Cambridge University Press.

Eichner, A. (1976). *The megacorp and oligopoly*. Cambridge: Cambridge University Press.

Eisinger, J. (2017). *The chickenshit club: Why the justice department fails to prosecute executives*. New York, NY: Simon & Schuster.

Frank, R. (2011). *The Darwinian economy: Liberty, competition and the common good*. Princeton, NJ: Princeton University Press.

Friedman, M. (1970). The social responsibility of business is to increase its profits. *New York Times*, September 13.

Galbraith, J. K. (1952a). *American capitalism*. Boston, MA: Houghton Mifflin.

Galbraith, J. K. (1952b). *A theory of price control*. Cambridge, MA: Harvard University Press.

Galbraith, J. K. (1954). *The great crash 1929*. Boston MA: Houghton Mifflin.

Galbraith, J. K. (1958). *The affluent society*. Boston, MA: Houghton Mifflin.

Galbraith, J. K. (1967). *The new industrial state*. New York, NY: New American Library.

Galbraith, J. K. (1970). *The liberal hour*. New York, NY: New American Library.

Galbraith, J. K. [1973] (1975). *Economics and the public purpose*. New York, NY: New American Library.

Galbraith, J. K. (1975). *Money: Whence it came, where it went*. Boston, MA: Houghton Mifflin.

Galbraith, J. K. (1990). *A short history of financial euphoria*. New York, NY: Penguin Books.

Galbraith, J. K. (1996). *The good society: The humane agenda*. Boston, MA: Houghton Mifflin.

Geissler, H. (2018). *Seasonal associate*. Cambridge, MA: MIT Press.

Gilens, M. (2012). *Affluence and influence: Economic inequality and political power in America*. Princeton, NJ: Princeton University Press.

Hacker, J., & Pierson, P. (2010). *Winner-take-all politics*. New York, NY: Simon & Schuster.

Hall, R. (2018). *New evidence on the markup of prices over marginal cost and the role of mega-firms in the US economy*. National Bureau of Economic Research. Cambridge, MA: Working Paper 24574.

Hansen, A. (1939). Economic progress and declining population growth. *American Economic Review, 29*, 1–15.

Harrington, M. (1962). *The other America*. New York, NY: Penguin.

Hemmer, N. (2016). *Messengers of the right: Conservative media and the transformation of American politics*. Philadelphia, PA: University of Pennsylvania Press.

Hession, C. (1973). Four reviews of John Kenneth Galbraith: Economics and the public purpose. *Journal of Economic Issues, 9*, 90–93.

Jensen, M., & Meckling, W. (1976). Theory of the firm: Managerial behavior, agency costs, and ownership structure. *Journal of Financial Economics, 3*, 305–360.

Johnston, D. C. (2005). *Perfectly legal: The covert campaign to rig our tax system to benefit the super rich – And cheat everybody else*. New York, NY: Penguin.

Johnston, D. C. (2008). *Free lunch: How the wealthiest Americans enrich themselves at government expense (and stick you with the bill)*. New York, NY: Penguin.

Keynes, J. M. (1936). *The general theory of employment, interest and money*. London: Macmillan.

Marglin, S., & Schor, J. (Eds.). (1992). *The golden age of capitalism: Reinterpreting the postwar experience*. Oxford: Oxford University Press.

Marx, K. (1976). *Capital: A critique of political economy* (Vol. I). Harmondsworth: Penguin Books.

Marx, K. (1978). *Capital: A critique of political economy* (Vol. II). Harmondsworth: Penguin Books.

Marx, K. (1981). *Capital: A critique of political economy* (Vol. III). Harmondsworth: Penguin Books.

Mayer, J. (2016). *Dark money*. New York, NY: Doubleday.

McCartin, J. (2012). *Collision course: Ronald Reagan, the air traffic controllers, and the strike that changed America*. Oxford: Oxford University Press.

Mishel, L., & Bivens, J. (2021). *Identifying the policy levers generating wage suppression and wage inequality*. Washington, DC: Economic Policy Institute.

Mishel, L., & Wolfe, J. (2019). *CEO compensation has grown 940% since 1978: Typical worker compensation has risen on 12% during that time*. Washington, DC: Economic Policy Institute.

Nyhan, B., & Reifler, J. (2010). When corrections fail: The persistence of political misperception. *Political Behavior, 32*, 303–330.

Orshansky, M. (1965). Counting the poor: Another look at the poverty profile. *Social Security Bulletin, 28*, 3–29.

Parker, R. (2005). *John Kenneth Galbraith: His life, his politics, his economics*. New York, NY: Farrar, Straus & Giroux.

Piketty, T. (2014). *Capital in the twenty-first century*. Cambridge, MA: Harvard University Press.

Pressman, S., & Scott, R. (2009). Consumer debt and the measurement of poverty and inequality in the US. *Review of Social Economy, 47*, 127–146.

Reisman, D. (1980). *Galbraith and market capitalism*. New York, NY: NYU Press.

Robinson, J. (1933). *The economics of imperfect competition*. London: Macmillan.

Schumpeter, J. (1942). *Capitalism, socialism and democracy*. New York, NY: Harper & Brothers.

Sharpe, M. (1973). *John Kenneth Galbraith and the lower economics*. White Plains, NY: International Arts and Sciences Press.

Shleifer, A., & Summers, L. (1988). Breach of trust in hostile takeovers. In A. Auerbach (Ed.), *Corporate takeovers: Causes and consequences* (pp. 33–56). Chicago, IL: University of Chicago Press.

Shleifer, A., & Vishny, R. (1990). The takeover wave of the 1980s. *Science, 249*, 745–749.

Smith, A. (1776). *An inquiry into the nature and causes of the wealth of nations*. Indianapolis, IN: Liberty Classics.

Stahl, J. (2016). *Right moves: The conservative think tank in American political culture since 1945*. Chapel Hill, NC: University of North Carolina Press.

Stanbury, A., & Summers, L. (2020). The declining worker power hypothesis: An explanation for the recent evolution of the American economy. *Brookings Papers on Economic Activity*, No.1, 1–77.

Stigler, G. (1954). The economist plays with blocs. *American Economic Review, 44*, 7–14.

Summers, L. (2016). The age of secular stagnation: What it is and what to do about it. *Foreign Affairs,* *95,* 2–9.

Task Force on Inequality and American Democracy. (2004). American democracy in an age of rising inequality. *Perspectives on Politics, 2,* 651–666.

Veblen, T. (1899). *A theory of the leisure class.* New York, NY: Macmillan.

Veblen, T. (1921). *The engineers and the price system.* New York, NY: B.W. Huebsch.

Weidenbaum, M. (1973). Four reviews of John Kenneth Galbraith: *Economics and the public purpose. Journal of Economic Issues, 9,* 87–90.

Weil, D. (2014). *The fissured workplace.* Cambridge, MA: Harvard University Press.

CHAPTER 3

CONSUMER SOVEREIGNTY IN THE DIGITAL SOCIETY

Alexandre Chirat

ABSTRACT

Do digital technologies of early 21st century capitalism promote or reduce consumer sovereignty? This chapter addresses this question by examining John Kenneth Galbraith's critique of consumer sovereignty during the post-war period of industrial society and looks at the insights he provides to understand the impact of platform capitalism on consumer sovereignty today. This chapter has the following sections: (1) I review the main postulates of Galbraith's theory; (2) I highlight the main differences between traditional advertising and online behavioral advertising; (3) I explain how online behavioral advertisement strengthens Galbraith's dependence effect and revised sequence theories; (4) I then discuss normative challenges raised by digital platform corporations to individual sovereignty; and (5) finally, I argue that platform capitalism is a mature form of Galbraith's "new industrial state."

Keywords: Consumer sovereignty; online behavioral advertising; digital economics; platform capitalism; digital platform corporations; John Kenneth Galbraith

Research in the History of Economic Thought and Methodology: Including a Symposium on John Kenneth Galbraith: Economic Structures and Policies for the Twenty-First Century
Research in the History of Economic Thought and Methodology, Volume 41C, 35–54
Copyright © 2024 by Emerald Publishing Limited
All rights of reproduction in any form reserved
ISSN: 0743-4154/doi:10.1108/S0743-41542024000041C003

INTRODUCTION

Contemporary societies are going through a digital revolution that is significantly changing their institutions and organizations. A ubiquitous part of digital technology is online advertisements. Online advertisements play a prominent and vital role in digital technology affecting organizations and consumers. Digital advertising, which can substitute or complement offline advertising, is taking a larger share of the advertisement market, rising from 15% in 2010 to 48% in 2018 (Silk & Berdt, 2020, p. 17). The leading digital platform corporation, Google (Alphabet), receives 85% of its earnings from its advertising activities (Helberger, Huh, Milne, Strycharz, & Sundaram, 2020, p. 379).

While digitalization has dramatically reduced information costs, it has also blurred the difference between advertising and other information-producing activities with its ability to microtarget groups or individuals, thanks to granular consumer data.[1] This makes the technology useful for advertisement and political campaigns (Dommett & Power, 2019). In the 2014 US midterm election, 1.8 billion dollars was spent on digital media campaigns, representing 20% of total media expenditure. In the 2018 midterms elections, it rose to 40%. This shows that digital advertisement and microtargeting play an ever-increasing role in influencing consumers, voters, and individual behavior. The question I want to pursue is the impact of the digital society on consumer sovereignty, particularly the role of online advertisements. To help explore this question, I turn to John Kenneth Galbraith and his work on the industrial state and consumer sovereignty.

The digital revolution is playing a significant role in moving capitalism from Galbraith's "new industrial state" (Galbraith, 1967) to "platform capitalism" (Boyer, 2022; Marciano, Nicita, & Ramello, 2020; Montalban, Frigant, & Jullien, 2019).[2] The emergence of online advertisements, which aim at "monitoring people's online behavior" (Helberger et al., 2020, p. 401), has raised concerns about consumer sovereignty, individual privacy, consumer protection, and antitrust laws. The same issues Galbraith was concerned about with the development of industrial corporations after World War II (Galbraith, 1958, 1967). One of Galbraith's primary concerns was how corporate industrialization impacted consumer sovereignty through advertisement. The same question should be asked today with platform capitalism. Yet, the scholarly work in digital economics focuses mostly on the effects of costs (Goldfarb & Tucker, 2019) and largely ignores the challenges that online advertisement poses to consumer sovereignty.[3] Efforts to look at the impact of digital advertisement on consumer sovereignty are found more in marketing, law, and information journals than in economics. And within these journals, all accept the mainstream definition of consumer sovereignty.

The principle of consumer sovereignty is that consumers' free choice determines the allocation of resources in competitive markets, which hinges on three hypotheses. First, the individual is the best judge of their preferences. Second, welfare is defined by preference satisfaction. Third, the individual seeks information to maximize the satisfaction of their preferences. The principle of consumer sovereignty is a "central normative principle in contemporary assessments of economic policies and systems" (Penz, 1987, p. 1). It has been at the core of mainstream economics, from classical welfare economics to contemporary behavioral economics (Hédoin, 2017; Infante, Lecouteux, & Sugden, 2016; Lecouteux, 2021; Lerner, 1972; Penz, 1987; Persky, 1993). Digital platform corporations like Google justify online advertisement as fitting within the boundaries of consumer sovereignty. Hal Varian, who operates as Google's chief economist, stated that competition between digital platforms is doing what it should. Google performs better than its competitor Bing, showing "fewer, more relevant ads at a lower cost per click" due to competition. He also claimed that "competition among tech firms is working well" (2021, p. 3). David Evans, who founded the consulting firm Market Platform Dynamics, also concluded in his literature review for *The Journal of Economic Perspectives*, "After all, the online advertising industry increases the likelihood that consumers will receive relevant ads and decreases the likelihood that they will waste time on irrelevant ads" (Evans, 2009, p. 57). From these experts, it appears that online behavioral advertisement generates the Leibnizian best of all possible digital worlds.

John Kenneth Galbraith might have demurred the "culture of contentment" and "conventional wisdom" of these economic experts.[4] However, more importantly, he would criticize their grasp of reality. Galbraith's analysis of corporate power, particularly in *The Affluent Society* (1958) and *The New Industrial State* (1967), constitutes a fruitful starting point for a fresh analysis of digitization and advertisement and their impact on consumers. Although Galbraith, like Veblen and other institutionalists, considered that any economic theory is bound to become obsolete because of historical changes, Galbraith's insights about the evolution of industrialization and its relation to consumer theory are as useful today as when he looked at industrialization and consumer sovereignty in the 1950s and 1960s. Galbraith helps us look at the impact of digital technologies on consumer sovereignty with a different lens that is much needed.

To look at the influence of digit online advertisement on consumer sovereignty, I will first review the main aspects of Galbraith's theory of consumption in the industrial age. I then discuss the main differences between traditional and online behavioral advertisement. Thus, I explain how online behavioral advertisement follows Galbraith's *dependence effect* and *revised sequence* and raises normative challenges to individual sovereignty. Lastly, I discuss some prospects on the importance of digital platform corporations and how it is a mature form of the "new industrial state" (Prospects on the Political Economy of Platform Capitalism Section).[5]

GALBRAITH'S THEORY OF CONSUMPTION AND ADVERTISING

Influenced by the works of Veblen (1923), Clark (1923), and Chamberlin (1965 [1933]), who shared a common interest in the integration of salesmanship practices and alteration of consumers preferences into economic analysis, Galbraith provides an examination of consumption, as a social fact, rather than an analysis of consumer behavior as an individual act.[6] His theory builds on the hypothesis of endogenous preferences that individual preferences are context dependent, shaped by patterns, and evolving. Galbraith's view of endogenous preferences did not accept the distinction in mainstream economics between true/false, rational/ irrational, and informed/uninformed preferences (Chirat, 2020). According to Galbraith, since preferences are partly the product of social persuasion, advertisement is more than just whether it is true or false (Galbraith, 1982).

Galbraith's theory of consumption in an industrial society is based on three main ideas. The first is the *dependence effect* (1958, p. 129). This effect depends on the assumption that some wants are conventionally judged more urgent than others within a given society. It argues that the less urgent wants are, the more susceptible they are to being molded by advertisement. The more affluent a society is, the more unsatisfied wants of little urgency there are. Galbraith's idea is that an increasing number of wants "depends on the process by which they are satisfied" in an affluent society. A rise in the standard of living makes the dependence effect more relevant.[7]

Galbraith's second fundamental tenet about consumption is his *social imbalance thesis*. He argued that "public services have failed to keep abreast of private consumption" in the United States. The consequence is "an atmosphere of private opulence and public squalor" (Galbraith, 1958, p. 191). His analysis of social imbalance comes from his *dependence effect*, where advertisement, besides providing information, shapes and alters consumers' wants (Chirat, 2020). Galbraith did not dismiss the importance of individual preferences but insisted that you also need to look at the economic, historical, and social patterns that shape them. For example, in the United States, advertisement focuses on private over public consumption, contributing to a social imbalance between private and public goods. In addition, consumers can only demand what the market supplies. Yet public goods are inadequately supplied compared to private goods. That, in part, is why consumer sovereignty is not an accurate description of how resources are allocated within an industrial society.[8]

This leads us to the third central tenet of Galbraith's theory of consumption, which he called *the revised sequence* (1967). In *The New Industrial State*, Galbraith argued that in an economic system ruled by large corporations, "producer sovereignty" rules. The supply side of the "market" is the real driver of the economic process. The consumer is free to choose, but only between goods corporations have chosen to produce. Consumers confront a restricted choice set. Consumer sovereignty means the power to determine the choice set, which corporate power restricts. That is why advertisement plays a vital role in corporate power over consumers (Chirat, 2022a). It decides the choice set and, through advertisement, persuades consumers that their preferences are satisfied by the type of goods they produce.

In classical economics, advertisement is considered more informative than persuasive.[9] As an informative activity, it provides consumers with knowledge and thus allows them to make better-informed decisions. Nonetheless, the leading representatives of the neoclassical synthesis in the post-war era, such as Paul Samuelson in his *Economics* (1964) or James Meade (1968) and Robert Solow

(1967) in their reviews of *The New Industrial State*, argued that advertisement is a wasteful activity. Advertising competition is wasteful since customers of one firm are attracted to another and vice versa.[10] For this reason, Meade and Solow argued that advertisements should be taxed. Galbraith challenged both the classical and neoclassical arguments on advertisements. First, Galbraith endorsed the view of his friend Nicholas Kaldor, who said that "all advertising is persuasive in intention and all is informative in character" (1950). What type of advertisement we see and how it is presented is not simply based on trying to match goods with consumer preferences but also to form intimate links with how corporations want to arrange our desires for their products. Second, Galbraith challenged the idea that advertisement competition is a waste for firms.[11] Following Veblen (1923), Galbraith explained that advertisement affects the economic system at three levels: firm, industry, and macroeconomics. Advertisements increase the demand for goods the firm wants to produce at the expense of better-quality substitutes. For corporations, advertisement is a means to reduce market uncertainty and create a specific level of demand for their products. It thus helps corporations' technostructure achieve the ends of their planning and investments. It also plays an "organic role" in an economic system where macroeconomic growth is the ultimate goal, with consumption pushing it.

WHAT IS DIFFERENT WITH ONLINE BEHAVIORAL ADVERTISING?

To understand Galbraith's critique of advertisement and consumer sovereignty in an industrial state and how it relates to a digital society, we must look at the difference between traditional and online (behavioral) advertisement. Goldfarb (2014) claims that the literature discussing online advertisement does not "suggest a new purpose for advertising." However, he adds that "the fundamental economic difference between online and offline advertising is a substantial reduction in the cost of targeting" (2014, p. 115). What is not mentioned digital advertising can increase the exploitation of consumers' vulnerabilities more than traditional advertising methods (Susser, Roessler, & Nissenbaum, 2019), for "manipulation no longer concerns biases generally present in the population but biases specific to each micro-segment of consumers or even to each consumer" (de Marcellis-Warin, Marty, Thelisson, & Warin, 2022, p. 262). It does this by transforming an impersonal social act of persuasion into a highly personalized one.

Since the digital economics literature takes for granted that the main difference between online and offline advertisement is the precision of its targeting particular individuals raises Galbraith's concern about whether advertisement is informative or persuasive. Some experts praise online behavioral advertisements for the information it provides. It is "more informative" than traditional advertisement because of trying "to improve the informativeness of advertising" (Tucker, 2012, p. 326). Informativeness refers to the idea that an ad provides information on the material and technical characteristics of the product. But Tucker's statement remains questionable, even if targeting advertising could help consumers confront an information overload created in a digital society. The link between the use of data and the amount of informativeness advertisement offers is not straightforward. First, data are collected by digital platform corporations to target consumers more specifically. That means the information provided is biased and based on individual prejudices and the corporation's goals.

Second, following Woodcock (2018), digital technologies' drastic reduction in information cost "renders most advertising obsolete as a tool for conveying product information." Consumers can easily acquire product information online by themselves, so "advertising remains useful for firms only as a tool for persuading consumers to purchase advertised products" (Woodcock, 2018, p. 272). Third, empirical studies suggest that digital advertisements delivered through social media affect the "linguistic style" and the "emotional contagion" rather than the informativeness of the message (Evans, Phua, Lim, & Jun, 2017; Lee & Theokary, 2021; Lou & Yuan, 2019). All these arguments favor the relevance of Kaldor's (1950) opinion that "all advertising is persuasive in intention."

Some have argued that digitalization empowers consumers. Kucuk (2016) stresses how some digital devices and practices improve the rights of the consumer as defined by the 1960 consumers' Bill of Rights, namely the "right to be informed," the "right to choose," the "right to be heard" and the "right to safety" (2016, p. 519). Helberger et al. (2020, p. 380) claimed that "Consumers in the computational advertising ecosystem are not only media content receivers and target audience of ads but also take more active roles, namely, the role of the advertiser or creator and active distributor of ad content." The system of consumer recommendations, which is fundamental in the functioning of platforms as various as Airbnb, Amazon, and Google, illustrates the active role that consumers can play in the digital society.

Consumers provide their comments and recommendations not just to close friends and family members but to other consumers searching for online information. Helberger et al. (2020) add that consumers are also

> more influential than before because the implicit and observed data they generate, which are inferred from observed behavior rather than data supplied by the consumer themselves, are critical input and enablers for the algorithmics process and feedback loops that help to adjust advertising to personal preferences. (2020, p. 380)

This benefits consumers' welfare by improving the quality and relevance of the information they receive, thanks to the digital platform's attention to consumers' past behaviors and experiences.

Critics can challenge such a vision of such an active consumer. First, the targeting process relies on the appropriation, aggregation, and evaluation of data by digital platform corporations, which raises the question of respect for consumer privacy. This concern is even more notorious as privacy preferences are highly context dependent (Acquisti, Brandimarte, & Loewenstein, 2015; Yeung, 2017). The infringements on individual privacy as well as the opacity of Google's algorithms are such that Zuboff (2019) diagnosed the emergence of "surveillance capitalism," which "aims to predict and modify human behavior as a means to produce revenue and market control" (Zuboff, 2015, p. 75). Second, the shift from an industrial society with mass advertising to a digital society with mass targeted advertisement is not necessarily synonymous with greater autonomy. Targeted advertising can indeed reduce "choice and awareness of competing products and services that are not being recommended, making it difficult for providers of alternative services and products to reach consumers" (Helberger et al., 2020, p. 380). This is all the more relevant with the internet of objects and "algorithm consumers" who "simply replace humans in making such [consumption] choices" (Gal & Elkin-Koren, 2017, p. 313). Third, high personalization generates feelings of alienation and heteronomy (Boerman, Kruikemeier, & Zuiderveen Borgesius, 2017; Plangger & Montecchi, 2020). Fourth, if it is true that "targeting works when subtle" (Lewis & Reiley, 2014, p. 21), then online behavioral advertising is inversely correlated with consumers' knowledge and autonomy. Following Susser et al. (2019), one might consider that online behavioral advertising is a manipulative practice *par excellence*.[12] Fifth, even search advertisement, which requires active requests emanating from consumers, impairs consumers' agency since search platforms can control or influence the result of the search process itself (Goldfarb & Tucker, 2019). In light of these observations, Galbraith's concepts of *the dependence effect* and *the revised sequence* are still relevant to understand how resources are allocated in the digital society as they were in an industrial one.

The dependence effect states that an increasing number of wants "depends on the process by which they are satisfied" is more relevant in the digital society since the process hinges on the data collection by digital platform corporations generated by the satisfaction of past wants. Galbraith emphasized that advertisements alter wants to satisfy corporations' objectives.[13] The effect of an online behavioral advertisement does precisely that. Behavioral economists like Richard Thaler and Cass Sunstein (2008) of nudge agree (de Marcellis-Warin et al., 2022; Frischmann, 2022; Yeung, 2017). Recently, Sunstein has redefined nudge as "private or public initiatives that steer people in a particular direction but that also allow them to go their own way" (2022, p. 659).[14] This is precisely what traditional advertisement, as well as behavioral advertisement, do. Yet, since online behavioral advertising relies on continuous feedback, Yeung (2017) claims that it corresponds to an "hypernudge ... by configuring and thereby personalizing the user informational choice context, typically through algorithmic analysis of data streams from multiple sources and claiming to offer predictive insights concerning the habits, preferences, and interests of targeted individuals," online behavioral advertising enables to "channel user choices in directions preferred by the choice architect," namely digital platform corporations (Yeung, 2017, p. 119). Moreover, targeting also opens the way toward personalized pricing policy mediated through algorithms designed to segment demand (Thornton & Danaher, 2018). Such discriminatory pricing policy might impair consumer welfare because corporations can confiscate consumer surplus (de Marcellis-Warin et al., 2022, p. 262).[15]

Galbraith's theory of consumption led to the conclusion that the consumer has freedom of choice among a given choice set in the affluent society. However, they were not sovereign since sovereignty precisely means the power to determine such a choice set. He argued that power lay in the hands of corporations in an industrial society. We can find the same concerns in a digital society. First, the choice set is still determined by corporations. But with digital platform corporations, they can operate a double selection (Dholakia, Darmody, Zwick, Dholakia, & Fırat, 2021), not only as advertising publishers but more generally as information producers. They determine the choice set presented to consumers (boosted choice set) and discretionary design the presentation of that set (frame of the choice environment). For example, Ariely and Lynch (2000) demonstrated that in the online wine market, price becomes a less important determinant of consumers' choice if the price does not rank among the information immediately available. Whereas mass advertising sustains corporation sovereignty by determining the available choice set, mass personalized advertising enables digital platform corporations to reshape the choice set made available by traditional corporations, as illustrated by Fig. 3.1.

The activities of digital platform corporations, which act as information producers, generate a process of selecting a subset of the available choice set produced by traditional corporations. Fig. 3.1 illustrates a specific subset (black box) of conventional corporations' choice set of products (gray box). Moreover, they select the presentation frame of such boosted choice set (discontinuous line). The satisfaction of wants thanks to consumption generates data (arrows) on consumed products (point in the black box), which traditional corporations use to target their future choice set of products. Meanwhile, through data extraction and analysis, digital platform corporations exert contextual and behavioral targeting to select the choice set they boost and how they frame it. Based on continuous feedback, this process is consequently prone to generate a reduction of choice open to consumers (narrower boxes). Because of consumer targeting, digital platform corporations eventually seem prone to generate "filter bubbles" (Pariser, 2011).[16] Studying online news consumption, Flaxman, Goel, and

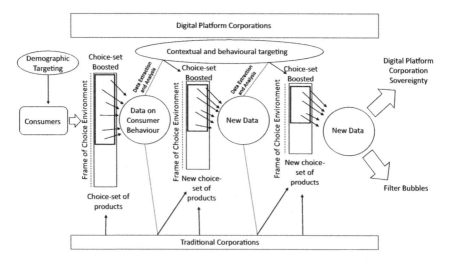

Fig. 3.1.   The Dynamics of the Consumers' Space of Choice in the Digital Society.

Rao (2016, p. 318) observed that "articles found via social-media or web search engines are indeed associated with higher ideological segregation than those an individual reads by directly visiting news site." However, they also stressed that online news consumption increases the exposition "to opposing perspectives" and that consumers have potential access to a wide range of both products and information on products than before.

This is the *raison d'être* of digital platform corporations as information producers since opening the space of choice by removing physical constraints on consumption generates demand for reducing it. It also follows Woodcock's (2018) diagnosis that advertising has become obsolete as a provider of information. Yet, gathering new information about news or products requires spending an incredible amount of time online gathering, processing, and checking information. In addition, the process does not free the consumer from the power of digital platform corporations that control the results of search engines. This allows the filtering of the informational content given to consumers and creates the discretionary frame to exploit consumers' cognitive biases at a very personalized level. This is how digital platform corporations exert sovereignty over the allocation of resources and provide an incentive structure that discourages consumers' freedom of choice.

This does not mean that consumers are puppets of digital platform corporations. In *The Powerful Consumer* (1960), George Katona, a pioneer of behavioral economics with Herbert Simon, challenged Galbraith's thesis of consumption behavior in an affluent society. Katona disagreed with Galbraith's representation of the consumer as a passive agent. Katona's "powerful consumer" refers to consumer's income and affluence. With abundance, Katona believes that consumer choices are more likely to depend on their willingness to buy and thus on their discretion since their consumption behavior is less constrained by biological necessities.[17] The consumer is even more powerful in the digital society since living standards have risen and information costs have dropped. In addition, some consumers with significantly high numerical literacy can use devices such as adblockers to de-moderate the effect of behavioral advertising. Still, this begs the question of why consumers must spend so much time and resources navigating and protecting themselves from manipulative platforms and whether they can win the battle. The spread of behavioral advertisements also raises several other normative concerns.

NORMATIVE CONCERNS RAISED BY BEHAVIORAL ADVERTISING

We know that the digitalization of the economy transforms economic, social, and political structures. There are good reasons to question the legitimacy of its influence. The test for economists who adhere to consumer sovereignty is whether it allows the best possible satisfaction of individuals' preferences and welfare. The digital society has failed the test for the same reasons Galbraith gave for the industrial society, that is, endogenous preferences, dependence effect, and revised sequence. Galbraith provided alternative criteria to evaluate consumer sovereignty in an industrial society that we can use in a digital society. Joan Robinson once argued that Galbraith's economics "lacks the moral beauty of the old orthodoxy" (1952,

p. 928). Not providing a criterion as clear as the Pareto principle explains her judgment. Nonetheless, in *American Capitalism* (1952), Galbraith provides a normative stance: There needs to be a balance of power between industrial corporations and other economic agents such as small businesses, unions, farmers, and consumers. Neoclassical economics suggests how to deal with corporate power with antitrust laws. Galbraith questioned their efficiency (Chirat, 2022a). Oligopoly being the rule rather than the exception, he considered antitrust laws "anachronism." If useful, he saw them as insufficient and required, as during the New Deal and World War II, direct "social control of business" (Rutherford, 2015).

Within the digital society, the structure of digital platform corporations is oligopolistic. For this reason, antitrust laws have already been used several times. Yet, Google, Amazon, Facebook, Apple, and Microsoft and some others still enjoy vast market power. Such market power has already generated social control measures, such as establishing the General Data Protection Regulation (GDPR) in Europe and efforts to protect consumers' and citizens' privacy (European Commission, 2020, pp. 57–58). Such measures have proved to be insufficient to compensate for the power asymmetry between digital platform corporations and individuals. A recent proposal made by de Marcellis-Warin et al. (2022, p. 263), of using "counter-algorithms" to re-equilibrate "the informational balance to benefit consumers without aggravating their informational overload" echoes Galbraith's countervailing powers. The problem is, who would create and manage these counter-algorithms? The emergence of countervailing powers faces a specific problem in digital society. In *The New Industrial Society*, Galbraith explained that big unions could emerge spontaneously in front of the power of industrial giants. No countervailing force seems to have emerged and, more importantly, to organize itself within the digital society. The various movements of contestation against digital platform corporations have not given birth to organizations where workers and managers reached "social compromises" (Duménil & Lévy, 2018; Galbraith, 1967). In addition, there are no social groups united in their opposition to the activities of digital platform corporations, which would be able to form a "dominant social bloc" (Amable & Palombarini, 2022).

When countervailing power did not emerge spontaneously in front of the original power of corporations, Galbraith (1952) urged the state either to foster the building of countervailing powers or to regulate the activities of corporations directly. Yet, throughout his trilogy (Galbraith, 1952, 1958, 1967), he gradually departed from using the state to endorse a more radical view inherited from Veblen (Chirat, 2023). This change happened because he analyzed the bureaucratic symbiosis between industrial corporations and public agencies. Given the symbiosis in "market-led platform capitalism,"[18] countervailing actions undertaken by the state would depend on the concentration of the asymmetries with digital platform corporations and how successful the state can be.

A strong voice against Galbraith's view was Chicago economist George Stigler (1954), who criticized every book he wrote and the vagueness of countervailing power as a normative criterion. In a letter to Stigler, Galbraith responded that his "value criteria involve minimization of social tensions rather than maximization of real consumer income."[19] Galbraith saw the neoclassical normative criterion – the *principal* of consumer sovereignty – as appropriate for a widespread poverty world. "The increased real income of consumers was the simple test of improved welfare." But this is no longer the case since "an opulent society can afford to sacrifice material well-being for social contentment" (1954, pp. 2–3). Hence, he emphasized a social balance between public and private goods in *The Affluent Society* to achieve social contentment between different socioeconomic groups. While Galbraith stressed that the disparity between public squalor and private opulence was "no matter of subjective judgement," he explicitly lamented this imbalance by introducing a normative distinction between human needs in terms of their relative urgency (Chirat, 2022). Galbraith manifested a conventionalist approach of needs (Penz, 1987), namely that basic needs are those whose social conventions stipulate that without them, one cannot live with dignity. These same concerns are still relevant today in a digital society – how should platform capitalism respond to what the members of a society considered as basic human needs?

I have shown how digital platform corporations have the power to alter through boosting and framing the choice set panel we confront as consumers. The activities of digital platform corporations determine the social ends pursued in the digital society. This point is brought out by Cédric Durand, who convincingly argues that "Big data" are "institutions" mastering big data extraction and analysis to "pursue their ends, unrelated to those that the affected communities might pursue" (Durand, 2020, pp. 126–127). As Galbraith did for industrial corporations, digital platform corporations exert a de facto social responsibility and should be held accountable. Because of the practice of targeted advertisement and the use of "hypernudge," Yeung argues that online behavioral advertising contradicts the "core liberal idea of personality articulated with personal autonomy," which "demands that individuals be allowed to choose and pursue their different plans or paths of life for themselves without interference from others" (Yeung, 2017, p. 129).[20] The behavior of digital platform corporations might be condemnable on moral grounds regarding the means employed to interfere with individual preferences – notwithstanding the predatory means used by digital platform corporations to take over "behavioral surplus" (Zuboff, 2019) and their consequences on personal and social learning (Frischmann, 2022). The very process of microtargeting indeed contradicts the liberal ideal of autonomy and liberty. Galbraith's argument that individual preferences are partly endogenously determined explains the importance of social persuasion. His response is that we should first analyze the formation of preferences rather than take them for granted.[21] The more aware individuals are of the causes that determine their behavior, the freer they are. But such awareness requires investigation of the political economy of platform capitalism.

PROSPECTS ON THE POLITICAL ECONOMY OF PLATFORM CAPITALISM

To produce his "integral economics," Galbraith merged his theory of consumption with his institutionalist theory of the corporation as a planning unit ruled by a technostructure (Chirat, 2022a; Galbraith, 1984). He argued that the mature corporation aims at reducing market uncertainties. Administered prices and hierarchical (rather than market) coordination figured among the primary means to limit uncertainty and thus achieve its production plans. A significant component of a firm's uncertainty is expected demand. This explains why the technostructure of corporations supported state regulation of aggregate demand at the macroeconomic level and specific demand at the industry and firm levels through advertising expenditure (Galbraith, 1967). In the digital society, conditioning demand through online behavioral advertisement plays an organic role in limiting the effects of market uncertainty. We have seen that digital platform corporations lie at the heart of this process through data extraction, aggregation, and commercialization. The very business of digital platform corporations finds its origin as economic actors to curb uncertainty. I would even argue that the whole historical process toward modern civilization attempts to reduce uncertainty. And this trend will not stop. In this regard, platform capitalism appears as a mature form of the "new industrial state," one main difference being that digital platform corporations, rather than traditional corporations preside largely over the allocation of resources in the economy.

Traditional corporations, as advertisers, digital platform corporations, as content publishers, could have diverging interests. Levin and Milgrom (2010) stressed that advertising platforms might be interested in withholding granular data from advertisers to increase their revenues. In addition to information asymmetry, digital platform corporations also benefit from an asymmetry of power. For instance, Google, with its search engine listed at the top of the search results of its own services like price comparison tools rather than those offered by competitors (Calvano & Polo, 2021).[22] Moreover, two advertisers spending the same amount of money would not necessarily reach the same number of targets. Facebook uses a "pay to play" (rather than "pay to click") model for targeted advertisement, which is combined with an auctioning model prioritizing "content which is more engaging" (Dommett & Power, 2019, p. 263). The power of digital platform corporations exercised over traditional corporations and small businesses are also revealed in *Prediction Machines* (Agrawal, Gans, & Goldfarb, 2018). The authors emphasize how firms depend on analyzing data collected by digital platform corporations to control expected demand effectively. Firms that do not collect data should buy "the prediction that the data generates" to "identify high-value customers" and "avoid advertisement to low-value customers" (2018, pp. 175–177). Not doing so would put them at a competitive disadvantage. This is especially required for a newcomer in any industry since access to vast data is essential for entering the market (Agrawal et al., 2018, pp. 175–177).

The quantity of data required to improve the value of predictive analysis and targeted advertising provided by digital platform corporations raises the fundamental question of returns to scale and market power. In line with Chamberlin (1965 [1933]) and Schumpeter (1942), Galbraith argued that the nature of competition had changed since the last decade of the 19th century. Price competition has been gradually replaced by monopolistic competition, an oligopolistic market structure combined with product differentiation (Chirat & Guicherd, 2022). Galbraith (1967) saw the productive superiority of the mature corporation due to returns to scale, which sustain its market power as a means to reach the technostructure's objectives (Baudry & Chirat, 2018). Today, a wide consensus in digital economics claims "that large data bases can lead to natural economies of scale and network effects, which potentially generate market power" (Goldfarb, 2014, p. 125). Since the effectiveness of online behavioral advertising is, above all, based on the quantity of data collected and analyzed, "companies with larger (and unique) customer bases will increase their advantage over time without any innovations beyond effective use of an increasingly larger database" (Goldfarb, 2014, p. 125). We should recall that traditional advertisement created entry barriers (Bain, 1956), caused by two kinds of returns to scale: "lower prices paid for advertising message" and "greater effectiveness of a larger volume of messages in terms of its impact on potential buyers, which may be due to the increased impact of repeated messages" (Comanor & Wilson, 1979, p. 467). Online behavioral advertising leverages these features of traditional advertising.

The economic system of the digital society ultimately experiences a double concentration process. First, the online advertising industry is highly oligopolistic. In 2020, Google represented over three quarters of search advertising, and Google and Facebook accounted for more than 50% of all digital advertisements (Rauch, 2021, p. 149). Second, online behavioral advertising favors established corporations with the means to be big advertisers or publishers since the more data collected, the more efficient targeted advertising will be (Lewis & Rao, 2015). This channel explains the "superstar effect" (Elberse & Oberholzer-Gee, 2006). Increasing returns to scale and concentration on both the advertisers and the publishers' sides have mixed theoretical effects on mark-ups and, thus, prices (Eeckhout & Veldkamp, 2022). In the industrial society, Tibor Scitovsky (1962) argued that returns to scale and oligopoly "destroy the main merit of the market economy," as described by Milton Friedman (1962) and others, of consumer sovereignty. Data and online behavioral advertising can neglect consumer preferences since they can reallocate production toward more profitable goods and services. Thus, the functioning of the economy within the digital society directly runs counter to the implementation the principle of consumer sovereignty, which has been the cornerstone of welfare economics and the main argument for a legitimate free-market economy (Chirat, 2022b).[23]

The effects of an oligopolistic market structure on innovation are complex. Contrary to Schumpeter, Galbraith never equated the entrepreneurial with innovation, which in an industrial state falls in the hands of engineers in the technostructure (Baudry & Chirat, 2018). Large industrial corporations foster innovation because of their market power, which allows them to spend money on R&D. Because of the profits they generate, large corporations might go on shaping the technological and organizational future. But they might also be victims of laziness and routinization that some economists attribute to monopolies. The course of history remains open. What is certain is that the innovations that gave birth to the digital society were developed by government agencies or in close relationship with them, as explained by Mazzucato in *The Entrepreneurial State* (2013).[24] The analysis of the "bureaucratic symbiosis," especially of the industrial–military complex in the cold war context, between private corporations and public administrations, is at the heart of Galbraith's analysis of 20th century American capitalism. Galbraith's symbiosis has to be considered to understand the success of digital platform corporations, thanks to the support of military and intelligence services during the post-cold war period (Zuboff, 2019).

CONCLUSION

This chapter has argued that the activities of digital platform corporations have reduced consumer sovereignty by partly determining the available choice set that consumers face. In addition, it has been argued that the bureaucratic symbiosis between digital platform corporations and governments extends to the political realm. An example was the tight relationship between the Obama Administration and Google's technostructure (Zuboff, 2019) and the Cambridge Analytica scandal (Susser et al., 2019). For the same reasons digital platform corporations infringe on consumer sovereignty, they also infringe on citizen sovereignty. Digital platform corporations have the hand tools to alter the result of elections or referendums.[25] Mounk (2018) argues that their political involvement has reinforced the polarization and democratic deconsolidation observed in Western countries. Like online targeting of consumers, which is prone to generate a polarization of consumer choices through filter bubbles, online targeting of citizens favors political and ideological polarization that can impair the functioning of the democratic process. Because preferences are endogenous, Galbraith concluded that political propaganda could no longer appear as an imperfection of democracy but a constitutive feature (Chirat, 2022b). The business model of corporations such as Google and Facebook fosters a particular kind of propaganda of being "sensitive to popularity but indifferent to truth" (Rauch, 2021, p. 125).

NOTES

1. Goldfarb and Tucker defined digitalization as "the representation of information in bits" (2019, p. 3).
2. I use the expression "platform corporation" for two main reasons. First, following Galbraith, I use corporation, rather than firm, since I refer to large (successful) companies. Second, the qualificative "platform" allows to distinguish corporations whose core activities lay in digitalization from "traditional" corporations, in particular industrial ones. The main platform corporations are the GAFAM and BATX.
3. To see the issue raised up, one has to turn his eyes toward papers, sometimes written by economists but published in journals in the fields of marketing, law, information and big data (see Darmody & Zwick, 2020; de Marcellis-Warin et al., 2022; Dholakia et al., 2021; Grafanaki, 2017; Helberger et al., 2020; Marciano et al., 2020; Susser et al., 2019; Yeung, 2017; Zuboff, 2015).
4. I am tempted to add that Galbraith would also warn us, as he did in the industrial society context (1967), of the risk that vested interests of platform corporations invade the "Educational and Scientific Estate." Dealing with that problem of economists capture, Zingales interestingly explains that "one factor that can reduce capture is access to data that is independent from industry" (2013, p. 2). Digital economics is one of the fields in economics where it is rarely the case, in particular with respect to empirical studies on online

advertising. For instance, Lewis and Rao (2015), who published a noteworthy contribution in *The Quarterly Journal of Economics*, were working for Amazon, Netflix, and Google for the former and Microsoft and Booking for the later.

5. This paper also contributes to a literature stressing the contemporary relevance of Ken Galbraith's economics. Dunn put forward its accuracy with evidence from the Tobacco Industry and the Food Industry (Dunn, 2010; Dunn & Anderson, 2006). Lamdin (2008) highlighted its empirical relevance, by stressing the positive correlations between changes in advertising expenditures, consumer credit, and consumption of goods and services, especially durables. In the framework of a Dynamic Stochastic General Equilibrium (DSGE) model of the economy, Molinari and Turino (2018) also observed that an increase in advertising leads, in the long run, to an increase in worked hours, Gross Domestic Product (GDP) and investment – "the underlying mechanism operating through a work and spend channel." Lastly, Dutt (2008) recalled that many recent studies have challenged "the fact that increases in consumption and income – at least significantly – affect happiness as evaluated by the consumers themselves" (2008, p. 236).

6. It is based on previous paper, where the complete justification of what follows stands (Chirat, 2020).

7. Obviously, as Galbraith already explained, his concept does not mean that poverty has disappeared in affluent societies.

8. Galbraith figured among the postwar social scientists who conceptualized the main features, as an ideal type, of the industrial society (see Chirat, 2019).

9. On the functions of advertising, especially the opposition between information and persuasion, see Kaldor (1950). For a synthesis on more recent developments, see Bagwell (2007). Interestingly, Woodcock (2018) highlights that the US Supreme Court has endorsed this "informative view of advertising in 1976, extending First Amendment protection to advertising on the explicit ground that a 'free enterprise economy' requires 'informed' consumers" (2018, p. 2273).

10. As early as 1923, Veblen explained that advertising is a zero-sum game between competitors of an industry only if the size of the industry market is given. In the context of an infant industry, he emphasized that the first-mover advantage in a market can be enhanced by advertising because a product is then likely to be directly associated with a particular brand. He then explained that advertising expenditures are contained within limits. The lower limit is set by the compositional effect of the competitive behavior of the players. A company cannot lower its advertising budget too far below that of others. As for the upper limit, it depends on the evolution of marketing costs in relation to sales prices, since a firm must maintain a certain level of profit (Veblen, 1923, pp. 303–305).

11. Galbraith also considers that advertising generates a form of waste, but this waste is not due to a pure economic loss. It is rather due to its consequences on the allocation of resources (the social imbalance).

12. Whereas persuasion and coercion work by appealing to the target's capacity for conscious decision making, manipulation attempts to subvert that capacity. It neither convinces the target (leaving all option open) nor compels the target (eliminating all options but one). Instead, it interferes with the target's decision-making process in order to steer them toward the manipulator's ends (2019, p. 17).

13. See, for instance, Lerner's paradigmatic defense of consumer sovereignty (Lerner, 1972).

14. This catch-all definition of nudge erases the idea of nudge as a paternalist device promoting the well-being of the nudged agent. Advertising is a nudge used in the interest of the nudging agent. For these reasons, the term "sludge" or "dark nudge" has been used to refer to it. See, for instance, de Marcellis-Warin et al. (2022).

15. The important costs of exit in platform capitalism might also impair consumers welfare since they do not benefit from "the central mechanisms of competition in free markets: free choice among alternative offers" (Marciano et al., 2020, p. 349).

16. "When you enter a filter bubble, you're letting the companies that construct it choose which options you're aware of. You may think you're the captain of your own destiny, but personalization can lead you down a road to a kind of informational determinism in which

what you've clicked on in the past determines what you see next – a Web history you're doomed to repeat. You can get stuck in a static, ever narrowing version of yourself – an endless you-loop" (Pariser, 2011, p. 14).

17. On Katona and Galbraith relationship, see Edwards (2014) and Chirat (2022a).

18. Here, I refer to Boyer's expression of "market-led platform capitalism" in order to distinguish US platform capitalism from Chinese platform capitalism, which is led by a state party. For more details, see Boyer (2022).

19. Letter from Galbraith to Stigler, November 24, 1953, John Kenneth Galbraith personal papers, Series 3, Box 9.

20. From an ecological conception of rationality, Gigerenzer (2015, p. 361) also critics libertarian paternalists for putting "the blame on individuals' minds rather than on external causes, such as industries that spend billions to nudge people into unhealthy behavior."

21. Cass Sunstein (2017) has proposed his own reformulation of the notion of consumer sovereignty and political sovereignty. He precisely argued that consumer sovereignty implies that "individual tastes" are "fixed or given," whereas political sovereignty does not. Since Sunstein's suggestion that the digital society is not at odd with consumer sovereignty but only with citizen sovereignty rests on such challengeable definition of consumer sovereignty, I did not discuss it here.

22. Hence, some condemnations in Europe for abuse of dominant position, by the European Commission (in 2017 and 2019) and the Autorité de la Concurrence in France (in 2021).

23. This claim contradicts the "long tail" effect diagnosed by Anderson (2006) regarding cultural industries. Discussing the empirical relevance of Anderson's thesis, Benghozi and Benhamou (2010) reach the conclusion that "the wealth of diversity on offer can lead to a narrowing of the range of choices, as consumers turn away from the vast number of choices available." The increasing use of online behavioral advertising might explain this tendency. Interestingly, recent empirical studies on music streaming corroborate the idea that platform corporations alter consumers choices (Aguiar, Waldfogel, & Waldfogel, 2021), even if the effect on diversity appears mixed for this particular market (Bourreau, M., Moreau, F., & Wikström, P. (2022).

24. On the mutation from Galbraith's new industrial state to Mazzucato's entrepreneurial state, see Nogueira-Centenera (2020).

25. Referring to some empirical studies, this power of altering political outcome is presented as inexistent by Mercier (2020, p. 139). The treatment of the effects of behavioral advertising in general are, however, too slight to be fully convincing, especially when Mercier argued that "if advertising effectiveness is so difficult to measure, it is not for technical reasons but because ads have small effects at best" (2020, p. 141). The issue of the effects, at least in the economic realms, of targeted advertising cannot be treated in isolation and at the individual level only, as shown by Galbraith's political economy.

REFERENCES

Acquisti, A., Brandimarte, L., & Loewenstein, G. (2015). Privacy and human behavior in the age of information. *Science, 347*(6221), 509–514.

Agrawal, A., Gans, J., & Goldfarb, A. (2018). *Prediction machines: The simple economics of artificial intelligence*. Brighton, MA: Harvard Business Press.

Aguiar, L., Waldfogel, J., & Waldfogel, S. (2021). Playlisting favorites: Measuring platform bias in the music industry. *International Journal of Industrial Organization, 78*, 102765.

Amable, B., & Palombarini, S. (2022). *Multidimensional social conflict and institutional change*. New Political Economy, 1–16.

Anderson, C. (2006). *The long tail: Why the future of business is selling more for less*. New York, NY: Hyperion.

Ariely, D., & Lynch, J. G., Jr. (2000). Wine online: Search costs affect competition on price, quality, and distribution. *Marketing Science, 19*(1), 83–103.

Bagwell, K. (2007). The economic analysis of advertising. *Handbook of Industrial Organization, 3*, 1701–1844.

Bain, J. S. (1956). *Barriers to new competition*. Cambridge, MA: Harvard University Press.

Baudry, B., & Chirat, A. (2018). John Kenneth Galbraith et l'évolution des structures économiques du capitalisme: D'une théorie de l'entrepreneur à une théorie de la firme? *Revue Économique, 69*(1), 159–187.

Benghozi, P. J., & Benhamou, F. (2010). The long tail: Myth or reality? *International Journal of Arts Management*, 43–53.

Boerman, S. C., Kruikemeier, S., & Zuiderveen Borgesius, F. J. (2017). Online behavioral advertising: A literature review and research agenda. *Journal of Advertising, 46*(3), 363–376.

Bourreau, M., Moreau, F., & Wikström, P. (2022). Does digitization lead to the homogenization of cultural content? *Economic Inquiry, 60*(1), 427–453.

Boyer, R. (2022). Platform capitalism: A socio-economic analysis. *Socio-Economic Review, 20*(4), 1857–1879.

Calvano, E., & Polo, M. (2021). Market power, competition and innovation in digital markets: A survey. *Information Economics and Policy, 54*, 100853.

Chamberlin, E. H. (1965 [1933]). *The theory of monopolistic competition* (8th ed.). Cambridge, MA: Harvard University Press.

Chirat, A. (2019). La société industrielle d'Aron et Galbraith: Des regards croisés pour une vision convergente? *Cahiers D'economie Politique, 1*, 47–87.

Chirat, A. (2020). A reappraisal of Galbraith's challenge to consumer sovereignty: Preferences, welfare and the non neutrality thesis. *The European Journal of the History of Economic Thought, 27*(2), 248–275. E

Chirat, A. (2022a). *L'Économie intégrale de John Kenneth Galbraith (1933–1983)* Paris: Classiques Garnier, coll. bibliothèque de l'économiste.

Chirat, A. (2022b). Démocratie de la demande versus démocratie de l'offre: Reconstruction et interprétation des analogies démocratie-marché. *conomia. History, Methodology, Philosophy, 12*(1), 55–91.

Chirat, A. (2023). When Berle and Galbraith brought political economy back to life: Study of a cross-fertilization (1933–1967). *History of Political Economy, 55*(4), 639–676.

Chirat, A., & Guicherd, T. (2022). Oligopoly, mutual dependence and tacit collusion: The emergence of industrial organisation and the reappraisal of American capitalism at Harvard (1933–1952). *The European Journal of the History of Economic Thought, 29*(1), 112–145.

Clark, J. M. (1923). *Studies in the economics of overhead costs*. Chicago, IL: University of Chicago Press.

Comanor, W. S., & Wilson, T. A. (1979). The effect of advertising on competition: A survey. *Journal of Economic Literature, 17*(2), 453–476.

Darmody, A., & Zwick, D. (2020). Manipulate to empower: Hyper-relevance and the contradictions of marketing in the age of surveillance capitalism. *Big Data & Society, 7*(1), 2053951720904112.

de Marcellis-Warin, N., Marty, F., Thelisson, E., & Warin, T. (2022). Artificial intelligence and consumer manipulations: From consumer's counter algorithms to firm's self-regulation tools. *AI and Ethics, 2*(2), 259–268.

Dholakia, N., Darmody, A., Zwick, D., Dholakia, R. R., & Fırat, A. F. (2021). Consumer choicemaking and choicelessness in hyperdigital marketspaces. *Journal of Macromarketing, 41*(1), 65–74.

Dommett, K., & Power, S. (2019). The political economy of Facebook advertising: Election spending, regulation and targeting online. *The Political Quarterly, 90*(2), 257–265.

Duménil, G., & Lévy, D. (2018). *Managerial capitalism: Ownership, management and the coming new mode of production*. London: Pluto Press.

Dunn, S. P. (2010). *The economics of John Kenneth Galbraith: Introduction, persuasion, and rehabilitation*. Cambridge: Cambridge University Press.

Dunn, S. P., & Anderson, S. J. (2006). JK Galbraith's challenge to the accepted sequence: The management of the consumer. *Revista Econômica, 8*(2), 337–351.

Durand, C. (2020). *Technoféodalisme: Critique de l'économie numérique*. Brooklyn, NY: Zones.

Dutt, A. K. (2008). The dependence effect, consumption and happiness: Galbraith revisited. *Review of Political Economy, 20*(4), 527–550.

Edwards, J. M. (2014). Consumer power and market control: Exploring consumer behaviour in affluent contexts (1946–1980). *The European Journal of the History of Economic Thought, 21*(4), 699–723.

Eeckhout, J., & Veldkamp, L. (2022). *Data and market power*. Working Paper No. 30022. National Bureau of Economic Research, Cambridge, MA.

Elberse, A., & Oberholzer-Gee, F. (2006). *Superstars and underdogs: An examination of the long tail phenomenon in video sales* (Vol. 7). Boston, MA: Division of Research, Harvard Business School.

European Commission. (2020). Directorate-General for research and innovation. In A. Ezrachia & M. Stuckeb (Eds.), *Digitalisation and its impact on innovation*. Luxembourg: Publications Office of the European Union.

Evans, D. S. (2009). The online advertising industry: Economics, evolution, and privacy. *Journal of Economic Perspectives, 23*(3), 37–60.

Evans, N. J., Phua, J., Lim, J., & Jun, H. (2017). Disclosing Instagram influencer advertising: The effects of disclosure language on advertising recognition, attitudes, and behavioral intent. *Journal of Interactive Advertising, 17*(2), 138–149.

Flaxman, S., Goel, S., & Rao, J. M. (2016). Filter bubbles, echo chambers, and online news consumption. *Public Opinion Quarterly, 80*(S1), 298–320.

Friedman, M. (1964). *Capitalism and freedom*. Chicago, IL: University of Chicago Press.

Frischmann, B. (2022). Nudging humans. *Social Epistemology, 36*(2), 129–152.

Gal, M. S., & Elkin-Koren, N. (2016). Algorithmic consumers. *Harvard Journal of Law & Technology, 30*, 309.

Galbraith, J. K. (1952). *American capitalism: The concept of countervailing power*. Oxford: Basil Blackwell.

Galbraith, J. K. (1954). Countervailing power. *The American Economic Review, 44*(2), 1–6.

Galbraith, J. K. (1958). *The affluent society* (40th anniversary ed.). Boston, MA: Houghton Mifflin.

Galbraith, J. K. (1967). *The new industrial state* (4th ed.). Princeton, NJ: Princeton University Press.

Galbraith, J. K. (1982). *The anatomy of power*. Boston, MA: Houghton Mifflin.

Galbraith, J. K. (1984). Galbraith and the theory of the corporation. *Journal of Post Keynesian Economics, 7*(1), 43–60.

Goldfarb, A. (2014). What is different about online advertising? *Review of Industrial Organization, 44*(2), 115–129.

Goldfarb, A., & Tucker, C. (2019). Digital economics. *Journal of Economic Literature, 57*(1), 3–43.

Grafanaki, S. (2017). Drowning in big data: abundance of choice, scarcity of attention and the personalization trap, a case for regulation. *Rich. JL & Tech., 24*(1), 1–66.

Hédoin, C. (2017). Normative economics and paternalism: The problem with the preference-satisfaction account of welfare. *Constitutional Political Economy, 28*(3), 286–310.

Helberger, N., Huh, J., Milne, G., Strycharz, J., & Sundaram, H. (2020). Macro and exogenous factors in computational advertising: Key issues and new research directions. *Journal of Advertising, 49*(4), 377–393.

Infante, G., Lecouteux, G., & Sugden, R. (2016). Preference purification and the inner rational agent: A critique of the conventional wisdom of behavioural welfare economics. *Journal of Economic Methodology, 23*(1), 1–25.

Kaldor, N. (1950). The economic aspects of advertising. *The Review of Economic Studies, 18*(1), 1–27.

Katona, G. (1960). *The powerful consumer; Psychological studies of the American economy*. New York, NY: McGraw-Hill.

Kucuk, S. U. (2016). Consumerism in the digital age. *Journal of Consumer Affairs, 50*(3), 515–538.

Lamdin, D. J. (2008). Galbraith on advertising, credit, and consumption: A retrospective and empirical investigation with policy implications. *Review of Political Economy, 20*(4), 595–611.

Lecouteux, G. (2021). Behavioral welfare economics and consumer sovereignty. In C. Heilmann & J. Reiss (Eds.), *The Routledge handbook of philosophy of economics* (pp. 56–66). London: Routledge.

Lee, M. T., & Theokary, C. (2021). The superstar social media influencer: Exploiting linguistic style and emotional contagion over content? *Journal of Business Research, 132*, 860–871.

Lerner, A. P. (1972). The economics and politics of consumer sovereignty. *The American Economic Review, 62*(1/2), 258–266.

Levin, J., & Milgrom, P. (2010). Online advertising: Heterogeneity and conflation in market design. *American Economic Review, 100*(2), 603–607.

Lewis, R. A., & Rao, J. M. (2015). The unfavorable economics of measuring the returns to advertising. *The Quarterly Journal of Economics, 130*(4), 1941–1973.

Lewis, R. A., & Reiley, D. H. (2014). Online ads and offline sales: Measuring the effect of retail advertising via a controlled experiment on Yahoo! *Quantitative Marketing and Economics, 12*(3), 235–266.

Lou, C., & Yuan, S. (2019). Influencer marketing: How message value and credibility affect consumer trust of branded content on social media. *Journal of Interactive Advertising, 19*(1), 58–73.

Marciano, A., Nicita, A., & Ramello, G. B. (2020). Big data and big techs: Understanding the value of information in platform capitalism. *European Journal of Law and Economics, 50*(3), 345–358.

Mazzucato, M. (2013). *The entrepreunarial state: Debunking public vs private sector myths*. London. Anthem Press.

Meade, J. E. (1968). Is "the New Industrial State" inevitable? *The Economic Journal, 78*(310), 372–392.

Mercier, H. (2020). *Not born yesterday. The science of who we trust and what we believe*. Princeton, NJ: Princeton University Press.

Molinari, B., & Turino, F. (2018). Advertising and aggregate consumption: A Bayesian DSGE Assessment. *The Economic Journal, 128*(613), 2106–2130.

Montalban, M., Frigant, V., & Jullien, B. (2019). Platform economy as a new form of capitalism: A régulationist research program. *Cambridge Journal of Economics, 43*(4), 805–824.

Mounk, Y. (2018). *The people vs. democracy*. Cambridge, MA: Harvard University Press.

Nogueira-Centenera, A. (2020). Empresarios, innovación y Estado en John K. Galbraith y Mariana Mazzucato. *Revista de Economía Institucional, 22*(42), 109–125.

Pariser, E. (2011). *The filter bubble: How the new personalized web is changing what we read and how we think*. New York, NY: Penguin.

Penz, G. P. (1987). *Consumer sovereignty and human interests*. London: Cambridge University Press.

Persky, J. (1993). Retrospectives: Consumer sovereignty. *Journal of Economic Perspectives, 7*(1), 183–191.

Plangger, K., & Montecchi, M. (2020). Thinking beyond privacy calculus: Investigating reactions to customer surveillance. *Journal of Interactive Marketing, 50*, 32–44.

Rauch, J. (2021). *The constitution of knowledge: A defense of truth*. Washington, DC: Brookings Institution Press.

Robinson, J. (1952). Review of American capitalism: The concept of countervailing power. *The Economic Journal, 62*(248), 925–928.

Rutherford, M. (2015). Institutionalism and the social control of business. *History of Political Economy, 47*(Suppl. 1), 77–98.

Samuelson, P. A. (1964). *Economics*. New York, NY: McGraw-Hill Book Company.

Schumpeter, J. A. (1942). *Capitalism, socialism and democracy*. New York, NY: Harper.

Scitovsky, T. (1962). On the principle of consumers' sovereignty. *The American Economic Review, 52*(2), 262–268.

Silk, A., & Berndt, E. R. (2020). *Aggregate advertising expenditure in the US economy: What's up? Is it real?* No. w28161. National Bureau of Economic Research, Cambridge, MA.

Solow, R. M. (1967). The new industrial state or son of affluence. *Public Interest, 9*, 100–108.

Stigler, G. J. (1954). The economist plays with blocs. *The American Economic Review, 44*(2), 7–14.

Sunstein, C. R. (2017). *# Republic*. Princeton, NJ: Princeton University Press.

Sunstein, C. R. (2020). Sludge audits. *Behavioural Public Policy, 6*(4), 654–673.

Susser, D., Roessler, B., & Nissenbaum, H. (2019). Online manipulation: Hidden influences in a digital world. *Georgetown Law Technology Review, 4*, 1.

Thaler, R. H., & Sunstein, C. R. (2008). *Nudge*. New Haven, CT: Yale University Press.

Thornton, P., & Danaher, J. (2018). *On the wisdom of algorithmic markets: Governance by algorithmic price*. Working Paper https://philpapers.org/archive/THOOTW-2.pdf.

Tucker, C. E. (2012). The economics of advertising and privacy. *International Journal of Industrial Organization, 30*(3), 326–329.

Varian, H. R. (2021). Seven deadly sins of tech? *Information Economics and Policy, 54*, 100893.

Veblen, T. B. (1923). *Absentee ownership and business enterprise in recent times: The case of America*. New York, NY: B.W. Huebsch.

Woodcock, R. A. (2018). The obsolescence of advertising in the information age. *The Yale Law Journal, 127*, 2270–2341.

Yeung, K. (2017). 'Hypernudge': Big data as a mode of regulation by design. *Information, Communication & Society*, *20*(1), 118–136.

Zingales, L. (2013). *Preventing economists' capture.* Chicago Booth Research Paper, No. 13-81, pp. 1–35

Zuboff, S. (2015). Big other: Surveillance capitalism and the prospects of an information civilization. *Journal of Information Technology*, *30*(1), 75–89.

Zuboff, S. (2019). *The age of surveillance capitalism.* New York, NY: Public Affairs.

CHAPTER 4

JOHN KENNETH GALBRAITH'S SOCIAL BALANCING THEORY IN THE 21ST CENTURY

Eric Scorsone

ABSTRACT

John Kenneth Galbraith's social balance theory is an important theme in many of his books, particularly The Affluent Society, The New Industrial State, *and* Economics and the Public Purpose. *Galbraith's social balance theory states that forces driving private consumption in an industrial society will out-pace the development and provision of public goods and services with consequences on the well-being of society (Stanfield, 1996, p. 49). The theory leads to several questions: (1) What is the specific relationship between private and public goods and consumption? (2) What is optimized with social balancing? (3) Does the relationship between private and public goods change over time? and (4) How do we evaluate the types of public goods we need? This chapter explores these questions and examines the type of public goods we need today to serve our communities better. For example, police presence and activities in many minority communities are now viewed negatively, as evidenced by the "defund the police" movement. Conversely, some have advocated for greater public spending on community mental health programs and new initiatives to deal with racism in communities.*

Keywords: Social balance; federal spending; public goods; techno structure; affluent society; societal well-being

Research in the History of Economic Thought and Methodology: Including a Symposium on John Kenneth Galbraith: Economic Structures and Policies for the Twenty-First Century
Research in the History of Economic Thought and Methodology, Volume 41C, 55–71
Copyright © 2024 by Emerald Publishing Limited
All rights of reproduction in any form reserved
ISSN: 0743-4154/doi:10.1108/S0743-41542024000041C004

INTRODUCTION

John Kenneth Galbraith's most famous book, *The Affluent Society,* was
published in 1958 with four additional editions. A core theory of the book
is the social balance theory. A famous quote from the book summarizes his
theory perfectly:

> the family which takes its mauve and cerise, air-conditioned power steered and power braked
> automobile out for a tour passes through cities that are badly paved, made hideous by lit-
> ter, blighted buildings, billboards and posts for wires that should long since have been put
> underground. They pass on into a countryside rendered largely invisible by commercial art.
> (Galbraith, 1958, p. 192)

Galbraith observed that post-war industrial society prioritized private goods
over public goods, leading to a social imbalance. America's ever-burgeoning
private economy was not in balance with the public goods needed to improve
social welfare, particularly persistent poverty. *The Affluent Society* was written
at the height of the Cold War with increased corporate influence and the beginning of a new stage in social welfare. Historically, there have been three phases
in government social welfare programs. The dominant view in the 19th century
of the government's role is to provide social security through military and law
enforcement (night watchmen function) and provide basic infrastructure and
public works. A second phase began in the late 19th century and continued well
through the first half of the 20th century with social welfare legislation first
introduced by German Chancellor Bismarck. Social welfare programs included
old-age insurance, workers' accident insurance, survivor's pensions, unemployment insurance, government-provided health insurance, and family allow-
ance plans (Rimlinger, 1971). Other countries followed, particularly during
the Great Depression of the 1930s when wide scale adoption of social welfare
programs was universally accepted in Western economies. A third phase began
after World War II with environmental regulations, civil rights, and expanding
social welfare programs like Medicare and Medicaid in the 1960s with President
Johnson's *Great Society.*

These different phases can be partially tracked by examining the US government's spending over time. The following Chart 4.1 depicts the overall change in
US federal government spending from the late 1800s through the early 21st century. The period of 1850 through 1900 is averaged together but represents almost
no real growth or change in expenditures.[1] Federal spending did not noticeably
increase during the progressive era of the 1900s and 1910s. Spending bumped
up in World War I but then fell back down. As expected, there was a colossal
spike in government spending during World War II and then a significant reduction in the late 1940s. Government spending saw a steady upturn in the 1950s.
The Korean War and Cold War were partly to explain but also ongoing investments in public infrastructure and social welfare programs.[2] Galbraith argued
that despite increasing government spending in the 1950s and 1960s, relative deprivation existed between different populations and economic groups, causing a
social imbalance.

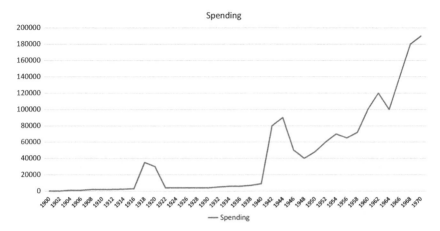

Chart 4.1. US Aggregate Federal Spending (1850–2022).

J.K. GALBRAITH'S THEORY OF SOCIAL BALANCE

Galbraith created the social balance theory in response to the significant economic growth in the US economy after World War II. Several factors created a social imbalance between private and public consumption. Galbraith looked specifically at two, which he called the *dual economy* and *consumer dependence* that underpin his social balance theory. The Galbraithian *dual economy* is divided into two sectors. The first sector he called the planned economy (name used in *Public Purpose and Economics*) or the technostructure (name used in *The New Industrial State*), and the second sector represented small firms in the market economy. The market economy comprised small producers subject to price-taking behavior with little power over suppliers or consumers. They constituted the largest part of the economy and wielded the least power. Conversely, the planned economy comprises large firms that exert market power and engage in strategic planning to secure that power. Large firms wield dominance relative to consumers and other producers. Galbraith spent much of his career documenting the nature and use of corporate power and how to countervail it to achieve a social balance.

The definition of small businesses has varied over time, but generally, they have few employees and are price takers. Large businesses, on the other hand, have large revenues, can generate sales, and have many employees. Data provide a context of corporations' changing economic structure and power in the United States. In 1955, General Motors held the Number 1 position in business ranking; US Steel, Number 3; and General Electric, Number 4. By 1970, General Motors remained Number 1, General Electric was still 4th, and US Steel fell to 12th. From 1955 to 1970, corporate power changed toward technology-driven firms like AT&T and IBM. In 1955, AT&T ranked 15, and by 1970, it ranked 11. IBM moved from 61 in 1955 to a ranking of fifth in 1970. By 2021, the firms of *Fortune 500* changed dramatically from industry to technology and service. Traditional powerhouses of American industry, such as General Motors, had fallen to 25th. The biggest companies now were retailers such as Walmart and Amazon, along with health insurance and health-care companies like CVS, United HealthCare, McKesson, and Amerisource. Today, we have a class of highly influential companies known as the "big five," which include Microsoft, Amazon, Alphabet (Google), Meta (Facebook), and Apple. These companies significantly influence the makeup and dynamics of the US economy.[3]

The big five emphasizes another important Galbraithian term, *the dependence effect*. The dependence effect states that consumer preferences are not fixed but are shaped by the producer side of the market. That is, consumer demand is partly endogenous to the firm's marketing and influence. This power is enhanced even more today in the era of "surveillance capitalism," a term by Shoshana Zuboff to describe the new powers technical firms have over consumers in a digital society (Zuboff, 2019, p. 8). Companies of the mid-20th century could only imagine having the algorithmic power and pricing discrimination abilities of the technology companies of the 21st century. The *dual economy* and the *dependence effect* helped create the conditions for social imbalance. Firms in the planning or technostructure have expertise in driving and motivating consumer demand for private goods over public consumption for their own benefit. Although modified in the 21st century, the Galbraithian *dual economy* and the *dependence effect* remain intact today.

THE AFFLUENT SOCIETY INTRODUCES
SOCIAL BALANCING THEORY

Social balancing first appeared in *The Affluent Society* in Chapter 27. In Part 2 of the chapter, Galbraith gives us the definition: "It will be convenient to have a term which suggests a satisfactory relationship between the supply of privately produced goods and services and those of the state, and we may call it social balance" (Galbraith, 1958, p. 255). A few pages later, he summarizes the problem: "... failure to keep public services in minimal relation to private production and use of goods is a cause for social disorder or impairs economic performance" (Galbraith, 1958, p. 259). Galbraith cites two problems caused by social imbalance. First, industrialization creates externalities like pollution and social problems like inequality. Second, the economy's overall micro and macro performance suffers with lower job growth, higher inflation, and a weak supply and demand link, like in the housing market.

Galbraith explores the connection between the dependence effects on social balancing by looking at the consequences of advertisements on consumers' demand. He writes, "the conventional wisdom holds that the community, large or small, decides how much it will devote to its public services" (Galbraith, 1958, p. 197). However, because of corporate power, there's a tendency to underrepresent public needs or have them influenced by corporate interest groups. This tends "to keep public services in minimal relation to private production and ... a cause of a social disorder or impair economic performance" (Galbraith, 1958, p. 197). Galbraith goes on to say that through forms of "persuasion," the entrepreneur remains a romantic figure for most Americans, perhaps going back to the ideals of Jeffersonian democracy while "public bureaucracy" and the government is to be scorned. Galbraith rebukes this "myth" and asks us to consider how true it is in a modern industrial state: "Even public services to avoid disorder must be defended. By contrast, the man who devises a nostrum for a nonexistent need and then successfully promotes both remains one of nature's nobleman" (Galbraith, 1958, p. 204).

Ron Stanfield (1996) provides an important perspective on Galbraith's theory of social balancing. Stanfield notes that Galbraith was first going to write a book about poverty and then realized that wealth and affluence was the issue that was going to be ignored in economics (Stanfield, 1996, pp. 41–42). While mainstream economists focused on undifferentiated economic growth from the private sector, Galbraith examined the cost of growth and private consumption and its impact on social welfare. He saw the production of wasteful and harmful private goods and insufficient public goods. As Americans overconsume food, debt, cars, and energy, they fail to address those without the most basic commodities.

Galbraith's social balance theory, as expected, drew both sympathetic and unsympathetic critics. Economists sympathetic to Galbraith, like Robert Heilbroner, had doubts about his social balance theory. In a review of *The Affluent Society,* Heilbroner paid particular attention to the social balancing theory:

> I do not think it is possible to construct such a theory if we must do so within the rules of the game that have become conventional for our discipline ... thus I am not sanguine with regard to the possibility of formulating a theory of social balance on par with models of capital crises or stagnation.(Heilbroner, 1989, p. 374)

He concluded that social balancing is not a theory but a metatheory.

Public choice scholars also criticized Galbraith for ignoring the inefficiencies with which public goods are provided. Harold Demsetz (1970) wrote there are two traditional characteristics of public goods: exclusion and joint consumption. Public goods, he argues, are typically joint product goods where different prices can be charged to different consumers. Hence, private producers can provide public goods "efficiently," so it is not only the government that can provide them (1970, p. 293). Henry Wallich (1961) concedes that Galbraith might be right that consumer preferences are misallocated. The answer he saw is for consumers to reexamine their choices and reallocate.

F.A. Hayek also addressed Galbraith's social balancing in 1961. Hayek called the dependence effect a "non sequitur." Hayek's critique is that

> if the producer could, in fact, deliberately determine what the consumers will want, Professor Galbraith's conclusions would have some validity. But though this is skillfully suggested, it is nowhere made credible, and could hardly be made credible because it is not true. (Hayek, 1961, p. 346)

Finally, critics claim that Galbraith's social balance theory opposes established theories like the environmental Kuznets curve (Acemoglu & Robinson, 2002). The curve represents increased environmental degradation initially, but with economic growth and affluence, environmental degradation improves over time as consumers demand more and better public goods.

GALBRAITH'S RETHINKING
OF SOCIAL BALANCING

Galbraith published *The New Industrial State* (1967) almost 10 years after *The Affluent Society* (1958). It introduces Galbraith's dual economy theory, where two separate economic sectors exist with different levels of development, technology, and power. A technostructure dominates the sector with large corporations. In Chapters 26 and 27, Galbraith looks at the relationship between the technostructure and the state and how it relates to social balance. He highlights the key areas that the technostructure is interested in 1) labor supply, 2) regulation of aggregate demand, 3) underwriting of technology, and 4) defense spending. The technostructure supports, for its interest, certain types of public goods. While Galbraith does not mention social balancing specifically, he is interested in how the dual economy affects the relationship between the state and sectors of the economy. His next book, *Economics and the Public Purpose* (1973), further extends his social balancing theory, though with a different name. In both of these books, we see how Galbraith modified his social balancing hypothesis. He explains how an industrialized dual economy changes the social balance.

The technostructure represents the "planned part" of his dual economy, and competitive markets of hundreds of thousands of small, often service-based firms represent the other half. Small firms cannot influence the state in any major fashion, and they have minimal control over consumer preferences or suppliers regarding market power and preference shifting. The planned economy, with its technostructure, operates with two main principles: the protective response and affirmative purpose. The protective response is designed to ensure 1) the technostructure's ongoing existence and 2) prevent external interference. This protective response is tied to the affirmative purpose of the growth and ongoing development of the firm's operational financial enlargement. Galbraith recognizes that these purposes may be in conflict with each other, and he expects that different industries will deal with the conflict in different ways. Understanding the twin purposes of the planning system is key to understanding the relationship between the technostructure and social balance theory. He writes, "the technostructure also extensively influences the purchase of public goods in accordance with its needs" (Galbraith, 1973, p. 141). He summarizes the outcome of the influence of the planning system on the government and the public bureaucracy this way: "How economic resources – capital, manpower, materials – are to be allocated to production, both in private and public sectors of the economy, depends heavily though of course not exclusively on, producer power" (Galbraith, 1973, p. 144). Here, we see the changes in Galbraith's thinking from *The Affluent Society* (1958), where the public sector is not absolutely deprived relative to the private economy. Rather there is relative deprivation of the public sector depending on its relationship to the planning economy. This is the maturation of Galbraith's social balancing theory.

Why does this relative deprivation occur? He hypothesizes that the state (government) is underfunded only in specific categories or relative deprivation of certain areas or parts of the government. The planning system or technostructure is incentivized to drive the state in a particular direction: "the government, through its procurement and in its providing for the various needs of the planning system, plays a vital role in advancing the purposes of the planning system" (Galbraith, 1973, p. 241). The planning system also enables certain myths to protect themselves from attack and build support among the public. Galbraith further writes that "the subordination of the state to the individual purpose which makes producer and public interest identical is a disguising myth" (1973, p. 256).

He addresses two key points in how the technostructure maintains its power with the state. The first is how power and money shape democratic politics. The technostructure must continue convincing people that the current system works, allowing them to maintain their power. Galbraith believed that the public needs to be fully aware of the mismatch and the disguising impact of the enabling myths through what he calls "public cognizance." Second, they must maintain a strong relationship with the public bureaucracy. The net result is a deprivation of key public goods and services and an overly stimulated private sector combined with certain parts of the public sector.

We can now see how Galbraith's social balancing theory evolved. Typically, the private economy of firms and households operates with a balance of goods and services as each drives supply and demand for the other. Galbraith writes, "it has long been recognized that tolerably close relationship must be maintained between the production of various kinds of products" (Galbraith, 1958, p. 192). The original social balancing theory is based on the absolute deprivation of the public sector compared to the private sector. Families could afford a new car with the latest features but drove on poor roads and in the smoke-filled air. The economy needed to be more balanced in providing an overall perspective on all types of economic goods. The modified social balancing theory provided additional perspective on how this process works and the overall results observed in society. In the revised theory, the social balance was one of relative deprivation rather than absolute deprivation. Certain parts of the public sector are underfunded or underprovided. This under-provision occurred because of the structure of the economy. The actors in the system reinforce this imbalance and further perpetuate myths to ensure that government officials and the public will buy into this self-reinforcing system.

LATER WORKS AND SOCIAL BALANCE THEORY

Galbraith did not explicitly mention the social balancing hypothesis in his later books, such as the *Culture of Contentment* (1992), *The Good Society* (1997), and *Reaganomics* (Galbraith & McCracken, 1983). However, *The Culture of Contentment* does make reference to social balancing:

> social expenditures favorable to the fortunate, financial rescue, military spending and of course interest payments ... has shown by far the greatest increase. Expenditures for welfare, lost-cost housing, health care for those otherwise unprotected, public education and the diverse needs of great urban slums is now viewed as a burden of government. (Galbraith, 1992, pp. 25–26)

And in his other later writings, we see the social balancing theme of the relative growth of certain government spending like defense compared to welfare and other lower-income household programs, even as the private economy grows. He extends his modified social balancing theory by adding more context, like the relationship between taxes and government spending, especially with various income classes. Galbraith writes,

> so government with all of its costs is pictured as a functionless burden, which for the fortunate, to a considerable extent, it is. Accordingly, it and the sustaining taxes must be kept to a minimum; otherwise, the individual's liberty will be impaired. (Galbraith, 1992, p. 46)

Galbraith wrote these lines in the aftermath of the Reagan and Bush presidential administrations. He noted that specific selective sectors and certain activities are well funded and supported by the government, like defense spending and the savings and loan industry bailout. At the same time, other parts of public services are stagnant or curtailed. His modified social balancing theory is extended not just to the interests of the technostructure but also to wealthy households who can express preferences and shape government activity.

As we can see, Galbraith's social balancing theory has evolved in his writing. In the 1950s, he envisioned a clear and absolute state of deprivation or imbalance between private and public investment and spending. He saw that US society overemphasized the consumption of private goods and underemphasized the need to reduce economic externalities and invest in public goods. Over the next 30 years, his argument evolved as he observed that privileged groups were incentivized to boost certain government activities and investments for their benefit and undermine others on ideological grounds. This led to a new hypothesis of relative deprivation or social imbalance based on the power expressed by these groups, which included the large business establishment (technostructure or planning system) and members of the high-income household community (represented by Reaganomics).

INITIAL EVIDENCE FOR THE
SOCIAL BALANCE THEORY

Undoubtedly, there will be debate about the empirical testing of Galbraith's social balancing theory. One question would be the relative spending per sector. Is it about the provision of goods, the quality of public goods, or even something else? Some of these approaches will be easier to assess empirically than others. In the rest of this chapter, I will examine various kinds of evidence regarding the Galbraith theory of social balancing. Can we provide any statistical evidence regarding how well Galbraith's thesis (original or modified) holds up in the period 1962 through 2022 at a federal level? In 1958, when *The Affluent Society* came out, total government spending in the United States (federal, state, and local) was approximately $119 billion, 24% of the US gross domestic product (GDP). In 1973, when *Economics and the Public Purpose* appeared and close to the end of the Vietnam War, the government spent $421 billion or 29.5% of the US GDP. By 2021, The US government spending increased to $9.3 trillion at the height of the Covid-19 pandemic with a peacetime record of 40% of the US GDP, barely surpassing World War II. In the aggregate, government expenditures have increased substantially. It should be noted that before the global pandemic in 2018, total government spending represented 32.9% of GDP.

We now need to look at private economy changes and consumption over time. In 1958, personal consumption expenditures were $289 billion or 60% of GDP. By 2021, this figure had risen to over $15.9 trillion or 68% of GDP. Before the global pandemic, personal consumption expenditures had represented 72% of the total GDP; personal consumption expenditures rose 5,600%, while government expenditures rose over 5,500%. We see that total government spending kept pace with the private economy from 1958 through 2021. (Government spending gained a substantial share of the economy during the global pandemic compared to the private sector.) However, focusing on aggregate spending in the public and private economy doesn't answer the Galbraithian question. In 1958, when *The Affluent Society* was published, there was an imbalance between public and private spending. The public sector would have to increase its overall economic share in the next few decades to restore social balance. This happened recently during the global pandemic and will most likely be temporary. The aggregate evidence needs to provide a clear-cut answer to the Galbraith theory. If it does, it leans toward a solution supporting the Galbraithian social imbalance through the 20th and 21st centuries.

There's another issue to consider as well. Galbraith modified his social balance theory to focus on the relative deprivation of certain parts of the public sector, especially the technostructure. Galbraith's modification to social balancing requires examining government spending trends across major categories. There is an increase across all categories, from defense spending (which Galbraith might have expected) to social welfare programs, social insurance, education, and community development. No area of major federal spending declined over that time in absolute terms. This question can be examined from the relative shares of the total federal budget. Table 4.1 illustrates that, in general, most federal spending categories increased much more than the inflation rate over time.

The overall data show that government spending across all categories has increased substantially in the past few decades. At first glance, this might seem to indicate that Galbraith's ideas of social balancing are simply wrong. However, we also know that Galbraith modified his ideas over time. The expectation might be that some categories grow faster than others.

A modified Galbraithian social balancing seems in order based on this evidence. It is true that some categories, such as Medicare and health services and welfare and income security, grew far faster than other categories. This may be in line to some extent with the idea that health care is fundamentally about financing private businesses, and they will support increases in government spending. Some categories grew slower than inflation, including natural resources, environment, and agricultural programs. The slow growth of environmental programs seems to fit with the general theme of Galbraith's social balancing thesis but less well with the slower growth in agricultural spending.

Both sides of the argument can claim that Galbraith was right or wrong, depending on the interpretation of this evidence. First, aggregate government spending has kept pace with the private economy. Second, the share of government

Table 4.1.   Percent Change in Federal Government Spending by
Functional Area in Nominal Terms (1979–2021).

Major Federal Spending Categories	Percent Change in Nominal Spending (%)
Military and defense	522
International affairs	807
Science, space and technology	549
Energy	−22.8
Natural resources and environment	249
Agriculture	323
Commerce and housing	121
Transportation	705
Community and regional development	250
Education and training	686
Health services	3,547
Medicare	2,829
Welfare and income security	1,840
Social security	952
Veterans affairs	997
General government	137
Justice	157

Source: US Office of Management and Budget Historical Tables.

spending in most categories increased markedly, although there is some evidence that some functional areas have grown more than others. Galbraith's modified social balancing argued that the planning system or technostructure favors some government spending over others, such as government-provided goods that promote stability and stable growth. This might include economic development incentives, certain types of infrastructure, facilitation of credit services, technical education, and similar efforts.

While federal spending tells one story, local government spending is that which daily and directly impacts citizens. At an aggregate level, local government spending has also increased rising from under 5% of GDP in 1950 to over 10% in 2015 (Page-Hoongrajok, Mason, & Jayadev, 2019). At first glance again, this may refute the Galbraith social balancing idea. However, it is also clear that there is a great deal in inequity between communities and what they can spend on local public services. There may be little doubt that low-income communities suffer from a lack of provision of public goods in the United States. Note the bankruptcy of the city of Detroit in 2013 and its inability to provide basic public services (Bomey, 2017).

COMPETING VIEWS OF THE
THEORY OF SOCIAL BALANCE

Before and after Galbraith's work, there were alternative views on the relationship between the public versus private sectors. Adolph Wagner examined the size of government relative to the private economy in Germany in the late 19th century. Wagner theorized that the government would grow as the private or national economy grew. His model saw the government and its public goods as income elastic (Koester & Priesmeier, 2013). He assumed that people would vote for increasing public services and goods with economic growth. Building on Wagner's work, The Buchanan–Wagner (Richard Wagner) hypothesis (Buchanan & Wagner, 1977) stated that a modern government heavily depends on debt financing, especially at the federal level. Public spending will increase faster or faster than the general economy because a debt-financed government is perceived as cheaper than tax funding. Debt is a form of deferred taxes, and citizens operate under a state of "fiscal illusion" regarding current government costs. Both the original Wagner and Buchanan–Wagner hypotheses argue that public spending increases faster than private spending.

In addition, you have public choice economists who argue that the government and the public sector grow faster than the general economy. They forecast a different type of social imbalance of too much government spending, not too little. The public choice school maintains that bureaucrats will attempt to maximize their budgets, leading to faster government spending. Thomas Borcherding, wrote in 1985, "any scholar of U.S. fiscal history must address one simple but central point ... Why did Americans choose to spend one-twelfth of their income through the public sector at this century's beginning, but over one-third today?" (Borcherding, 1985, p. 359). Borcherding takes direct aim at Galbraith: "the new view of government as selfishly redistributive though unrealistic is a useful prophylactic to the public interest fiscal theories of Galbraith (1958)" (Borcherding, 1985, p. 378).

What Galbraith and public choice economists have in common is that the state will be driven by conventional wisdom or vested interests to favor certain forms of regulation or public spending, thus resulting in relative deprivation. They differ in whom those vested interests are composed. It should be said that Galbraith was not enamored of the public bureaucracy. He wrote in *Economics and the Public Purpose* that "the second source of public power is bureaucratic symbiosis" and "the various specialists of the private bureaucracy work readily with their opposite numbers in the public bureaucracy pooling information for a jointly achieved decision" (Galbraith, 1973, p. 16). There is also literature from the Left that questions Galbraith social balance theory. They argue that the state extracts wealth and income from its most vulnerable citizens. This is a public version of Galbraith's dependence effect. The difference is that the state uses power for coercion and taking property. Public law enforcement has often acted to violate the rights of African American citizens, including the taking of life. This has led some Black activists to call for "defunding police" and shifting those resources for community needs and other social services. This is an example of Galbraithian relative deprivation. The wealthy approve public money for police enforcement while fighting against resources to combat police brutality and social services. Another example is the government's taking of homes and property for not paying taxes, as happened in Detroit. Law Professor Bernadette Atuahene writes in the *California Law Review* that "Predatory cities are urban areas where public officials systematically take property from residents and transfer it to public coffers, intentionally or unintentionally violating domestic laws or basic human rights" (Atuahene, 2020, p. 1).

The overall criticism of Galbraith's social balancing theory is that there is no linear or straightforward relationship between spending and outcomes or service quality. The government may invest or spend large sums of money, but such spending may need to be more efficient or misdirected in some cases. This may mean that government spending does not translate into the quality of series that should be present such as well-paved roads, timely police, fire response, adequate environmental protection, or other public services. Another problem is the geographic, racial, or income-based distribution of public services and infrastructure. Blighted buildings and poor roads may be concentrated in some communities instead of others. There may be relative deprivation of public services both in absolute terms and in terms of specific communities. These challenges will be explored in later sections as we assess Galbraith's concept of social balancing for the 21st century.

SOCIAL BALANCING IN
THE 21ST CENTURY

A key question is the relevancy of social balancing theory in the 21st century. Given the importance of the dual economy to social balancing (technostructure versus market system), is it still applicable in an information-age economy – an economy described as "capitalism without capital"? At one level, the United States still has a dual economy. According to the Bureau of Labor Statistics, in 2022, 150 million people were employed in the United States. Of these, 40% were in firms with more than 1,000 workers, which represents only 0.21% of the total number of firms in the United States (12,000 versus a total number of over 5 million firms). In 2022, the "Fortune 500" had a US employment level of 13.5 million (about 7% of total US employment), an average of just over 60,000 employees, which generated over $6 trillion in revenue.[4]

These firms likely represent Galbraith's technostructure as much as any other, representing a dual economy. The question is whether they have the same level of influence as Galbraith's modified version of social balancing.

The evidence suggests not only that the US economy is a dual economy, but based on Galbraith's criteria, the technostructure or planning system is even more powerful today than in his own time. The "big five" who dominate the US economy do so not only with employment and revenue but also influence on business practices and business culture. Shoshana Zuboff, in "The Age of Surveillance Capitalism," provides new data on how this new technostructure works. In the early 2000s, Google used its extensive user data to mine for new information related to targeted advertising. Google had initially collected users only to improve its search engine but started to use its data sets to increase profits. Zuboff writes that

> these behavioral data available for uses beyond service improvements constituted surplus, and it was on the strength of this behavioral surplus that the young company would find its way to the sustained and exponential profits that would be necessary for survival. (Zuboff, 2019, p. 75)

Zuboff focused on a 2003 patent by Google known as "Generating User Information for Use in Targeted Advertising." The other big five members followed.

Google has extensively engaged in Galbraith's protective response, especially in Washington, DC. Galbraith defined the protective response as "the technostructure has two protective needs – it must secure its existence ... it must minimize the danger of external interference" (Galbraith, 1973, p. 93). Google (Alphabet) was among the top 20 corporate lobbying efforts at nearly $10 million in 2022 and over $150 million since 2015. Other members of the big five have spent in similar ways. The next question is how these companies shape or reshape social balance. Members of the "Big Five" have asked for legislation to support certain public spending, including the following:

1. Domestic education and training for future employees.
2. Favorable immigration policies for potential employees.
3. Investments in infrastructure such as broadband and, in some cases, traditional infrastructure like roads.

There's a clear connection between the protective and affirmative responses and broadband access. Growing access to broadband means more consumers and data points for these companies. Both education investments and liberal immigration policy favor these companies in attracting and retaining a strong workforce. This is not different from the public goods and investments the technostructure supported in *The New Industrial State* (1967). We see a dual economy, but now we need to ask if there is a social imbalance? The overall US economy expanded from $3.2 trillion in 1960 to over $20 trillion in 2021. The government sector's share of the economy and GDP went from 24% in 1960 to a much lower 17% in 2022. Spending levels alone do not necessarily capture all the critical aspects of Galbraith's social balancing theory, which also focuses on the quality of public sector goods and evaluating their contribution to social welfare. The following sections will examine health care, public infrastructure, environment, and climate. These examples will help us assess the relevancy of Galbraith's social balancing theory in the 21st century.

THE PUBLIC AND PRIVATE FACES OF US HEALTHCARE SYSTEM

Healthcare spending and income security are now the dominant forms of government spending in the United States, including state and local governments. Does such spending fit within Galbraith's social balance theory? Much of federal spending goes directly to business or technostructure interests. Medicare and Medicaid spending is done on behalf of patients and sent directly to healthcare providers such as physicians, hospitals, and other organizations. Health care is unique in that federal and state spending makes up a large part of the revenue base of private and not-for-profit providers. The Commonwealth Fund provides a comprehensive and non-partisan view of the US healthcare system

(Commonwealth Fund, 2022). In 2021, they compared the US system to other high-income countries. Three facts stand out about the US system:

1. Its high cost compared to other systems.
2. Aggregate outcomes show several inefficiencies.
3. Its healthcare measures are second in the ranking.

The US system is very good for those who can afford and have access to it, but the aggregate healthcare measurements are low because many cannot afford health insurance and lack access. Galbraith would ask how many people lack essential services while others have excellent care. The expenditures and the imbalance of care fit Galbraith's view of a mismatch between available healthcare goods and those in need of such services.

PUBLIC AND PRIVATE INFRASTRUCTURE

The quality of public infrastructure, such as roads, bridges, water, and sewer systems, is certainly an area where the United States needs help to maintain capacity and quality. At first glance, this type of infrastructure might interest the planning sector. The American Society of Civil Engineers (ACSE) has provided grades for American infrastructure for several years (ACSE, 2023). The most recent grade was a "C minus." It did vary by type of infrastructure. For example, bridges were a "C" level, while dames received a "D." Ports and railroads received a "B" grade, while public parks, roads, schools, and stormwater systems received a "D" grade. These grades can also be accessed via a state-by-state breakdown. It is still being determined whether the planning system can support these public goods, especially as constituted today. The point emphasizes Galbraith's concerns about the country's imbalance between public and private spending. In addition, it illustrates the relative deficiency of public infrastructure and its impact on low-income households. The Flint water crisis in 2015 is an excellent example of the government's failure to maintain infrastructure and actively work to undercut the public health of its citizens (Clark, 2018).

ENVIRONMENT, CLIMATE, AND SOCIAL BALANCE

Galbraith was one of the first economists in the United States to assess the potential damage and impact of environmental problems on American well-being as a cost of excessive private consumption. Environmental protection and natural resource conservation need better measures to implement policies and distribute public expenditures. With some indicators, the United States has improved its environmental measurements, such as ambient air pollution, anthropogenic lead emission, greenhouse gas emissions, and toxic air emissions, which have shown improvement (Environmental Protection Agency, 2023). Since the 1970s, the United States has significantly reduced ambient air pollution; however, in the last

10 or 20 years, this success has been tempered and stagnated. Another example is the acidity levels in lakes and streams. Since the 1970s, the United States has seen reductions. However, performance has only slightly improved in the last decade or so. This mixed result indicates that there has been progress in some key environmental indicators. Still, it has slowed appreciably, and parts of the country and specific communities face significant environmental pollution and injustice. Using Galbraith's modified social balance theory, we can see an imbalance in dealing with environmental pollutants. Again, we observe a pattern of relative deprivation in the degree of environmental protection as with other public goods.

CONCLUSION

John Kenneth Galbraith is one of the most important American economists of the 20th century. His work on the social balancing theory has significantly contributed to economic thinking and practice. Many economists have challenged Galbraith's social balancing by the growth of the nation's public sector over the past 50 years. A new brand of public choice economists argue that the government has grown faster than the overall economy as politicians and bureaucrats seek greater shares of the economy. The government's budgets did increase substantially after World War II, and the government share of the economy grew at the federal, state, and local levels in the United States. However, by the 1960s, Galbraith recognized that a large part of that growth came from the insistence of private industry, particularly from the technostructure or planning system for certain types of public sector spending that benefited their profits and self-interest.

Galbraith's original hypothesis of social balancing in 1958 pointed to a group of Americans that suffered deprivation and communities that faced underinvestment relative to other areas. In the 1960s, he came up with a reinterpretation of his social balancing theory that showed relative deprivation. Specific segments of American society face underinvestment and aggressive strategies to extract wealth and resources from the poor and middle class through private financial instruments and business scams. At the same time, low-income households face deprivation in a relative sense compared to wealthier communities. This deprivation is a lack of public investment and an inability to finance private substitutes.

A social balancing theory for the 2020s and beyond must account for the many structural economic changes since the mid-20th century. Today, the economy still has a dual structure where tech companies dominate. These tech companies have encouraged generations to think of themselves as independent agents who can express themselves through various products and services. It is a scale and scope of the Veblen conspicuous consumption and Galbraith dependence effect on a scale that could not be imagined 50 years ago. The consumer is now the product, as depicted in Zuboff's surveillance capitalism. In essence, Galbraith's dual economy and dependence effect are even more. New technical corporate structures today engage in Galbraith's affirmative and protective responses. Companies have declared a new version of freedom and libertarianism while relying on the government to shield them from liability and a protective response to their business model of digital surveillance; companies like Amazon lobby in favor of issues such as copyright and patent protections and to protect themselves from antitrust efforts that both political parties have occasionally put forth.

What are the implications for the balance between the public and private sectors? There is an argument that tech entrepreneurs believe in the power of innovation first and foremost. They support ventures like government research and development, charter schools, and other variations of new approaches to public ventures (Ferenstein, 2017). They are heavy supporters of free and open barriers for people, goods, and products to ensure a steady flow of labor, products (hardware often produced overseas, like Apple), and new consumers. A new social balancing theory must account for this new structure of politics and power between Silicon Valley and the government. Based on key sectors, such as health care and environmental protection, the United States faces social imbalance in the 21st century. The social imbalance has more to do with how specific social provisions and public goods are available concerning certain social groups. A point not noted by Galbraith, at least not until his much later work, is that the more affluent classes can afford to privately finance social protections and social goods, when necessary, whereas others cannot. The best example is the American healthcare system, the largest industry in the United States. For those with access to the system, it is a world-class system that can remediate many important illnesses. At the same time, for others, there is a significant lack of access to care in even the most basic form. African American infants and mothers still face a high death rate comparable to a developing nation. Compared to Galbraith's model, it is less a lack of overall public versus private wealth and provision but rather a relative deprivation, especially for specific communities and classes of households.

Is Galbraith's social balancing theory still relevant in the 21st century? The answer is yes; it is still relevant. A new social balancing theory must account for our more nuanced view of the positive and negative perspectives on the government's role in the economy. Some leaders in the Democratic Party have advocated for a new emphasis on government power in ideas such as the New Green Deal, stronger antitrust of the tech sector, basic income, and job guarantees. These policies will be part of new forums to redress the social imbalance and new forms of government structure and operations to address social imbalances in the 21st century.

NOTES

1. It is less clear regarding federal spending on infrastructure using debt as this is not available from the US Office for Management and Budget. This type of spending also occurred frequently at the state and local government level in terms of infrastructure.

2. Earlier in the 19th century, local governments had some responsibility for what would be termed social insurance poverty alleviation programs, but there is less known about these programs, and there were often very repressive in nature and nonuniform across countries. The US government did have a very large civil war pension program that acted as a form of social insurance in the latter half of the 19th century. Otherwise, the United States was a laggard in adopting these programs compared to Western Europe.

3. Stankiewicz, K. (2021, October 29). Bye-bye FAANG, hello MAMAA – Cramer reveals a new acronym after Facebook's name change. *CNBC,* January 20.
4. See the following data: https://www.bls.gov/web/cewbd/table_f.txt. This represents an increase from 31% in 1993. https://www.bls.gov/web/cewbd/table_f.txt. https://www.shrm. org/executive/resources/articles/pages/companies-with-immigrant-roots.aspx

REFERENCES

Acemoglu, D., & Robinson, J. A. (2002). The political economy of the Kuznets curve. *Review of Development Economics, 6*(2), 183–203.

American Society of Civil Engineers. (2023, September 15). *ASCE's 2021 American Infrastructure Report Card: GPA: C-.* https://infrastructurereportcard.org/

Atuahene, B. (2020). Predatory cities. *California Law Review, 108,* 107.

Bomey, N. (2017). *Detroit resurrected: To bankruptcy and back.* New York, NY: Norton and Co.

Borcherding, T. E. (1985). The causes of government expenditure growth: A survey of the US evidence. *Journal of Public Economics, 28*(3), 359–382.

Buchanan, J. M., & Wagner, R. E. (1977). *Democracy in deficit: The political legacy of Lord Keynes* (Vol. 8). New York, NY: Academic Press.

Clark, A. (2018). *The poisoned city.* New York, NY: Metropolitan Books.

CommonWealth Fund. (2022, December 20). https://www.commonwealthfund.org/publications/fund-reports/2021/aug/mirror-mirror-2021-reflecting-poorly

Demsetz, H. (1970). The private production of public goods. *The Journal of Law and Economics, 13*(2), 293–306.

Environmental Protection Agency. (2023, January 20). https://www.epa.gov/report-environment

Ferenstein, G. (2017). The disrupters. *City Journal,* Winter.

Galbraith, J. K. (1952). *American capitalism.* Boston, MA: Houghton Mifflin Company.

Galbraith, J. K. (1958). *The affluent society.* Boston, MA: Houghton Mifflin.

Galbraith, J. K. (1967). *The new industrial state.* Boston, MA: Houghton Mifflin Company.

Galbraith, J. K. (1973). *Economics and the public purpose.* Boston, MA: Houghton Mifflin Company.

Galbraith, J. K. (1992). *The culture of contentment.* Boston, MA: Houghton Mifflin.

Galbraith, J. K. (1997). *The good society.* New York, NY: Harper Business.

Galbraith, J. K., & McCracken, P. W. (1983). *Reaganomics.* Boston, MA: Collier Macmillan.

Hayek, F. A. (1961). The non sequitur of the "Dependence Effect." *Southern Economic Journal, 27*(4), 346–348.

Heilbroner, R. (1989). Rereading the affluent society. *Journal of Economic Issues, 23*(2), 367–377.

Koester, G., & Priesmeier, C. (2013). Does Wagner's law ruin the sustainability of German public finances? *FinanzArchiv/Public Finance Analysis, 69*(3), 256–288.

Page-Hoongrajok, A., Mason, J. W., & Jayadev, A. (2019). The evolution of state-local balance sheets in the United States, 1953–2013. *Journal of Post Keynesian Economics, 42*(1), 90–113.

Rimlinger, G. (1971). *Welfare policy and industrialization in Europe, America and Russia.* New York, NY: John Wiley and Sons.

Stanfield, R. (1996). *James John Kenneth Galbraith.* London: Palgrave Macmillan.

Wallich, H. (1961). Private vs public. *Harper's Magazine,* October.

Zuboff, S. (2019). *The age of surveillance capitalism.* New York, NY: Public Affairs.

CHAPTER 5

JOHN KENNETH GALBRAITH ON THE MILITARY–INDUSTRIAL COMPLEX

Adem Yavuz Elveren

ABSTRACT

The goal of this chapter is to reexamine the nature and structure of the military–industrial complex (MIC) through the works of John Kenneth Galbraith. MIC, or military power as he prefers, is a coalition of vested interests within the state and industry that promoted the military power in the name of "national security" for their interests. Galbraith's theory of giant corporations helps us understand the role of military corporations in the MIC. Moreover, he is a critical scholar in examining this topic because he was a political insider in the Roosevelt, Kennedy, and Johnson administrations and a prominent public intellectual against the Vietnam War. Against this background, this chapter has three parts. After explaining the development of military Keynesianism with respect to the main economic thoughts, it examines the history of the MIC and its impact on economic priorities during and after the Cold War through Galbraith's works. Finally, this chapter discusses MIC's relevancy today and evaluates Galbraith's prophecies.

Keywords: Military–industrial complex; Cold War; military Keynesianism; military corporations; Vietnam War; economic priorities

Research in the History of Economic Thought and Methodology: Including a Symposium on John Kenneth Galbraith: Economic Structures and Policies for the Twenty-First Century
Research in the History of Economic Thought and Methodology, Volume 41C, 73–92
ISSN: 0743-4154/doi:10.1108/S0743-41542024000041C005

INTRODUCTION

Military Keynesianism, a policy of using military expenditure (MILEX here-after) as a countercyclical economic tool and part of government spending, is still in use, even after the Cold War. As we enter the 21st century, 40 years after the fall of the Soviet Union, we need to revisit MILEX and its impact on the United States' economic structure and the power it wields in the world. During the Cold War, an elaborate military–industrial complex (MIC) between the state and industry determined MILEX policies. From the 1950s into the 1960s, John Kenneth Galbraith became concerned with how military Keynesianism was used and manipulated by the MIC and its impact on social balancing between private and public goods in the United States (Galbraith, 1958, 1967). To fully under-stand the nature and dynamics between MILEX and MIC during and after the Cold War, we turn to the writings of John Kenneth Galbraith.

The root of the term MIC goes back to the writings of C. Wright Mills (1956). It first became popular with President Dwight Eisenhower's well-known Farewell Address in 1961. The speech did not define the MIC precisely or how it operated. However, the speech did recognize its role in Cold War economic priorities.[1] John Kenneth Galbraith came up with a more precise meaning of the MIC (or what he called *military power*) by defining it as a coalition of vested interests within the state and industry that promoted the MIC in the name of "national security" for their interests (Galbraith, 1967, 1969a).[2] During the Cold War, the MIC estab-lished itself as an autonomous structure that justified military Keynesianism poli-cies for perceived or actual external threats. Galbraith saw such policies as part of the new industrial state where major contractors, dependent on government support, dominated the military market. Their size, influence, and control made it difficult for new firms to enter the market and displace incumbents in core areas of arms production (Dunne & Sköns, 2010). This led to the interdependence between large military corporations and government interests. Galbraith focused on their interdependence and its consequence during the Cold War era and after.

This chapter analyzes the development of military Keynesianism, the history of the MIC, and its impact on economic priorities during and after the Cold War through the writings of John Kenneth Galbraith. Although Galbraith did not analyze militarism or the effects of MILEX *per se*, his theory of giant corpora-tions helps us understand the role of military corporations in the MIC structure after World War II (WWII). Galbraith's perspective is unique since he was a polit-ical insider in the Roosevelt, Kennedy, and Johnson administrations and a major voice against the Vietnam War. The structure of this chapter is the following: First, I explain the meaning of military Keynesianism. I then analyze the nature and structure of the MIC through the works of John Kenneth Galbraith. Finally, I look at the relevancy of MIC today, followed by a conclusion.

MILITARY KEYNESIANISM

The beginning of military Keynesianism in the United States started with the country's decision to enter WWII.[3] Franklin D. Roosevelt's New Deal programs did not achieve full employment before the war for various reasons. With the

United States at war, the government created a demand for military goods that required full employment. This led to a view among some Marxists and Liberals (Baran & Sweezy, 1966; Melman, 1985) that MILEX can be used not only as "a time-limited economic effort to achieve a political goal (winning World War II)" but as a "means for governmental control of the economy" (Melman, 1985, p. 16). Starting in the 1950s, an ideological consensus developed on the Left that military Keynesianism was not merely sustainable but essential for economic growth and stability in a capitalist society. Military expenditure boosted aggregate demand to offset economic stagnation by increasing capital stock utilization, creating employment, and increasing short-run economic growth. Military spending was now a component of government spending via the income multiplier effect like any other form of government spending.

Kalecki was one of the first economists to recognize a critical "advantage" of military Keynesianism over other government expenditures such as health or education services (Kalecki, 1955, pp. 580–581; Toporowski, 2016, 2017). "[T]he construction of schools, hospitals and even roads is of limited scale" because they "compete with the private sector and reduce the rate of capitalist profits, which obviously has a negative impact on private investment," there-fore, their economic effect "will be weaker in the long run, and besides this, will draw immediate political opposition from monopolies damaged (by such competition)." Kalecki contended that "[a]rmaments play a specific role precisely because they are unproductive" (Kalecki, 1955, p. 581). Baran and Sweezy (1966) agreed with Kalecki by arguing that MILEX can absorb the surplus in the economy, contrary to other types of government expenditure that increase the economy's productive capacity.

There are two main views regarding the economic effects of MILEX from the Left. The first view is that military Keynesianism has a positive effect by increasing aggregate demand. The other view is that the effect is negative because MILEX eventually reduces the economy's productive capacity by crowding out public and private investment. Regarding the positive effect, Marxists view the operation of the MIC and the pursuit of profit by individual corporations as determined by the capitalist system's laws of motion and the capitalist class' interests (Smith, 1977). According to Baran and Sweezy (1966), MILEX prevents an undercon-sumption economic crisis by absorbing the surplus in the economy. Baran and Sweezy's argument is in line with Kalecki's. A similar view is Michael Kidron's permanent arms economy approach, which suggests that MILEX prevents the economy from overheating (Kidron, 1970).

Marxists offer five reasons MILEX performed better than civilian government expenditure (Baran & Sweezy, 1966; Reich, 1972). First, it is easily manipulated by the state. Second, weapons are rapidly used or rendered obsolete, guaranteeing endless demand. Third, MILEX is supported by powerful ideological arguments for fighting communism and worldwide insurgencies. Fourth, US military power helps to reinforce American political and economic hegemony. Fifth, welfare state expenditure is not preferred to military expenditure because it expands the civil-ian state sector, redistributes income, and turns labor market regulations in favor of labor. Military production can also be exported. This is important because the wasteful effects of MILEX are externalized through exports.

When there is unemployment and low profits the government must spend on something ... [F] or twenty-five years serious recessions were avoided by following this policy. The most convenient thing for a government to spend on is armaments ... It was the so-called Keynesians who persuaded successive [U.S.] presidents that there is no harm in a budget deficit and left the military-industrial complex to take advantage of it. (Robinson, 1972, pp. 6–7, quoted in Cypher, 2015, p. 457)

Because MILEX is wasteful, this inefficiency maintains high-profit rates by absorbing surplus, counteracting the economic crises inherent to the capitalist system. Joan Robinson emphasized this convenience of MILEX in the Richard T. Ely Lecture,[4] for which she was invited by Galbraith, where the MIC was one of the major topics of her lecture on the "second crisis" of economic theory.[5]

The liberal school of thought, on the other hand, led by Seymour Melman[6] (see also Dumas, 1986; Kaldor, 1981), claims that the impact of MILEX is negative. The military sector creates economic inefficiencies by crowding out productive civilian investment (Dumas, 1986; Kaldor, 1981; Melman, 1970, 1985; Rosen, 1973). Liberal argued that MILEX decisions

emerge not from a consensus on some national interest, but from bargaining and compromises between a variety of special interests. Because the various interests have unequal power and information, the decisions tend to be biased in favor of the groups with the largest stakes in military expenditure, the military-industrial complex. (Smith, 1977, p. 64)

Since the liberal school's analysis is based on "class-free national interest," it concludes that the removal of politicians with a hardline agenda and the use of liberal fiscal and monetary policies would be enough to promote civilian over military production (Georgiou, 1983; Smith, 1977). Although the liberal school considers militarism as irrational and immoral and doesn't represent the interest of the general public, they naïvely argue that "closer monitoring of R & D" and "more public accountability" are sufficient to deal with it (Georgiou, 1983). Except for Melman, the liberal school ignores MILEX's specific economic role.

The core reaction against Keynesian economics from the Marxists was their critique of military Keynesianism (Barker, 2019; McColloch, 2017). The military sector is embedded in the capitalist system and indispensable for capitalism to achieve economic stability without increasing welfare state expenditures (Toporowski, 2017). For liberals such as Melman (1965), the MIC is a parasite of capitalism. The MIC, which arose during the dual crises of the Great Depression and WWII, became a massive network of expanded political power, arms producers, and increased state authority that established well-entrenched interest groups – a powerful and extended network serving the interests of unions, giant corporations, and subcontractors, the military, and gave politicians votes (Duncan & Coyne, 2013).

GALBRAITH ON THE MIC[7]

Galbraith's influence on US economic policies started during WWII. He was head of price controls during the war (with Chester Bowles). He also "created the conditions under which saving in the form of government bonds became credible"

(Galbraith, 2004, p. 295). At the war's end, he continued his government involvement by assessing the allies' strategic bombing campaign against Germany with a distinguished group of economists, including Nicholas Kaldor, E. F. Schumacher, Edward F. Denison, Paul Baran, and Tibor Scitovsky. Galbraith worked at the heart of the American MIC and had significant knowledge of the German MIC as well. In 1945, he interrogated the Armaments and War Production minister in Nazi Germany, acquiring firsthand knowledge of war production and the relationship between state agencies and industrial contractors. Galbraith also prepared a 10-point plan in 1946, which anticipated the Marshall Plan advocated by Secretary of State George Marshall in 1947 to rebuild Europe (Dunn & Pressman, 2005, p. 167; Galbraith, 1946).[8]

Galbraith's influence continued after the war as an adviser to Presidents John F. Kennedy and Lyndon B. Johnson. He served as ambassador to India under Kennedy and sent the president telegrams and letters advising against increased US involvement in Vietnam, the planned Bay of Pigs operation in Cuba, and carrying out Central Intelligence Agency (CIA) operations in India (Dunn & Pressman, 2005; Galbraith, 1969b, 1998b). After the death of Kennedy, Lyndon Johnson appointed him to the White House Task Force against poverty. During Johnson's presidency, Galbraith became a strong voice against the United States' involvement in Vietnam. And "a strong and highly visible dissenter" in the arms race with the Soviet Union and the use of military Keynesianism (Cypher, 2008, p. 39; Galbraith, 1967). He saw military Keynesianism as creating a severe public sector imbalance. Galbraith rejected the general view that the United States had to increase MILEX because the Soviet Union was spending at least as much on its military. Instead, he advocated negotiations over nuclear arms development. In the 1950s, 1960s, and 1970s, Galbraith spoke out against the expansion of MIC and its harmful economic impact (Dunn & Pressman, 2005, p. 168; Galbraith, 1969b, 1998a, 2017). In *The Affluent Society* (1958), he argued that militarism "plays a deeply functional role in underwriting technology" for the benefit of MIC and the American people (1958, p. 257).

Galbraith provides a detailed discussion on the effects of MILEX in *The New Industrial State* (1967).[9] According to Galbraith, the arms race had a "deeply organic relation to economic performance." A consumer goods economy cannot allocate enough resources to research and development, whereas the military sector can "sustain such effort on a vastly greater scale." The consequence is that significant private and public development comes from military research, such as air transport, computer, and nuclear energy. Any private sector product can only achieve such beneficial research at this scale with public support for technological development. MILEX, Galbraith argued, "has done more to save us from the partial technological stagnation inherent in a consumer goods economy" (1958, p. 259). Without "publicly supported [military] research," technical progress in American industry would have been significantly slower. Nevertheless, he maintains that "this is a hideously inefficient way of subsidizing general scientific and technical development" (1958, p. 259).

Galbraith saw the Marxian view that a capitalist economy suffers from a chronic lack of aggregate demand and needs military expenditures as wrong.

Different types of public spending can also stimulate aggregate demand. However, he recognized the importance of their argument during the Cold War, where MILEX played a unique role in increasing aggregate demand. His view was similar to Baran and Sweezy's that MILEX stimulated aggregate demand because other types of public expenditure could not match the large-scale expenditure of military goods at that time. Hence, military Keynesianism – a term he did not use – stabilized the economy (Cypher, 2008). Over time, his view changed from that of Paul Samuelson and other economists that "the same effect could easily be obtained by shifting the outlays to civilian purposes or returning them to private use"[10] (Galbraith, 1967, p. 230). He explained why the view is simplistic: "Income released to or taken from private expenditure will only serve effectively to regulate demand if the public sector is large and the resources released or absorbed are large enough to count" (Galbraith, 1967, p. 203). Besides insufficient volume, "there is also that of underwriting technology and therewith the planning of the industrial system" (Galbraith, 1967, p. 231). He argues that civilian public expenditures, such as on schools, parks, and the poor, have a different effect because they lack MILEX's relation to technology (Galbraith, 1967, p. 231). In addition to underwriting technology, Galbraith also claims that MILEX innovation may have civilian purposes, referring to a spillover effect (Galbraith, 1967, p. 339). For Galbraith, "[i]f a large public sector of the economy, supported by personal and corporate income taxation, is the fulcrum for the regulation of demand, plainly military expenditures are the pivot on which the fulcrum rests" (Galbraith, 1967, p. 229). He emphasized that businesspeople strongly support MILEX because public defense and space exploration expenditure meets international policy goals (Galbraith, 1967, pp. 228–229). There is a symbiotic relationship between military corporations and the state.

Galbraith explains this symbiotic relationship – the dynamics of how the MIC operates – by analyzing the role of a new industrial class: *the technostructure*. He argued that, with the rise of the modern corporation,

> the emergence of the organization required by modern technology and planning and the divorce of the owner of the capital from the control of the enterprise, the entrepreneur no longer exists as an individual person in the mature industrial enterprise. (Galbraith, 1967, p. 71)

According to Galbraith, decisions are not made by *management* but by the "the guiding intelligence – the brain – of the enterprise." He considers this new class, the new decision-making group, *the technostructure*, similar to Veblen's distinction between *business* and *industry*. Power is exercised in society, particularly between the state and giant corporations. Galbraith's concept of *the revised sequence* is another key part of his theory: "[T]he accommodation of the market behavior of the individual, as well as social attitudes in general, to needs of producers and the goals of the technostructure is an inherent feature of the system" (Galbraith, 1967, p. 212). Rather than going from consumers to the products they demand, controls run the other way – in a *revised sequence*. Thus, he argued that it is not true that defense requirements are purely a national policy independent of the needs of the industrial system. Instead, the state, through its military and related procurements, serves to accommodate the needs of the industrial system, which means that the industrial design is no longer an independent entity. It exerts a certain degree of control over public and national policy to accommodate its interests (Galbraith, 1967, p. 232). The consequence is that "[t]he military power has reversed the constitutional process in the United States – removed power from the public and Congress to the Pentagon" (Galbraith, 1969a, p. 61). Image building is the key part of this process because it provides a reason to justify or rationalize the continued high MILEX. The Cold War, Galbraith argues, played that role for about two decades (Galbraith, 1967, p. 326), along with other interventions in Africa and Central America and in the Middle East against Iraq in 1991 (Galbraith, 1992, pp. 140–141).

Galbraith argued that the state guarantees a corporation capital to develop advanced technology through military and related procurements (1967, p. 308). Such investments entail long-term specialized allocation of capital and labor protected against cost increases (Galbraith, 1967, p. 308). In contrast, entrepreneurial corporations do not need such long-term planning because they use simpler technology and make smaller capital commitments. It is giant military corporations with the technostructure that require such protection to eliminate planning uncertainties (Galbraith, 1967, p. 225). Government procurements thus stabilize demand for the industrial–military system by offering long-term contracts with assurances against demand change (Galbraith, 1967, pp. 309–310). This "leads the technostructure to identify itself closely with the goals of the armed services" (Galbraith, 1967, p. 310). Moreover, this mechanism does not operate only within the Department of Defense but also in other major agencies, such as the National Space Agency, the Atomic Energy Commission, and the Federal Aviation Agency (Galbraith, 1967, p. 315), creating a symbiotic relationship between military corporations and the state. Galbraith discusses this relationship in *Economics & Public Purpose* (1973) of how roles are assigned between these two entities and how this symbiotic relationship functions:

> The public bureaucracy, citing the need for new weapons, can seem to be speaking out of a disinterested concern for public security. Its control over intelligence allows it, as necessary, to exploit public and congressional fears as to what the Soviets are doing or might be doing ... The private bureaucracy has the freedom and financial resources not available to the public bureaucracy for making strategic political contributions, for mobilizing union and community support, for lobbying, for advertising and for public and press relations. (Galbraith, 1973, p. 284)

Weapon firms and the Department of Defense must engage in reciprocal recruitment of top members of the technostructure (Galbraith, 1973, p. 143; also see Galbraith, 1969a, pp. 20–21). Similarly, at the organizational level, while the weapon firms developing and building aircraft achieve their "affirmative goal of growth with the concurrent reward to their technostructures," the public bureaucracy in charge of such contracts is "similarly rewarded by the development and possession of a new generation of planes" (Galbraith, 1973, p. 143). Galbraith persistently warned of the dangers of the power of military corporations over the state and argued for reforms to address the symbiotic relationship that generates inefficient outcomes for the general public through the inequitable distribution of public expenditure between arms and social infrastructure, health, and education. In this regard, paraphrasing Marx, he declared that "[t]he modern state ... is not the executive committee of the bourgeoisie, but it is more nearly the executive committee of the technostructure." He suggested space competition might be an admirable substitute for weapons production (Galbraith, 1967, p. 341). That is, while being the first to reach Saturn may not represent the ideal use of public resources, at least such a competition would not be extremely dangerous, in contrast to the conventional and nuclear arms races (Galbraith, 1967, p. 341).

In *How to Control the Military* (1969a), Galbraith analyzes the MIC deeper. He contends that *the revised sequence* is more critical when power passes to the Pentagon or military corporations producing weapons than General Motors (Galbraith, 1969a, p. 5). Galbraith asks us to recognize that large military contractors that conduct almost all of their business with the Pentagon are not "private firms" but basically "public extensions of the Pentagon" (Galbraith, 1969a, p. 7). This is the core of Galbraith's view on the MIC, which he prefers to call *military power*. He contends that "the Services, not their industrial suppliers, are the prime wielders of this power" (Galbraith, 1969a, p. 7). However, the military power is more than the services and its contractors because it includes the intelligence agencies, university scientists, defense-oriented research institutes, and "the organized voice of the military in the Congress" (Galbraith, 1969a, pp. 23–24). The problem is "not conspiracy or corruption but unchecked rule" because being unchecked allows the MIC to serve bureaucratic needs rather than national needs to reinforce its power (Galbraith, 1969a, p. 24). Galbraith, therefore, advocates the nationalization of top military corporations (Galbraith, 1969a, p. 7, 1969c, p. 162, 1973, pp. 284–285).

The main factors that enabled the MIC to gain its power during the Cold War, according to Galbraith, are the following: (1) a fear of communism; (2) secrecy of the knowledge surrounding Soviet weaponry; (3) the economic effects of MILEX; and the (4) the absence of either liberal or conservative opposition to the MIC. These factors are closely associated with three beliefs: First, any danger caused by the arms race is less harmful than any agreement with the Soviets because they would exploit it. Second, because the fight against communism is humanity's ultimate battle, the arms race must be pursued, no matter how dangerous it becomes. Third, the national interest is supreme, so not even the risk of Armageddon should prevent the development of new weapons because they serve this national interest (Galbraith, 1969a, pp. 17 & 18). Democrats and moderate liberals were careful not to question the excessive power of this symbiotic coalition between the military corporations and the military services because of the fear of being accused of being soft on communism. Anyone who criticized the MIC was considered a possible Soviet spy. Moreover, the economic situation served to reinforce the MIC's power. Since MILEX helped to sustain employment and the danger of economic stagnation made it impossible to criticize the MIC from an economic viewpoint (Galbraith, 1969a, p. 38). Although liberal economists thought that spending on education, housing, welfare, and civilian public works would be a better alternative to MILEX, the lack of public support prevented them from promoting their ideas (Galbraith, 1969a, p. 41).

In conclusion, Galbraith provides a vital account of understanding the MIC as an insider and public intellectual.[11] His core conclusion is that military power should be returned from the Pentagon to the public and Congress. He outlined how to accomplish this task in *How to Control the Military* (Galbraith, 1969a, pp. 52–62). Galbraith's views on the effects of MILEX developed by looking carefully at the role of MILEX in underwriting technology and its increased negative impact on the economy. For instance, whereas he argued that MILEX boosted the American economy during WWII, it later became a decisive restraining factor for economic development. In line with Melman, he emphasized the excessive allocation of resources and technical experts to the military sector (Galbraith, 1988, 1994). Galbraith's evaluation of the role of the MIC provides us with major insights into its development, threat, and relevancy in economic policies.

GALBRAITH'S INSIGHTS ABOUT THE MIC

Today's MIC still follows Galbraith's analysis. History has proved that Galbraith's concern over *the revised sequence* was fully justified, with many aspects of MIC theory remaining unchanged and expanded since the end of the Cold War (Dunne & Sköns, 2010). The link between the MIC and universities, which began during the Cold War (Chapman & Yudken, 1992; Dunne & Sköns, 2010; Giroux, 2007), has strengthened (Smart, 2016). Major contractors continue to dominate the market and heavily influence government policy. These contractors, in turn, depend on domestic government support despite the internationalization of the military industry. New firms cannot displace incumbents in core areas of arms production (Dunne & Sköns, 2010). The MIC, therefore, continues to be relevant today in explaining how vested interests determine MILEX.

While the end of the Cold War led to a steady and significant decline in MILEX, which dropped to 2.9% in 2000, the September 11 attacks and the subsequent global war on terrorism triggered an increase, as we see in Figs. 5.1A and 5.1B, with MILEX as a share of gross domestic product (GDP), as a share of the budget and as per capita for available years.

The "threat of communism" during the Cold War has been replaced by the "threat of terrorism" and other worldwide conflicts maintaining the demand for increasing arms production. By its nature, arms production is a very stable and profitable business. First, the sector is a monopsonist market with one dominant customer, the government, and a small number of suppliers. The sector has one of the highest concentration ratios. For example, *the four-firm concentration ratio* (CR4) of ammunition manufacturing (except for small arms) has increased from 52.9% in 2002 to 82.2% in 2017. CR4 is

> calculated by adding the market share of the four largest firms in a given industry. A CR4 number of higher than 50 percent is generally considered to be a concentrated market, with numbers ranging above 75 percent considered to be oligopolistic. (statista.com)

Having the government as the only customer offers substantial advantages. Second, since defense contracts provide long-term commitments and arms producers are strategically important actors in the business, they remain almost

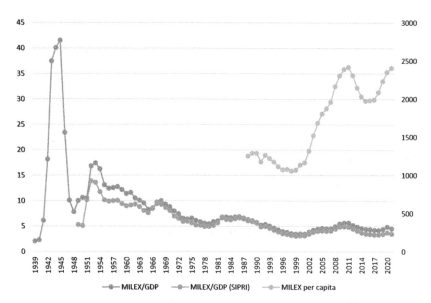

Fig. 5.1A.   MILEX of the United States (1939–2021). *Sources*: MILEX/GDP
from https://www.usgovernmentspending.com/, MILEX/GDP (SIPRI)
and MILEX per capita from SIPRI (right axis).

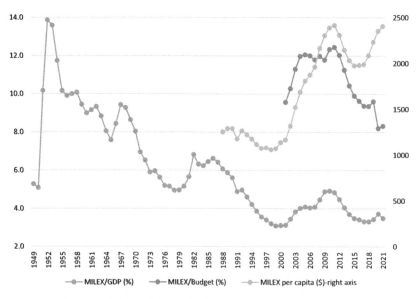

Fig. 5.1B.   MILEX of the United States (1949–2021). *Source*: SIPRI.

unaffected by business cycles and are very likely to be bailed out by the government if needed (Dunne & Sköns, 2010). Third, their profit rates are increased by having monopoly power in the business (Peltier, 2021). Finally, adapting the circuit of the capital model in Foley (1982) by incorporating the military sector, Elveren (2022) shows that profit rates are likely to be higher in the military than civilian sector due to a shorter realization lag in the former. Realization lag refers to the average period required to turn value as finished products into sales flow.

War, or militarization, yields a steady high profit for arms producers. The link is direct. Regarding Galbraith's revised sequence, defense firms have a high capability of creating demand for their products. First, weapons are rapidly used or rendered obsolete due to advances in the weaponry produced by the "enemy." This arms race guarantees endless demand. Second, defense firms promote more hawkish foreign policies, reinforcing militaristic values in the political, social, and economic domains. They also promote direct military interventions or destabilization of other countries through proxy forces, foreign-sponsored coups, and foreign and colonial occupation, thereby hindering diplomatic and peaceful solutions (Burke, 1998, p. 1; Elveren & Moghadam, 2022, p. 2). A key role is played by the close ties of defense firms with major think tanks that promote these hawkish foreign policies (Marshall, 2020). Besides the direct influence of arms producers on (foreign) policy, the globalization and outsourcing of production and increasing financialization have also contributed to militarization (Akçagün & Elveren, 2021; Marshall, 2020). There has been a convergence between the financial class and arms producers, reinforced by a highly militaristic foreign policy in the United States, which guarantees consistent investment in arms technologies and high returns for finance capital (Marshall, 2020).

Global financial capital has become increasingly part of the defense sector because it finds militarization indispensable since arms production is a major source of profits, while militarization is an extremely useful tool to expand financialization by protecting and expanding markets. Therefore, giant financial corporations have increased their power over the military sector by buying defense firms or acquiring their stock to become a major component of the MIC (Akçagün & Elveren, 2021; Herrera, 2013). Considering these strong ties between militarization and financialization, Akçagün and Elveren (2021) used alternative financialization variables, the profit rate in the financial sector, and several parametric and non-parametric methods to demonstrate a significant relationship between them in the United States for 1949–2019. The study proves that higher militarization is associated with higher financial profit rates.

Since the end of the Cold War, ownership has become increasingly concentrated through mergers and acquisitions, subcontracting and internationalization (Dunne & Sköns, 2010). Such mergers have increased the power of those arms producers in line with the massive increase in their size. Meanwhile, subcontracting has become more important since they began working with specialist civilian producers to obtain components at lower costs, particularly in electronics and information technology (IT). Moreover, during the 2000s, asymmetric guerrilla-type conflicts, together with the growth of "homeland security," made communications and surveillance technologies increasingly important (Smith, 2009).

This paved a way for what Foster and McChesney (2014) refer to as "surveillance capitalism." The growth of homeland security and intelligence gathering has militarized the global data industry (Marshall, 2020).

Subcontracting and internationalization have expanded and strengthened the link between the military and civilian sectors (Dunne, Garcia-Alonso, Levine, & Smith, 2007a, 2007b; Dunne & Sköns, 2010), particularly in relation to the internationalization of ownership and supply chains. Nevertheless, despite such internationalization, arms producers still depend on the governments of the countries where they operate (Dunne & Sköns, 2010). The MIC has become much more global in the United States and across Europe due to economic developments. State-industry relations in the military sector have changed remarkably due to mergers in the 1990s, transatlantic networks (e.g. USA–UK), the increased role of private contractors,[12] and expanded national and international outsourcing to civil companies (Dunne & Sköns, 2010). However, national governments still play the dominant role, and actors with vested interests are still a powerful lobbying group (Dunne & Sköns, 2010, p. 289).

In his early writings, Galbraith noted a spillover effect of MILEX-mediated innovation for civilian purposes while discussing underwriting technology. In contrast, Dunne and Sköns (2010) argued that for certain sophisticated technologies, the spillover effect had been reversed due to developments in many civilian technologies. Thus, while military technology led until the 1980s, civilian technology led military technology in several areas by the 1990s, particularly electronics for IT and mobile phones. Technology transfer now runs from the civilian to the military sector. Furthermore, civil and military technologies have diverged, for example, in the case of jet engines (Hartley, 2017, p. 56). Despite this, governments have continued to subsidize weapon systems development (Mazzucato, 2013, pp. 73–79). In fact, what matters more is how worthwhile the spillover is rather than whether there is still a spillover. In other words, the mere existence of spillover does not indicate its market value or prove that subsidies pay off because other industries can also create spillover effects (Hartley, 2017, p. 19). Potentially, that is, the same technology could be produced at a lower cost without relying on military spillover (Smith, 2009, p. 167).

In his later writings, Galbraith focused more to the limits of MILEX. As Richard Parker notes, Galbraith's "skepticism about military power and spending became a fixture of his work and his idea of economic analysis" (Parker, 2005, p. 196). Galbraith preferred to substitute other public spending for MILEX because it was both desirable and feasible. In his later writings, Galbraith also emphasized the long-term negative impacts of MILEX on the economy's productive capacity. He underscored the opportunity cost of excessive MILEX to the United States by pointing to the outstanding development of Japan, Germany, and other countries with well-developed welfare states.

While it appears desirable to substitute MILEX with higher social spending, such as health and education spending, there has been no major discussion of whether this is feasible. Baran and Sweezy (1966, p. 154) argued that Galbraith's proposition to replace the warfare state with the welfare state was desirable but not workable. Baran and Sweezy, and other Marxists recognized that, in contrast to social spending, excessive MILEX does not conflict with the interests of the capital class. This is because, in addition to its strategic and ideological uses, MILEX maintains high private sector profits because it does not redistribute income or alter labor market regulations in favor of labor. On the contrary, "wasteful" MILEX maintains high-profit rates by absorbing surplus, thereby counteracting the economic crises inherent to the capitalist system (Baran & Sweezy, 1966).

There is a sizeable amount of empirical literature on the effect of MILEX on the economy (Dunne & Uye, 2010; Yesilyurt & Yesilyurt, 2019). Detailed literature reviews suggest that more recent studies using advanced econometric methods have tended to find a negative impact (Dunne & Tian, 2013). Another strand of the empirical literature taking a Marxist perspective has investigated whether MILEX counteracts the tendency of profit rates to decline. Based on analyses of 24 Organization for Economic Cooperation and Development (OECD) countries and 32 major countries during 1963–2008 and 1963–2016, Elveren and Hsu (2016, 2018) and Elveren (2019), respectively, reported two major findings. First, MILEX has increased profit rates overall, although not since 1980. Second, while MILEX weakly increases profit rates in arms-exporting countries (e.g. the United States) it depresses them in non-arms-exporting countries (e.g. Turkey).

Finally, Galbraith always retained his opposition to hawkish foreign policies. Based on experience in the United States Strategic Bombing Survey (USSBS), Korea, and Vietnam, he concluded that there are strict limits to military power and hence to justifications for using it. Richard Parker notes three essential lessons Galbraith took from the USSBS (Parker, 2005, p. 188). First, he acknowledged the limits of linear programming models. For instance, when governments attempt to control inflation, their mathematical models fail to capture the outcomes of political battles between the state, firms, workers, and consumers, where each economic actor wants to maximize their interest. This leads to unanticipated solutions to "unfair" outcomes (Parker, 2005, p. 189). Second, elegant linear programming models also fail in strategic military planning. This is because economics deals with human relationships that involve institutions and power. Inevitably, therefore, elegant theories of perfect theoretical clarity cannot work, given reality's complex and uncertain nature. Third, Galbraith argues that democratic societies need the government to deal with growth, fluctuation, and income distribution because the market cannot create equilibrium – notwithstanding the claims of Marshallian economics (Parker, 2005, p. 190).

Galbraith consistently opposed overt and covert provocations, including the Bay of Pigs raid, the CIA's futile operations in Tibet, and escalations in Vietnam and other places. Unfortunately, the United States has pursued militarist interventions across the globe. The Bush Doctrine of 2002, of "preventive war," claims that the United States does not have to "wait for threats to fully materialize." Accordingly, the US military has been involved in conflicts in 25 countries since 2001, including Afghanistan, Iraq, and Libya, and maintains three times as many overseas bases as all other countries combined (Vine, Deppen, & Bolger, 2021). In addition, its massive military budget is about three times that of the second-highest spender, China, and larger than the next nine biggest military spenders combined. Since 2001, US development aid to Afghanistan has been 36.07 billion dollars, while its spending on the top five military contractors is 2.1 trillion dollars (https://watson.brown.edu/costsofwar/).

Conventional wisdom in US foreign policy is that its armed forces make the United States and other parts of the world more secure. However, wars in Afghanistan and Iraq, military assistance to countries like Israel, Egypt, and Jordan, and to armed proxy groups in Syria and Libya have not fulfilled US promises to suppress terrorism, curb disorder, and promote democracy and human rights (Pillar, Bacevich, Sheline, & Parsi, 2020). Rather, these militarist interventions have been extremely costly, with the loss of US troops, civilian casualties, and refugees. Of 750 US bases across 80 countries, 19 are in authoritarian countries and 8 in semi-authoritarian (Vine et al., 2021), providing de facto support to repressive regimes and prolonging instability rather than promoting democracy (Pillar et al., 2020; Vine et al., 2021).

Although President Trump pursued a sort of anti-militaristic election campaign, particularly against US involvement in Iraq, after taking office, he delayed the US withdrawal from Syria, increased US forces in war zones, and proposed a Pentagon budget for 2018 and 2019 that exceeded even the Pentagon's own expansive expectations. President Trump's confusing foreign policies represent a power struggle with the MIC. On the one hand, Trump worked to defuse tensions and reduce the sense of insecurity that has maintained the MIC in North Korea and Russia. He closed several military bases in Afghanistan, Iraq, and Syria. On the other hand, he reinforced Washington's hostile attitudes toward Beijing that began during the Obama administration, intensifying a great-power competition (Swaine, Lee, & Odell, 2021, p. 32). Trump deferred to several symbolic interventions in Syria. Regarding Iran, he withdrew from the internationally supported denuclearization agreement despite the opposition of his first national security team. He provoked a confrontation with Iran by ordering the assassination of its top general. The United States, under Trump, did not seriously resist the US interventionist foreign policy. Trump's national security strategy continued those under previous presidents, calling for strengthening the United States' role in the The Middle East and North Africa (MENA) region, South Asia, and Europe (Cordesman, 2018). Overall, Trump's policies reiterated Reagan's policy of reducing taxes on corporations and the rich while substantially increasing MILEX, albeit with a significantly more authoritarian touch. President Biden's foreign policy is still evolving. It seems to be taking a mixture of caution and firmness with China.

China's economic and military rise has changed the balance of power in East Asia (Swaine et al., 2021, p. 8). China's average GDP growth has been significant since its economic reforms in 1978. It has become the major trading partner of East Asian countries and provided investment and technology transfers to many countries in the region. Moreover, by establishing its own "World Bank," China has become a significant funding source for East Asian and African countries. While expanding economic ties with other countries, China has spent around 2% of its GDP on its military force over the last decades. It is now "capable of credibly contesting the longstanding dominance of U.S. military forces in maritime East Asia" (Swaine et al., 2021, p. 3). In contrast, the United States failed to provide enough economic support to East Asian countries after the international financial crises of 1998 and 2008. Consequently, even if American power is not declining, Asian countries perceive it to be doing so (Swaine et al., 2021, p. 12). Furthermore, ill-considered US policies have forced these countries to choose between the United States and China (Swaine et al., 2021; Wertheim, 2020). Although the balance of power in East Asia is changing in favor of China, it is far from achieving regional military dominance (Wertheim, 2020).

The United States should therefore accept and respond to China's rise with a new strategy that shifts its foreign policy toward regional diplomacy and cooperation (Swaine et al., 2021). Cooperation with regional actors should include economic, military, and human security provisions. This would involve expanding economic trade and foreign aid, building a cooperative agenda to address maritime insecurity and the proliferation of weapons of mass destruction, and dealing with pressing human security issues, including eroding democracy and human rights, the current pandemic, and climate change (Swaine et al., 2021, p. 3). Although Galbraith would certainly oppose provocations in the Taiwan Strait, as part of a more balanced approach of reassurance and deterrence, the United States must firmly restate its One China policy and endeavor to limit the militarization of the Taiwan Strait (Swaine et al., 2021, p. 4). Similarly, the United States must make steady and coordinated efforts toward ensuring peace and denuclearization of the Korean Peninsula. Such policies would prevent the arms races that Galbraith strongly criticized during the Cold War.

Russia is also a major regional power, aiming to expand its influence in the former Soviet region and build an alliance with China. As with its approach to China, the US administration should be realistic about Russia's presence as a power and respect its interests. Wertheim (2020) suggests that this includes "avoiding hostile governments in its 'near abroad,' and participating in core European security and diplomatic discussions." The current conflict between Ukraine and Russia over the Donbas region is also a major dispute between the United States and Russia. Here, the United States should acknowledge two major facts (Lieven, 2022, p. 10). First, Russia exerts greater power than the United States over most former Soviet republics. Second, offering "unwavering" support for Ukraine is not a "dominant or rational strategy" for the United States because Ukraine would definitely lose any war with Russia. This would force the United States to join the fight against Russia or break its promises to Ukraine, suffering international humiliation and a loss of credibility. As with potential conflicts with China in East Asia, pursuing armed solutions will make Russia even more aggressive (Wertheim, 2020). Therefore, diplomatic rather than militaristic strategies are in the best interests of the United States, European Union (EU), and Ukraine (Lieven, 2022).

CONCLUSION

This chapter discussed the MIC in relation to John Kenneth Galbraith's insights on (military) power as an invaluable guide for examining the MIC today. He taught us that economic theory is limited in describing the complex and evolving relationships within institutions where power is a major element. Galbraith's broad and rational approach is critical to understand the MIC and its impact on the economy since military, foreign, and industrial policies are intertwined.

Galbraith's framework provides a better understanding than the standard neoclassical approach of explaining how MILEX has developed in the United States. The neoclassical view sees the state as a rational actor and treats MILEX as a public good, balancing the opportunity costs and benefits to maximize the "national interest." In contrast, Galbraith's *revised sequence* warns us to rethink the divergence between "national interest" and "the public's general interest." He underscored that this divergence results from the increasing role of *the military power*, which promotes the interests of military services and their industrial suppliers in the name of "national security."

NOTES

1. This speech had enormous influence by allowing people to agree with Eisenhower without fear of being labelled Marxists or soft on Communism at the height of the Cold War. In reference to this, Galbraith notes that "[f]or many years thereafter anyone (myself included) who spoke to the problem of the military power [e.g. the MIC] took the thoughtful precaution of first quoting President Eisenhower" (Galbraith, 1969a, p. 37).

2. Galbraith in *The Anatomy of Power* (1983) introduces a general theory of power and a theory of organization to reinforce his thesis regarding the autonomy of the MIC. He notes that "Support for a strong national defense is an expression of normal patriotism, no truly good citizen dissents. This highly successful conditioning is, however, only part of an even larger manifestation of power. The power the military embraces not only the significant source of power but, with extraordinary comprehensiveness and effect, all the instruments of its enforcement" (Galbraith, 1983, p. 153).

3. In several works, it appears that it is Michał Kalecki who coined "Military Keynesianism," and in some others, it is Joan Robinson. However, apparently, it is Richard Hofstadter, American historian (Barker, 2019).

4. It was renamed to the AEA Distinguished Lecture in 2020.

5. For Joan Robinson, military Keynesianism was the worst version of "bastard Keynesianism."

6. Both Cypher and Gold disagree with the main arguments of the liberal school. They argued that, first, the crowding-out argument is not valid; second, there was no long-term trade-off between military and civilian R&D; third, there was no evidence of insufficient scientists and engineers in the civilian sector because of excessive recruitment by the military; fourth, it was not plausible that "military contractor 'cost-maximizing' practices had spread into the sphere of production of the civilian economy"; and finally, there was no evidence that other advanced countries had outperformed the United States since the late 1960s due to higher MILEX in the United States (Adams & Gold, 1987; Cypher, 1985, 2015, p. 465; Gold, 1990).

7. This section is taken from Elveren (2019).

8. One major difference between Galbraith's plan and the Marshall Plan was that Galbraith argued for a durable peace between the United States and Russia.

9. Galbraith was given a two-term sabbatical when he was at Harvard University to continue to develop his ideas in *The Affluent Society*, finally published this in 1967 because he was serving as an adviser during Kennedy's presidential election, after which Kennedy appointed him as ambassador to India (Galbraith, 1969b, cited in Dunn & Pressman, 2005, p.167).

10. "There is nothing about [government] spending on jet bombers, intercontinental missiles and moon rockets that leads to a larger multiplier support of the economy than would other kinds of expenditure (as on pollution control, poverty relief and urban blight) … America's potential and actual growth rate, far from depending upon war preparations,

would be markedly *increased* by an end of the cold war" (Emphasis in original in Samuelson, 1970, p. 804, cited in Galbraith, 1973, p. 185).

11. Cypher (2008) argues that Galbraith's interpretation of the MIC was "vague and seemingly contradictory" (p. 39). By comparing *How to Control the Military* (1969a) and *Economics & the Public Purpose* (1973), Cypher argues that "instead of the military bureaucracy performing the dominating role within the military–industrial complex, he insisted that the military contracting firms and the military bureaucracy were equally powerful" (p. 40). In my opinion, although it is true that Galbraith did not provide a very explicit definition of the MIC, his position is not contradictory. Rather, his seemingly contradictory remark results from his "vague" definition. For instance, in *How to Control the Military*, he acknowledged this vague structure of the MIC, which shows that his view had not shifted, contrary to what Cypher argues. Regarding decisions on weapons or weapon systems, he notes that "[n]o one can tell where the action originates – whether the Services or the contractors initiate decisions on weapons – nor can the two be sharply *distinguished*" (Galbraith, 1969a, p. 26, emphasis added). In addition, regarding the symbiotic relationship between the Department of Defense and the weapon firms, he notes that "no conclusion can or should be reached as to where the initiative lies" (Galbraith, 1973, p. 144).

12. One consequence of the neoliberal paradigm, which assumes that the private sector is more efficient than the public sector, is the extension of the MIC, with private contractors operating unofficial armies (Cypher, 2007, p. 44). This predatory behavior has become the mainstream model for US military forces, especially since the Iraq War, generating new opportunities for private sector profit. In addition to providing armed security, the private sector also provides many other services, such as "research and analysis, various types of technical services – such as information technology, system support, and maintenance, repair and overhaul of military equipment – and operational support, including logistics and intelligence services" (Dunne & Sköns, 2010, p. 288).

ACKNOWLEDGMENTS

I would like to thank Ric Holt for his help and James K. Galbraith for his invaluable comments.

REFERENCES

Adams, G., & Gold, D. (1987). *Defense spending and the economy*. Washington, DC: Center on Budget and Policy Priorities.

Akçagün, P., & Elveren, A. Y. (2021). *Financialization and militarization: An empirical investigation*. Political Economy Research Institute Working Paper No. 545. University of Massachusetts, Amherst.

Baran, P., & Sweezy, P. (1966). *Monopoly capital: An essay on the American economic and social order*. New York, NY: Monthly Review Press.

Barker, T. (2019). Macroeconomic consequences of peace: American radical economists and the problem of military Keynesianism, 1938–1975. In *Including a Symposium on 50 Years of the Union for Radical Political Economics* (pp. 11–29).

Burke, C. (1998). *Women and militarism*. Geneva: Women's International League for Peace and Freedom.

Chapman, G., & Yudken, J. (1992). *Briefing book on the military-industrial complex*. Washington, DC: Council for a Livable World Education Fund.

Cordesman, A. H. (2018). *U.S. national security strategy in the MENA region*. Washington, DC: Center for Strategic & International Studies.

Cypher, J. M. (1985). A review of Robert Degrasse, military expansion, economic decline. *Journal of Economic Issues, 19*(1), 227–233.

Cypher, J. M. (2007). From military Keynesianism to global-neoliberal militarism. *Monthly Review, 59*(2), 37–55.

Cypher, J. M. (2008). Economic consequences of armaments production: Institutional perspectives of J.K. Galbraith and T.B. Veblen. *Journal of Economics Issues, XLII*(1), 37–47.

Cypher, J. M. (2015). The origins and evolution of military Keynesianism in the United States. *Journal of Post Keynesian Economics, 38*(3), 449–476.

Dumas, L. J. (1986). *The overburdened economy.* Berkeley and Los Angeles, CA: University of California Press.

Duncan, T. K., & Coyne, C. J. (2013). The origins of the permanent war economy. *The Independent Review, 18*(2), 219–240.

Dunn, S. P., & Pressman, S. (2005). The economic contributions of John Kenneth Galbraith. *Review of Political Economy, 17*(2), 161–209.

Dunne, P., Garcia-Alonso, M., Levine, P., & Smith, R. (2007a). Determining the defence industrial base. *Defence and Peace Economics, 18*(3), 199–221.

Dunne, P., Garcia-Alonso, M., Levine, P., & Smith, R. (2007b). The evolution of the international arms industries. In W. Elsner (Ed.), *Arms, war, and terrorism in the global economy today-economic analyses and civilian alternatives.* New Brunswick, NJ: Transaction Publishers and Zürich: LIT.

Dunne, P., & Sköns, E. (2010). *The changing military industrial complex.* In A. T. H. Tan (Ed.), *The global arms trade a handbook.* London and New York, NY: Routledge.

Dunne, P., & Tian, N. (2013). Military spending and economic growth: A survey. *The Economics of Peace and Security Journal, 8*(1), 5–11.

Dunne, P., & Uye, M. (2010). Military spending and development. In A. Tan (Ed.), *The global arms trade.* London: Routledge.

Elveren, A. Y. (2019). *The economics of military spending a marxist perspective.* New York, NY: Routledge.

Elveren, A. Y. (2022). Military spending and profit rate: A circuit of capital model with a military sector. *Defence and Peace Economics, 33*(1), 59–76.

Elveren, A. Y., & Hsu, S. (2016). Military expenditures and profit rates: Evidence from OECD countries. *Metroeconomica, 67*(3), 551–577.

Elveren, A. Y., & Hsu, S. (2018). The effect of military expenditure on profit rates: Evidence from major countries. *World Journal of Applied Economics, 4*(2), 75–94.

Elveren, A. Y., & Moghadam, V. M. (2022). Militarization and gender inequality: Exploring the impact. *Journal of Women, Politics & Policy, 43*(4), 427–445. https://doi.org/10.1080/15544 77X.2022.2034430

Foley, D. K. (1982). Realization and accumulation in a Marxian model of the circuit of capital. *Journal of Economic Theory, 28*, 300–319.

Foster, J. B., & McChesney, R. W. (2014). Surveillance capitalism monopoly-finance capital, the military-industrial complex, and the digital age. *Monthly Review, 66*(3). Retrieved from https://monthlyreview.org/2014/07/01/surveillance-capitalism/#fn61

Galbraith, J. K. (1946). *Recovery in Europe.* Washington, DC: National Planning Association.

Galbraith, J. K. (1958). *The affluent society.* Boston, MA: Houghton Mifflin.

Galbraith, J. K. (1967). *The new industrial state.* Boston, MA: Houghton Mifflin Company.

Galbraith, J. K. (1969a). *How to control the military.* New York, NY: Doubleday and Company.

Galbraith, J. K. (1969b). *Ambassador's journal: A personal account of the Kennedy years.* London: Hamilton.

Galbraith, J. K. (1969c). The big defense firms are really public firms and should be nationalized. *New York Times,* November 16.

Galbraith, J. K. (1973). *Economics and the public purpose.* Boston, MA: Houghton Mifflin.

Galbraith, J. K. (1983). *The anatomy of power.* London: Corgi Books.

Galbraith, J. K. (1988). The political asymmetry of economic policy. *Eastern Economic Journal, 14*(2), 125–128.

Galbraith, J. K. (1992). *The culture of contentment.* Boston, MA: Houghton Mifflin.

Galbraith, J. K. (1994). *A journey through economic time a firsthand view.* Boston, MA: Houghton Mifflin.

Galbraith, J. K. (1998a). *Letters to Kennedy* (Ed. J. Goodman). Cambridge, MA: Harvard University Press.

Galbraith, J. K. (1998b). More than vague dinner conversation. *New Statesman, 127*, 25–26.

Galbraith, J. K. (2004). The worldly philosophers and the war economy. *Social Research, 71*(2), 293–304.

Galbraith, J. K. (2017). *The selected letters of John Kenneth Galbraith* (Ed. Richard P. F. Holt). New York, NY: Cambridge University Press.

Georgiou, G. (1983). The political economy of military expenditures. *Capital & Class, 7*, 183–205.

Giroux, H. (2007). *The university in chains: Confronting the military industrial academic complex.* Boulder, CO: Paradigm.

Gold, D. (1990). *The impact of defense spending on investment, productivity and economic growth.* Washington, DC: Center on Budget and Policy Priorities.

Hartley, K. (2017). *The economics of arms.* Croydon: Agenda Publishing.

Herrera, R. (2013). Between crisis and wars – Where is the Unites States heading? *Journal of Innovation Economics & Management, 12*, 151–174.

Kaldor, M. (1981). *The baroque arsenal.* New York, NY: Hill and Wang.

Kalecki, M. (1955). The impact of armaments on the business cycle after the Second World War. In J. Osiatyński (Ed.), *Collected works of Michał Kalecki volume II capitalism: Economic dynamics.* Oxford: The Clarendon Press.

Kidron, M. (1970). *Western capitalism since the war revised edition.* Harmondsworth: Pelican Books.

Lieven, A. (2022). *Ending the threat of war in Ukraine.* Quincy Paper No. 6. The Quincy Institute for Responsible Statecraft, New York, https://quincyinst.org/

Marshall, S. (2020). *The defense industry's role in militarizing US foreign policy.* Middle East Research and Information Project No. 294. The Middle East Research and Information Project, Chicago.

Mazzucato, M. (2013). *The entrepreneurial state.* London: Anthem Press.

McColloch, W. (2017). Profit-led growth, social democracy, and the left: An accumulation of discontent. *Review of Radical Political Economics, 49*(4), 559–566.

Melman, S. (1965). *Our depleted society.* New York, NY: Holt, Rinehart and Winston.

Melman, S. (1970). *Pentagon capitalism: The political economy of war.* New York, NY: McGraw-Hill.

Melman, S. (1985). *The permanent war economy: American capitalism in decline.* New York, NY: Simon & Schuster.

Mills, C. W. (1956). *The power elite.* New York, NY: Oxford University Press.

Parker, R. (2005). *John Kenneth Galbraith his life, his politics, his economics.* New York, NY: HarperCollins Publishers.

Peltier, H. (2021). *Arms, tanks, and munitions: The relationship between profits and monopoly conditions.* Security in Context Working Paper Series No. 1. https://www.securityincontext.com/

Pillar, P., Bacevich, A., Sheline, A., & Parsi, T. (2020). *A new U.S. paradigm for the Middle East: Ending America's misguided policy of domination.* Quincy Paper No. 2. The Quincy Institute for Responsible Statecraft, New York, https://quincyinst.org/

Reich, M. (1972). Does the us economy require military spending? *American Economic Review, 62*(1/2), 296–303.

Robinson, J. (1972). The second crisis of economic theory. *American Economic Review, 62*(1/2), 1–10.

Rosen, S. (1973). *Testing the theory of the military–industrial complex.* Lexington, MA: Lexington Books.

Samuelson, P. A. (1970). *Economics* (8th ed.). New York, NY: McGraw-Hill.

Smart, B. (2016). Military–industrial complexities, university research and neoliberal economy. *Journal of Sociology, 52*(3), 455–481.

Smith, R. (1977). Military expenditure and capitalism. *Cambridge Journal of Economics, 1*(1), 61–76.

Smith, R. (2009). *Military economics: The interaction of power and money.* Basingstoke: Palgrave Macmillan.

Swaine, M. D., Lee, J. J., & Odell, R. E. (2021). *Toward an inclusive & balanced regional order a new strategy in East Asia.* Quincy Paper No. 5. Quincy Institute for Responsible Statecraft, Washington, DC.

Toporowski, J. (2016). Multilateralism and military Keynesianism: Completing the analysis. *Journal of Post Keynesian Economics, 39*(4), 437–443.

Toporowski, J. (2017). *Kalecki on technology and military Keynesianism.* SPRU Working Paper Series No. 2017-22. University of Sussex, Sussex.

Vine, D., Deppen, P., & Bolger, L. (2021). *Drawdown: Improving U.S. and global security through military base closures abroad.* Quincy Brief No. 16. The Quincy Institute for Responsible Statecraft, New York, https://quincyinst.org/

Wertheim, S. (2020). The price of primacy: Why America shouldn't dominate the world. *Foreign Affairs, 99*(2). https://www.foreignaffairs.com/articles/afghanistan/2020-02-10/price-primacy

Yesilyurt, F., & Yesilyurt, M. E. (2019). Meta-analysis, military expenditures and growth. *Journal of Peace Research, 56*(3), 352–363.

CHAPTER 6

THE SOCIAL CONSEQUENCES OF INFLATION AND UNEMPLOYMENT AND THEIR REMEDIES

John Kenneth Galbraith (1979)
(Introduction by Alexandre Chirat, Basile Clerc,
and Richard P. F. Holt)

ABSTRACT

In 1979, Galbraith wrote a manuscript titled "The Social Consequences of Inflation and Unemployment and Their Remedies." The manuscript was found in the John Kenneth Galbraith Personal Papers at the John F. Kennedy Library. The reasons for Galbraith to write the article might appear at first glance to be purely contextual. At the macroeconomic level, the United States was experiencing stagflation, a situation unseen since 1945, resulting in double-digit inflation rates and high unemployment. A policy debate was going on about the Phillips curve and whether there is a trade-off between inflation and unemployment. Milton Friedman challenged the Keynesian analyses of the Phillips curve in the mid-1960s (Friedman, 1977). Galbraith's 16-page draft manuscript provides us an incisive summary of Galbraith's views about the causes of stagflation and what can be done about it. He provides us with an alternative to the neoclassical synthesis of Samuelson and Solow and the neoliberal thinking of Milton Friedman and F. A. Hayek.

Keywords: Phillips curve; monetarism; neoclassical synthesis; stagflation; government policy; John Kenneth Galbraith

Research in the History of Economic Thought and Methodology: Including a Symposium on John Kenneth Galbraith: Economic Structures and Policies for the Twenty-First Century
Research in the History of Economic Thought and Methodology, Volume 41C, 93–106
Copyright © 2024 by Emerald Publishing Limited
All rights of reproduction in any form reserved
ISSN: 0743-4154/doi:10.1108/S0743-41542024000041C006

INTRODUCTION

In 1979, Galbraith wrote a paper entitled "The Social Consequences of Inflation and Unemployment and their Remedies."[1] The article was not published and later found with his letters, documents, and memorandums at the John F. Kennedy Library, where Galbraith's papers are archived. The article was written at a time when the United States experienced significant economic stagflation: high inflation, unemployment, and slow growth. A debate ensued among economists to explain how and why this occurred and what policies were needed to remedy it. The heart of the theoretical discussion was over the Phillips curve (Goutsmedt, 2022). Economist A.W. Phillips (1958) empirically studied the relationship between nominal wages and unemployment in Great Britain from 1861 to 1957. From Phillips observation, Samuelson and Solow (1960) hypothesized that there is an inverse relationship between inflation and the rate of unemployment. These orthodox Keynesian economists recommended using the Phillips curve framework to help shape public policy in regard to inflation and employment.

This led to an ideological tug of war between Monetarist and Keynesian economists starting in the 1960s. Milton Friedman argued that the Phillips curve was based on unsound assumptions. He argued that the traditional Phillips curve only held, at best, in the short run. In the long run, economic agents would adapt their expectations about future inflation based on current rates of inflation and unemployment. This would break the Phillips curve inverse relationship. Keynesian expansionary policies to deal with unemployment will sooner or later cause inflation. If the government follows policies to retract the economy to deal with inflation, it increases unemployment. Friedman's solution was not to use government intervention policies at all but to let the free market allocate labor and wages and have strict monetary policies to stabilize prices (Friedman, 1968). Galbraith's article addressed this dilemma. He criticized both "liberal" neoclassical and monetarist economists. The government needed policies that would not allow unemployment or significant price increases. In the 1940s, as head of price controls in the early years of World War II, Galbraith used price controls quite successfully. He suggested that they be used in the 1970s to deal with stagflation. Friedman's medicine of anti-inflationary monetary policy seemed crude and cruel to Galbraith and unnecessary. Tight-monetary policies can create a recession forcing people out of work and firms to go bankrupt. But there is no guarantee that a "planned recession" would lead to back to full employment and stable prices. History does matter, Galbraith insisted. The world does not necessarily follow the logical prescriptions of neoclassical models and rational expectations. In addition, even if the economy does come back to life four or five years later, you still have lost the real income from the recession, which can never be made up again – it's lost forever. Galbraith argued there are other options besides a "planned recession" to deal with inflation and unemployment.

Galbraith's manuscript provides us with an excellent summary of his response to Samuelson's and Solow's "neoclassical synthesis" and Friedman's monetarism. In response, he defends his "integral economics" (Chirat, 2022). Galbraith argued the only way you are going to have permanent control over inflation with neoclassical policies is by creating what Marx called the "industrial reserve army of the unemployed." Once the economy starts reaching full employment, sooner or later inflation will appear again. That meant for Galbraith a continuous sub-optimum state where policies are constantly juggling unemployment, inflation, and slow growth. In the essay's first sentence, Galbraith argued that "inflation is, extensively, a manifestation of economic and political power" (1979, p. 1). He explicitly analyzed inflation as a distributional conflict. In *American Capitalism* (1980), where he coined the concept of countervailing power, Galbraith saw inflation as a structural issue found in oligopolistic markets. The exercise of market power by large corporations and unions could lead to a price-wage spiral that benefited both at the expense of consumers and workers in competitive markets, those on a fixed income, and unemployed groups. Galbraith wrote, "if you are a cause of inflation, you aren't a victim" (1979, p. 7). In 1978, he wrote a letter to *The New York Review of Books* emphasizing that "for the poor and for people living in fixed incomes, inflation is the cruelest tyranny of all" (Holt, 2017, p. 478).

In addition to the distributional problem of inflation caused "by the competitive thrust for higher incomes," it can "coexist with serious unemployment" (1979, p. 3). Galbraith's analysis of inflation strongly echoes Gardiner Means' "administered inflation" and Abba Lerner's "sellers inflation" (Chirat & Clerc, 2023). Contrary to Samuelson's and Solow's neoclassical synthesis with such models as the 45° diagram or the Phillips curve, which attempts to merge Keynesianism with Walrassian general equilibrium (Samuelson, 1951), Galbraith stressed that inflation could appear before full employment had been reached. In response to Keynes (1940) and Hansen (1941), Galbraith argued for targeted price controls along with monetary and fiscal policies to reduce disposable income to limit the expectation of rising prices (Galbraith, 1941). Since Galbraith saw inflation as tied to market structures and economic power, income policies are needed to control it. This required a social agreement where price demands are not pushed onto society as a whole.

In an article Galbraith wrote after the war, "The Disequilibrium System" (1947), he argued with the pressure to move from an "unplanned" to a "planned economy," as the war required, "supplement or supplanted" forces for "determining economic behavior" would be needed (Galbraith, 1947, p. 287). This would consist of (1) more "control over the employment of economic resources," (2) near "universal control over prices," and (3) "an aggregate of money demand substantially in excess of the available supply of goods and services" (Galbraith, 1947, p. 287). This would create what he called the "Disequilibrium System." Subject to certain "margins of tolerance," which remains contextual, it would be beneficial during the war to have an aggregate demand higher than supply to foster production (Galbraith, 1947):

> If markets are uncontrolled, any near approach to full employment of normally employed workers must lead to advances of prices (readily increased under conditions of imperfect competition in a strong market) followed by increases in a continuing cycle. (Wages can as well be considered the initiating factor in this cycle as prices.) This process, which the last few months have made unpleasantly familiar, can occur even when there is no excess demand and quite possibly while substantial numbers -perhaps some millions- are unemployed. A mirage now being

> chased through the early peace is that a stable equilibrium is possible with full employment
> when there is bilateral monopoly in the factor markets and parallel monopoly power in the
> product markets. The Disequilibrium System represented a simple adaptation of present-day
> capitalism to the wartime requirement that all resources must be employed and under condi-
> tions of approximately stable prices and costs. (Galbraith, 1947, pp. 291–292)

The imbalance between aggregate demand and aggregate supply would create a "system of disequilibrium" where price controls counteract the effects of the imbalance between supply and demand. If "margins of tolerance" are exceeded, the effect becomes counterproductive (1952, p. 35). For Galbraith, these tolerance margins relate to the incentive to work. Beyond a certain level, the excess savings resulting from the combination of price controls and rationing would become such that the population would lose its motivation to work. However, Galbraith saw "margins of tolerance" differently depending on the situation. During World War II, tolerance margins could remain high, mainly thanks to patriotism to fight the war. During a partial mobilization, as in the Korean War, the margins would be narrower, and partial price controls should participate a closer balance of supply and demand (1952, p. 69).[2] It is understandable then that, in the situation of a peacetime economy, Galbraith could write that price controls "do not allow us to have more demand than can be supplied with goods and services at full employment and full capacity operations" (1979, p. 11), since the margins of tolerance are then practically non-existent. Galbraith's point is that under certain conditions and with specific policy goals, price controls are an invaluable tool to deal with problems like stagflation, as are other policy goals, like maximizing output for war production, showed. Ideology should not be a factor in deciding its use or how long it should be put into place:

> The rational course would indeed have been to keep both price control and the supporting con
> trols over distribution until equilibrium had been nearly restored and to avoid the disorganiza
> tion in the labor market and the Inflation of the last year. It is hard to suppose that anyone who
> sensed the country's mood could have believed there was a danger that these controls would
> become permanent. It is difficult also to assume that anyone could take seriously the idle talk
> that price and production controls were inhibiting production when a first-year student would
> have observed (first) that more stringent controls had but recently coincided with the most
> significant expansion in the national product in history and (second) that the economy was
> currently in a state of full or more than full employment. One finds it strange that conserva
> tives invited this disorganization. The gods must muse at the recklessness with which American
> capitalism is abused by its most vocal defenders. (Galbraith, 1947, p. 302)

Another essential part of the manuscript is devoted to criticizing conventional methods to handle inflation through reducing aggregate demand, namely tight-monetary policy, increasing taxes, and decreasing public expenditures (1979, p. 4).

Galbraith lamented that these policies, which he expressed doubt of their efficiencies with oligopolistic segments in the economic system (Galbraith, 1957), could only control inflation at the price of unemployment. In addition to being inefficient, the policies are unfair since "unemployment in the modern economy is not evenly distributed," affecting "first and foremost the most vulnerable groups," that is to say, the same groups – poor people, women, Afro-Americans – that suffer the most from inflation, leading Galbraith to claim in his taunting way that "monetarism is a disguised justification for suffering by the poor" (1979, p. 6).

Galbraith's criticism of conventional macroeconomic policies converges with his continued assault on economics as a system of belief (Galbraith, 1970). Like Marx before him, he regularly compared economics to religion (1979, p. 1) and emphasized the existence of an "orthodoxy" (1979, p. 6). A pillar of the secular religion of economics is the faith it granted to the market price system to allocate and distribute resources with efficiency and fairness. Unlike the faith, Galbraith claimed that certain circumstances require "some form of direct restraint on organized price and income enhancement" (1979, p. 7).

Galbraith did not consider price control as a miracle solution "to cure infla-tion" but rather as a means to "get much closer to full employment without hav-ing to resort to fiscal and monetary restraint and the resulting unemployment" (1979, p. 9). As mentioned earlier, Galbraith observed the efficiency of price con-trol during the war (Laguérodie & Vergara, 2008) and tried to understand the conditions that might make price controls an efficient tool of macroeconomic policies (Galbraith, 1947, 1952). The manuscript, however, makes clear its limita-tions: (Price controls) "do not allow us to have more demand that can be supplied with goods and services at full employment and full capacity operations" (1979, p. 11). For there to be a success, it needs to be accompanied by *New-Deal style* industrial planning. His analysis of inflation is still relevant today. First, the idea of inflation resulting from a distributional conflict between actors holding market power seems particularly appropriate to understand the resurgence of the current inflationary situation, both in the United States and Europe. Josh Bivens (2022) recently showed that more than half of the inflation in the United States since 2020 is the result of "historically high" profits. Such a situation occurs in the con-text of increasing concentration in the US economy, as documented by Thomas Philippon (2019). This supports Galbraith's observation of the oligopolistic structure of the US economy (1980). The inflationary shock in Europe results from the war in Ukraine with a distributional conflict. In some key sectors, the margin rate has been maintained or even increased because of costs, leading to cost of inflation being passed on to workers.[3] In addition, inflation primarily con-cerns sectors in which demand remains, for the most part, structurally inelastic (energy, transport, food, etc.).

Galbraith put forward in *American Capitalism* (1980) that within oligopolis-tic capitalism, the sectoral nature of demand – elastic or inelastic – impacts the heart of the distributional conflict within different sectors. Indeed, when demand is elastic, "the trial of strength between union and management" is mainly over profit sharing, as firms cannot raise prices. Galbraith believed it was a "healthy manifestation of countervailing power" (1980, p. 133). In contrast, inelastic demand gave "a radically different form" to bargaining since management did not fear a reduction in the volume of sales: "The firm that first surrenders to the union need not worry lest it be either the first or the only one to increase prices" (Galbraith, 1980, p. 133). In Europe, it applies less directly to the issue of rais-ing wages – given the low level of unionization – but rather to the question of windfall tax. If the rate of the last bracket of the exceptional tax is not set at 100% – which would mean controlling margins, a solution that is not currently considered either in Europe or in the United States – a firm in an oligopolistic situation facing inelastic demand could be led to pass on part of this cost increase in its prices. Galbraith may therefore lead us to view with caution, at least theoretically, proposals to tax windfall profit at a marginal rate far from 100% in oligopolistic sectors facing inelastic demand.

Moreover to his analysis of the causes of inflation, his proposals for remedies remain relevant. A parallel can first be drawn between the economic problems of World War II and the issues that economies face today with the need for an ecological transition. In both cases, the central question remains: how to reconcile a high level of employment and investment with insufficient supply – linked nowadays to the availability of metals and energy (Schnabel, 2022) – to allow a massive, rapid, and efficient reallocation for an ecological transition? In both cases, you do not want to combat inflation at the cost of increased unemployment, as the reconversion of economies requires maximum use of resources. Galbraith argued for extensive price controls, combined with effective rationing, in cases like this. This option allows to "dispense with the buffer of unemployed resources which would have been necessary for equilibrium stability and to substitute, through surplus demand, a positive pressure on resource use" (1952, p. 34). This method is also socially fairer than letting the market adjust itself, as it limits the realization of "windfall profits."[4] Apart from the "exceptional" case of the massive reallocation of the means of production needed for an ecological transition, Galbraith also leads us to consider income policy.

If we assume, following Galbraith, that conflicts over the distribution of income structure the inflationary dynamic, then the type of policy used is essential. Extending the international comparisons made by Galbraith in his manuscript, we note that the Federal Republic of Germany – which did not develop controls – occasionally chooses to combat its inflation at the cost of an increase in unemployment. Conversely, in France, where price controls were widely used, the level of inflation was certainly higher than in Germany (although wages remain indexed to the price index); however, the unemployment rate remained more stable (Dumez & Jeunemaitre, 1989, pp. 127–129).[5] The income policy advocated by Galbraith can thus effectively appear as an alternative to the use of unemployment as an instrument, favored by capitalists, for regulating distributional conflicts (Kalecki, 1943). Another way to use Galbraith's analysis from the manuscript is to look at contemporary inflation problems internationally. Galbraith does not deal with price controls on imported goods, perhaps because of the low level of openness of the United States at the time he was writing. Since this question has become relevant today, it would certainly be appropriate to continue the theoretical work undertaken by Galbraith on price controls by adding an international dimension to the analysis.[6]

NOTES

1. Unpublished manuscript, JKGPP, Series 5, Box 821. JFK Presidential Library.
2. The role of controls is then no longer to maintain an imbalance that stimulates production but to "prevent the interaction of prices and wages where the imperative of maximized production requires full use of current resources, particularly of labor" (Galbraith, 1952b, p. 69).

3. For France, see, for example, https://blogs.mediapart.fr/economistes-parlement-union-populaire/blog/100622/oui-l-inflation-s-explique-bien-par-une-boucle-prix-profits. For a study of the interaction between conflict inflation and a rise in international prices (or an exchange rate depreciation increase), see Morlin (2023). It shows that workers with low bargaining power will tend to absorb the final cost of a rise in international prices.

4. The introduction of sectoral price controls during World War I, for example, appears to have been to a large extent justified by the need to limit windfall profits. See Litman (1920, p. V) and Gray (1919, p. 253).

5. Following the oil shock, for instance, over the period 1973–1975, while prices rose by an average of 10.9% per year in France for 6.5% in West Germany, unemployment rose by about 1.3% in France for 4% in West Germany. For data on unemployment in Organization for Economic Cooperation and Development (OECD) countries since the 1960s, see, for example, Nickell, Nunziata, and Ochel (2005).

6. We can note here that, following an increase in the price of an imported commodity – energy, agricultural inputs, etc. – two types of control can be considered. First, an *ex ante* control (before the price in question is regarded within the cost structure of national firms), raises the question of distributional conflicts between nations. Second, an *ex post* control (after the price is considered within the cost structure of firms) presents a question of distribution between firms in the same sector insofar as it is necessary to consider the inequalities that result from returns to scale. This point can be partially resolved by setting up equalization mechanisms.

REFERENCES

Bivens, J. (2022). Corporate profits have contributed disproportionately to inflation. How should policymakers respond? *Economic Policy Institute*, *21*.

Chirat, A. (2022). *L'Économie intégrale de John Kenneth Galbraith (1933–1983)*. Paris: Classiques Garnier.

Chirat, A., & Clerc, B. (2023). Convergence on inflation and divergence on price control among post Keynesian pioneers: Insights from Galbraith and Lerner, avec Basile Clerc. *Journal of Post Keynesian Economics*, 1–47

Friedman, M. (1968). The role of monetary policy. *The American Economic Review*, *58*(1), 1–17.

Friedman, M. (1977). Nobel lecture: inflation and unemployment. *Journal of political economy*, *85*(3), 451–472.

Galbraith, J. K. (1941). The selection and timing of inflation controls. *The Review of Economics and Statistics*, *23*(2), 82–85.

Galbraith, J. K. (1947). The disequilibrium system. *The American Economic Review*, *37*(3), 287–302.

Galbraith, J. K. ([1952] 1980). *American capitalism: The concept of countervailing power*. Oxford: Basil Blackwell.

Galbraith, J. K. (1952). *Theory of price control*. Cambridge, MA: Harvard University Press.

Galbraith, J. K. (1957). Market structure and stabilization policy. *The Review of Economics and Statistics*, *39*(2), 124–133.

Galbraith, J. K. (1970). Economics as a System of Belief. *The American Economic Review*, *60*(2), 469–478.

Galbraith, J.K. (2014[1979]). *The social consequences of inflation and unemployment and their remedies*. RHETM, 103–108

Goutsmedt, A. (2022). How the Phillips curve shaped full employment policy in the 1970s: The debates on the Humphrey-Hawkins Act. *History of Political Economy*, *54*(4), 619–653.

Gray, L. C. (1919). Price-fixing policies of the food administration. *The American Economic Review*, *9*(1), 252–271.

Hansen, A. H. (1941). Defense financing and inflation potentialities. *The Review of Economics and Statistics*, *23*(1), 1–7.

Holt, R. P. (Ed.). (2017). *The selected letters of John Kenneth Galbraith*. Cambridge: Cambridge University Press.

Jeunemaître, A., & Dumez, H. (1989). *Diriger l'économie: L'Etat et les prix en France de 1936 à 1986*. Paris: Editions L'Harmattan.

Kalecki, M. (1943). Political aspects of full employment. *The Political Quarterly, 14*(4), 322–330.

Keynes, J. M. (1940). *How to pay for the war*. London: Macmillan.

Laguérodie, S., & Vergara, F. (2008). The theory of price controls: John Kenneth Galbraith's contribution. *Review of Political Economy, 20*(4), 569–593.

Litman, S. (1920). *Prices and price control in Great Britain and the United States during the World War*. New York, NY: Oxford University Press.

Morlin, G. S. (2023). Inflation and conflicting claims in the open economy. *Review of Political Economy, 35*(3), 1–29.

Nickell, S., Nunziata, L., & Ochel, W. (2005). Unemployment in the OECD since the 1960s. What do we know? *The Economic Journal, 115*(500), 1–27.

Phillips, A. W. (1958). The relation between unemployment and the rate of change of money wage rates in the United Kingdom, 1861–1957. *Economica, 25*(100), 283–299.

Philippon, T. (2019). *The great reversal: How America gave up on free markets*. Cambridge, MA: Harvard University Press.

Samuelson, P. A. (1951). Economic theory and wages. In D. McCord Wright (Ed.), *The impact of the union* (pp. 312–342). New York, NY: Kelley & Millman.

Samuelson, P. A., & Solow, R. M. (1960). Analytical aspects of anti-inflation policy. *The American Economic Review, 50*(2), 177–194.

Schnabel, I. (2022). A new age of energy inflation: climateflation, fossilflation and greenflation. Speech given at a panel on "Monetary Policy and Climate Change" at the ECB and its Watchers XXII conference, March 17.

THE SOCIAL CONSEQUENCES OF INFLATION AND UNEMPLOYMENT AND THEIR REMEDIES

JOHN KENNETH GALBRAITH

There is now a fairly general recognition in the industrial countries that inflation is, extensively, a manifestation of economic and political power. Relatively strong organizations have achieved a substantial measure of control over their incomes. They can advance these incomes or put up their prices, which are, of course, one dimension of income, without regard to the market. This recognition one must especially applaud so far as the United States is concerned. Here, the established religion of economics has its most powerful hold. And in the United States, organization is extensive and strong. The strongest of the organizations are the large corporations, a thousand of which now contribute around half of all private US production. All of these large firms, acting with regard to their common interest, have substantial control over their prices. They also distribute this power to those within the firm. The control by senior corporate executives over their own incomes, which is also implied in recent requests for restraint, is nearly total. Top executives of large American corporations have their salaries set by boards of directors which they themselves selected in a charade which should fool no one, though often it still does. And lesser executives, engineers, lawyers, and other specialists have a substantial bargaining position derived from personality, self-advertisement, or specialized talent.

Where there are large corporations, there are all but invariably strong unions. These too have a well-recognized ability to influence their incomes. That is their purpose. Where unions do not exist, there is the poor man's equivalent, which is the legislated minimum wage. (This is selected for attack as uniquely inflationary by scholars who, instinctively or otherwise, don't want to get involved with unions or corporations because they have a considerable capacity for self-defense.) Farm support prices give minimum income protection to producers of basic farm products. Public sector employees are not subject to classical market influences, although, like the minimum wage recipients, they do not enjoy the same legitimacy as corporate executives or ordinary trade union members and are currently only slightly ahead of the Mafia and the Ku Klux Klan as an object of condemnation and abuse in the United States.

The power to control prices and income now extends to Third World producers, the most notable manifestation of which is Organization of Petroleum Exporting Countries (OPEC). It will be subject to widespread imitation even though this may not be easy.

Thus, the group control of income, partial or great, is now widespread. The thrust for higher income by these different groups has, in turn, become a basic cause of inflation. This thrust takes on a competitive aspect as one group sees or senses the greatest advantage of others. It also has a very cruel aspect, for it leaves behind all of those – the young, the old, the minorities, the small businessmen – who are not so organized or protected.

The inflation caused by the competitive thrust for higher incomes I've just cited can coexist with very serious unemployment. In the United States, we now have a rate of inflation, caused primarily in this fashion, running above 10% annually, perhaps higher. Meanwhile unemployment, though improved in recent months, is still in the vicinity of 6% of an increasing labor force. And this figure disguises more than it reveals the true character of the unemployment problem. Unemployment among the vulnerable groups – women, the minorities, the young and those with a combination of these characteristics – is very much higher. And since these vulnerable groups are heavily concentrated in the central cities, unemployment has a heavy regional concentration in these areas. Among young, black or Spanish-speaking workers in the big cities, unemployment runs as high as 35% or 40%.

II

Inflation in all countries in the past has been attacked by one or another of three methods, all of which have their effect by curbing total spending in the economy. These are the measures celebrated by the textbooks and the economists of sound and reputable view. Monetary policy reduces spending from borrowed funds. Higher taxes reduce spending by private taxpayers. Reduced public expenditures reduce spending and demand from the public sector. None of these measures, when now applied, have marked initial effect on the general thrust by organizations for higher income. A tight-monetary policy or an astringent tax and expenditure policy works first to cut back on demand and therewith to cut back on employment. Only where there is substantial idle plant capacity and substantial unemployment is the general thrust for higher income abated by these traditional measures. So, a vital and increasingly indisputable point, the traditional methods of attacking inflation now work primarily as they increase unemployment. This is specifically true of monetary restriction, which, since it requires no legislation and is badly understood by the average citizen who supposes some higher magic is involved, tends to be the first line of defense against inflation.

As I've just noted, unemployment in the modern economy – the United States is an especially serious case – is not evenly distributed. The kinds of workers now unemployed are, to state the obvious, the least in demand. So, the orthodox monetary and fiscal measures against inflation, involving as they do an increase in unemployment, will affect first and most the most vulnerable groups. It has long been observed, in the United States in particular, that the young and black are the last hired and the first fired. This proposition is firmly grounded in the economics of the present situation. Any attack on inflation has obvious and grievous disadvantages if it increases unemployment. This is especially so if it removes hope for employment where joblessness is already chronic and serious.

There is a substantial constituency in all countries for curing inflation by unemployment. It is foolish for anyone to believe otherwise. Some members of this constituency hold that unemployment in the modern economy is inevitable. There is at least a certain honesty about his position. More urge the use of monetary policy against inflation in the belief that it works, as just suggested, through

---

The original manuscript begins with a Section 2, without being explicitly preceded by a Section 1. The original numbering has been retained here.

some magic intelligence of the Federal Reserve or other central bank. This is a dangerous and reactionary delusion against which all who speak for the socially deprived must be on guard. Were there are such monetary magic, it would long ago have been found and put into use. Monetary policy, to repeat, works by curbing expenditures, particularly to and by those industries that depend on borrowed money. It is only effective as it increases idle capacity and unemployment. What is called monetarism is a disguised justification for suffering by the poor. This is not Milton Friedman's avowed intention, to mention the most single-minded and eloquent of the advocates of monetary policy. But no one should doubt his service to the affluent or the rigor of his stand against the poor. He is rightly loved by the privileged.

III

From what I've just said comes the choice. Public officials can accept inflation. Or they can lessen or cure inflation by having unemployment, which will be especially bad among minorities and the young and, in the United States, in the central cities. Or they can find some way of tempering or preventing the direct competitive thrust for higher prices and income without resort to unemployment.

Inflation is not a tolerable solution. The strong groups that are the source of the competitive thrust for higher prices and incomes have a built-in protection against inflation. If you are a cause of inflation, you aren't a victim. The weak, including the old, the unorganized and those who live on savings, welfare, pensions, and other fixed income, bear the brunt. No decent society can so treat a large number of its citizens. Also were we ever to stop trying to prevent inflation, we would have a great deal of it. Unemployment, however it be defended in the abstract and however it may promote a more tractable labor force, is not a solution. As inflation strikes the weakest people in the society, unemployment solves it at the expense of the weakest people in the working force. Anyone with a sense of responsibility for, or any constituency in, people of average income or less will reject this solution.

IV

Until this point, recurring now for a moment specifically to the American scene, I am not in serious conflict with the administration of President Carter. It has rejected both unemployment and inflation. This has brought it to the advocacy of some form of direct restraint on organized price and income enhancement. And some groups, notably public employees, farmers, minimum wage recipients, and beneficiaries of public regulation, have been told rather firmly that their thrust for higher incomes must be curbed. But when it comes to the heart of the problem, which, of course, is the power of the large corporations and unions, the administration has so far had a failure of courage. So long as it postpones action, there will be danger that pressures for anti-inflationary action will lead to restrictions by the Federal Reserve, and thus to unemployment, as the remedy for inflation. Or public services and associated taxes will be attacked as the seemingly easy way of gaining relief from high prices and costs – something that is already occurring.

It is illogical and wrong to have a policy which excludes corporations and unions from specific concern merely because they are politically strong and articulate.

Recent polls on controls show that, by a substantial margin, the American people accept the firm action on wages and prices would be popular.

The only course that reflects sympathy for the least fortunate people in the modern industrial society is one that involves some form of income and price policy. This, needless to say, must be applied in a context of discussion and substantial consent. But there must be legal recourse against those who choose not to comply. Otherwise, the least cooperative, the most obdurate, would get the largest reward. There is also danger in voluntary measures that people in general and those involved as well will have an impression of accomplishment which will not, later on, be justified by the price indexes. There is danger in a purely rhetorical approach that the government will fool both the people and itself. These are the flaws in present policy.

The purpose of effective restraint on incomes and prices is not to cure inflation. It is to allow us to get much closer to full employment without having to resort to fiscal and monetary restraint and the resulting unemployment. It remains wholly necessary that total demand in the economy be generally equal to what can be supplied at full employment.

V

Conservatives hold as an article of faith that such an income and price policy cannot succeed. That is to say that either inflation or unemployment must succeed. In fact, controls succeeded brilliantly in the United States during World War II; they held the cost of living nearly stable through that enormous convulsion and totally so from 1943 to 1945. Industrial production more than doubled; manufacturing output more than tripled. Unemployment sank virtually to zero. When the controls were lifted and subsidies ended in 1946, there was a bulge of around 7% in living costs that year and of 12% the next. This is small compared with the recent peacetime experience. Controls also broke the inflationary spiral during the Korean War. Firm, clearly articulated price and labor standards, including a substantial measure of compulsion, held prices stable through the long expansion in production and employment in the first half of the 1960s. Mandatory controls were successfully employed by President Nixon. Though no satisfactory organization was set up either to administer or enforce them and they were in the charge of people who detested them, the controls, by the end of 1972, brought both unemployment and inflation down to well below5%. They also helped reelect Mr. Nixon, and they were then abandoned in early 1973 because at then-Secretary of the Treasury Schultz proclaimed, they were working. (Mr. Nixon's memoirs have Schultz regretting the hastiness of his action.) It does seem certain that too much demand was allowed to build up behind the Nixon price ceilings; controls, to repeat, allow us to approach full employment without inflation, but they do not allow us to have more demand than can be supplied with goods and services at full employment and full capacity operations.

So much for the American experience. The need for controls is affirmed by the fact that nearly all other countries are using them in one form or another. In Austria, Germany, and Switzerland, an income policy is implicit in the process of wage bargaining. These negotiations, which are industry- and country-wide, are conducted subject to a close concern for what will be consistent with stable prices. This procedure is complemented, in the so-called social market policy, by an understanding, explicit in Austria, that wage restraint will be matched by price restraint, and this is further enforced by heavy dependence on export markets. Britain has a highly developed system of wage and price restraints into which tax policy is integrated. France has a formal system of enforced restraints, which, unhappily, now works mostly on wages. The United States, along perhaps with the Italians, could well be the laggard in this general policy.

Switzerland, Austria, Germany, France, and other European countries are also aided in their national unemployment position by the fact that they draw heavily on an external working force, the inflow of which can be regulated with varying degree of efficiency. So, when workers are not needed in these countries, they remain in Turkey, southern Italy, Yugoslavia, Spain, Algeria, or Portugal. There, though unemployed or partly employed, they are not counted. The German, Swiss, Austrian, and (to some extent) French solution disguises but does not solve the employment problem. In the United States or Britain, the unemployed are within the country and must be counted.

VI

Controls or restraints in their useful sphere do not interfere with the operation of the market. That is because they become necessary only when the market has gone. They are made necessary by the very fact that organized power has displaced the market – that corporations, trade unions, and other organized groups acting independently or, like the farmers, with the state have replaced market control over prices. The prices of the thousand largest corporations in the United States are now privately controlled. Were the US government to put in a system of restraints, they would be fixing prices that, in effect, are already fixed. It is private fixing that makes necessary the public price restraints.

For a variety of reason, including the differing form of collective bargaining, the differing attitudes toward inflation (it is obviously more feared in Germany and Austria where the experience is more poignant than in the United States) and the differing role of foreign labor, the form of wage and price restraint that is part of an unemployment/inflation policy will be different in different countries. But superficial differences should not disguise basic similarity. In all industrial countries, there is retreat from the market; in all, this is part of a larger historical process; in all, with whatever variations, it requires an effective direct restraint on incomes and prices. The alternatives are inflation which inflicts the greatest suffering on the poorest and weakest people of the national community or measures to control that inflation which likewise afflict the vulnerable.

VII

The tasks here outlined do add to the responsibilities of the government. From this, there is no escape. However, the concentration of power that allows firms and groups to control their prices and incomes has also the effect of simplifying somewhat the administrative problem. That problem is confined to the large corporations, their high-salaried staff, collective bargaining contracts, farm support policy, and public pay. Where there is no power to raise prices, no controls are needed or useful. In the United States, no system of control would bother with prices of enterprises employing fewer than, say, 1,000 people or with unorganized workers. Farm price and income policy would be confined to consideration of the level of minimum prices. Fiscal and some monetary policy, to repeat, are still necessary to keep aggregate demand related to aggregate supply and thus to continue to control the prices and incomes of those who are still subject to the market, who have not achieved the power which made the control necessary.

It will be urged, and it is indeed urged, that any talk of control brings anticipatory price increases. This problem is rather easily solved. The baseline for controls should be set not at the time of the enactment of legislation but at some time well prior to the beginning of the active discussion. A uniform increase would then be allowed over the baseline. Consequently, no firm would have an advantage from anticipatory price increases.

It will also be urged that the controls work better for wages than for prices. This I strongly believe to have been the case with the Nixon controls in the United States. I do not believe, however, that this is necessary for a liberal and compassionate government. Nor should unions expect their members to absorb cost-of-living increases. If living costs do rise, then wages under any income policy should go up therewith. No system will bring perfectly stable prices. What we are seeking is not zero inflation but to avoid the gross and damaging price increases that are otherwise in prospect.

In recent months in the United States, farm and food prices have shown substantial increases. These increases need to be understood with some care. The period of monetary and fiscal recession which brought the Nixon/Ford inflation partially to an end did not arrest the increase in industrial prices; that continue right through the whole recession. But the recession did bring a sharp reduction in farm and commodity prices. The more liberal monetary and fiscal policies of the present administration have brought a compensating recovery. This relative increase has to be accepted. Maximum price controls are not appropriate or workable for this part of the economy.

VIII

I do not want to make the line of policy I here urge seem easy. Since possibly my experience in the matter is more complete than that of anyone now extant in the United States – I had charge of price control in the early years of World War II – I am disposed to minimize the complexity of the task. One comes to direction intervention on self-administered prices and incomes only because the alternatives – inflation and unemployment – inflict the greatest suffering on the weakest, more helpless, least articulate people in the society, although it is perhaps permissible to remind politicians that many of those people also do vote.

PART II

ESSAYS

CHAPTER 7

PARETO EFFICIENCY FROM LAUSANNE TO THE UNITED STATES: THE ROLE OF MAURICE ALLAIS

Irène Berthonnet

ABSTRACT

This chapter tells the story of how the concept of Pareto efficiency was shipped from Lausanne to the modern US theory of competitive general equilibrium, focusing on the specific role of Maurice Allais. It identifies similarities in both epistemological approach and theoretical achievements realized first by Pareto, then by Allais, and finally by Debreu and Arrow and Hahn. It also shows that these similarities are not casual, since historical circumstances account for the influence of Pareto on Allais and later of Allais on Arrow and Debreu.

Keywords: Allais; Pareto efficiency; general equilibrium; surplus; Arrow and Debreu and historical influence

1. INTRODUCTION

Although the familiarity between the Lausanne school of thought and the more contemporary general equilibrium theories seems obvious to lots of economists, little evidence of the historical conditions that explain the theoretical similarities is actually available. This chapter tells the story of how a key concept – Pareto

Research in the History of Economic Thought and Methodology: Including a Symposium on John Kenneth Galbraith: Economic Structures and Policies for the Twenty-First Century
Research in the History of Economic Thought and Methodology, Volume 41C, 109–129
Copyright © 2024 by Emerald Publishing Limited
All rights of reproduction in any form reserved
ISSN: 0743-4154/doi:10.1108/S0743-41542024000041C007

efficiency – was shipped from Lausanne to the United States, focusing on the specific role of Maurice Allais. Many other protagonists and circumstances have played a role in transferring Pareto efficiency from Lausanne to the United States, but the history told here allows to cast light on the bridges between French-Italian and American traditions of general equilibrium analysis. This perspective thus complements the existing work on the Vienna circle as the link between European and American general equilibrium theory (Cot & Lallement, 2006; Ingrao & Israel, 1990; Weintraub, 1983) and that on the London School of Economics (LSE) (Ingrao & Israel, 1990).

To demonstrate the continuity between European and US general equilibrium theory, this chapter identifies common points in both the theoretical achievements realized first by Pareto, then by Allais, and finally by Debreu and Arrow and in their epistemological approach. It focuses on how Pareto, Allais, and then Debreu and Arrow and Hahn have understood the Paretian criterion as a property of competitive general equilibrium devoid of any value judgment, rather than as a minimal norm for welfare economics. Beyond similarity of results, this chapter also explains the historical circumstances that created a linear influence from Pareto to Arrow, highlighting the determining role of Maurice Allais, both in the elaboration of the economic theory and as a source of influence on his successors.

The Pareto-efficiency criterion has been elaborated in Lausanne by Vilfredo Pareto, at the extreme end of the 19th century. Like many aspects of Pareto's work, Pareto efficiency has not been immediately successful. Whether this is due to the Marshallian domination in the Anglo-Saxon world, to the decline of the Lausanne school after Pareto, to his support to the fascist regime, or to the fact that Pareto did not train many students (Kirman, 2008) will not be discussed here. The object is rather to show that Pareto's efficiency criterion has been "re-discovered" in its original Paretian epistemological dimension in the 1940s. This might seem paradoxical considering the success of Pareto-efficiency inside welfare economics, but it will be shown that Maurice Allais has been the first to integrate the criterion in his "pure economics," thus carrying more faithfully the Paretian legacy. Allais indeed bases his demonstration of the maximum of social return theorem upon the Paretian criterion, and he has also been the first to give to the Paretian criterion its name of "efficiency." The rest of this chapter identifies how similar are Allais' contributions and Arrow-Debreu's, regarding the specific use of Pareto efficiency. This similarity can be at least partly explained in terms of historical influences, both of Allais on Debreu and then of Debreu on Arrow.

This chapter is organized in four sections. The first one introduces the work of Pareto and the early uses of the criterion inside new welfare economics, in order to highlight why the first book of Maurice Allais, *A la Recherche D'une Discipline Économique. L'économie Pure* (1952 [1943]), can be considered as a turning point in the history of Pareto efficiency. The second section focuses on Allais' introduction of the term of efficiency to refer to the Paretian criterion and on the epistemological motivations for doing so. Third section shows how Allais has been a fundamental influence on G. Debreu, and how this can account for the specific use of Pareto efficiency in his *Theory of Value* (1959) and later in Arrow and Hahn's *General Competitive Analysis* (1971). Last section concludes.

2. THE EARLY STORY OF
PARETO'S CRITERION: 1894–1943

Full paternity of an idea is always difficult to establish firmly, and many anticipations of the modern Pareto-efficiency criterion have been suggested by earlier economists: Dupuit (1844), Edgeworth (1881), and Walras (1900). Pareto's criterion of "maximum of ophelimity" is traditionally considered the first modern formulation because of its clarity and of its ordinal-based approach of utility, although the filiation with Walras is clear and although Edgeworth's contribution is still relevant insofar as the properties of Pareto efficiency are best shown through an Edgeworth box (Ingrao & Israel, 1990, pp. 257–258). For these reasons, we begin the story of the criterion with Pareto's formulation of a "maximum of ophelimity."

a. Pareto's "Maximum of Ophelimity"

Pareto originally introduced his famous criterion inside the field of what he called "pure economics." Pure economics were in Pareto's work the discipline which served as a first approximation to understand the laws of the social world, and which sketched a simplified and abstract representation of economic phenomena and their interdependencies. However, pure economics were not self-sufficient, since they had to be complemented by applied economics and sociology, in order to describe and explain accurately real phenomena (Ingrao & Israel, 1990; Marchionatti & Mornati, 2021). Like later his commentators (Bridel & Mornati, 2009), Pareto called himself a positivist: "I am much more of a positivist than Spencer, which means that I separate more faith from reason and experiment" (Pareto, 1897, letter to Adrian Naville, quoted by Marchionatti, 1999, p. 280). He wrote many times that social sciences would gain in relevance by using the logico-experimental method (Marchionatti & Gambino, 1997), because he considered it a guarantee of scientificity (Picavet, 2011). This implies abstract and formal economics, with empirical assumptions and verification of results (Marchionatti, 2006, pp. 547–548). Thus, only the final confrontation of theoretical results to facts would avoid value judgments and protect pure economics from normativity. This does not prevent pure economics from being an abstract and formal science, since they serve as the first basis that represents the social system:

> This way of approaching reality with theories which are always more in agreement with it, and which therefore usually become more and more complex, is called the method of *successive approximations*. (Pareto, 1898, pp. 106–107)[1]

This unusual epistemological framework shapes the specific status of Paretian pure economics as a first approximation: it is a formal and abstract analysis – and not an accurate description of reality – yet, it is not completely disconnected from reality since it forms the basic skeleton of a descriptive analysis, to be carried by sociology (Steiner, 1995). Pareto considers his pure economics as a purely positive discipline, thus meaning that it must not include political recommendations or economic prescriptions, for those are rather the object of politics than the object of science.

Pareto introduces his criterion inside pure economics, as a "maximum of ophelimity[2] for the community" (Schmidt, 1999). First presentation of the criterion is in an early text from 1894 (Pareto, 1894), but the complete and rigorous definition is presented in the 1909 *Manuel D'économie Politique*,[3] in which the criterion is introduced after the demonstration of general equilibrium (Mornati, 2013). Pareto shows that the "maximum of ophelimity" is a characteristic of competitive equilibrium and defines it this way:

> We shall say that the members of a community enjoy, in a certain situation, maximum ophelimity when it is impossible to move slightly away from this position in such a way that the ophelimity enjoyed by each member of the community increases or decreases. That is to say, every small displacement from this position must necessarily have the effect of increasing the ophelimity enjoyed by some individuals and decreasing that enjoyed by others, i.e., of being agreeable to some and disagreeable to others. (Pareto, 2014 [1906], p. 179)

In the *Traité de Sociologie Générale*, Pareto writes that the maximum of ophelimity is a scientific concept, void of any moral or value judgment (Pareto, 1916, pp. 1339–1340). It merely characterizes a specific state of the economy, the realization of which situation can be at most noted by the social scientist but is never a requisite demanded by any moral or ethical values. The status of the criterion is nonetheless important to Pareto, since in the *Manuel*, he wrote that the maximum of ophelimity is a fundamental matter in pure economics:

> If we denote by d the variations along a path – or a certain kind of path – when the individual acts according to type I, the condition of equilibrium is given by $\partial\Phi = 0$ This may or may not coincide with the preceding condition of maximum ophelimity. The aim of the study we have just undertaken has been precisely to look for conditions under which such a coincidence takes place.(Pareto, 2014 [1906], *Appendix to the 1909 French Version*, p. 383)

Some notions that Pareto had introduced in the *Manuel* have had a strong and immediate success, such as ordinal utility. But his overall project, and his criterion of maximum of ophelimity have not made the same impact. According to Allais (1981, p. 235), Pareto's *Manuel* has not been translated into English until 1972.[4] Schumpeter (1949, p. 148) explains the limited diffusion of Pareto's work in the Anglo-Saxon world by the Marshallian domination and Samuelson by the difficulty of reading it (Samuelson, 1971 [1947], p. 268). Other explanations have also been suggested, such as the small number of students he had trained (Kirman, 2008), and his connection to the fascist regime (Hicks, 1961). Nevertheless, all these authors acknowledge the first rank importance of Pareto's contributions for many modern notions in neoclassical economics and regret that it was not until his work has been used by others, that this value has been recognized. In this respect, Schumpeter attributes the rediscovery of the theory of value to Hicks and Allen (1934). Despite Pareto's introduction of the maximum of ophelimity in scientific positive economics, the first successes of the criterion have been in the field of welfare economics.

b. The Paretian Optimum in Welfare Economics

Many economists of the 1930s have written that until those years, Pareto's influence on general economic theory has been rather limited. Hicks wrote that he was "disturbed to find that in the twenty years which have elapsed since Pareto ceased his major contributions to economic theory, the tree which he planted has thrived so little" (Hicks, 1932, p. 299); Schumpeter (1949) and Georgescu-Roegen (1973) consider that his work has been really rediscovered in the 1930s. Although this traditional view has been discussed and nuanced by Marchionatti (2006),[5] and despite the fact that general equilibrium has always been taught in some economics departments in the United States, mostly due to Fisher's influence (Dimand, 2021), it is still true that Pareto's major impact on economics until the 1930s has been on welfare economics. First contribution is Barone's (1935 [1908]), who tried to give a new proof of the coincidence between Pareto's criterion and competitive equilibrium (though without explicitly mentioning the Paretian criterion). The criterion has also been used by the neoclassical socialists (Lange, 1937), since in its original form it applied both to competitive market economy and to planned economy and did not discriminate between private or collective property. In the late 1930s, new developments in welfare economics based on the Paretian criterion were also suggested by Lange (1932), Kaldor (1939), and Hicks (1939). Based on the critique that strict Pareto improvements are very unlikely, Hicks introduced the criterion of potential compensations, which is Paretian in its inspiration but less restrictive.

Thus, in the 1930s, "new welfare economics" have emerged as a normative discipline that tries to establish which policies can be considered scientifically as economically desirable (Backhouse, Baujard, & Nishizawa, 2021). Pareto's optimum plays a central role in this branch, being considered by most economists of the time as a non-normative but still evaluative basis for welfare analysis (Hands, 2012, p. 224), mostly because it was free from interpersonal comparisons of utility: the ordinalist turn changed the perspective on social well-being (Ingrao & Israel, 1990, p. 225). Beyond the diversity of approaches that can be identified in welfare economics (Mongin, 2006), the Paretian optimum has often been considered as a minimal efficiency condition, based on which theoreticians have tried to elaborate a justice theory (Desreumaux, 2008). As advanced by d'Aspremont (1995), the Paretian criterion has been used as a departure point for welfare economics: "'New welfare economics' have used Pareto's concept as its departure point for trying to elaborate a more precise determination of the social optimum" (d'Aspremont, 1995, p. 219).

As shown by Schumpeter (1949), it is paradoxical that welfare economics have been using the Paretian criterion as an efficiency basis: considering how Pareto himself felt about justice and science, it is actually contradictory to use his criterion as a basis for a theory of justice. Indeed, Pareto originally refused to discuss ethics and justice, which he considered as nonscientific. Therefore, the first economic theories that have built upon the Paretian criterion belonged to a field of research which had nothing to do with the original framework in which the "maximum of ophelimity" was introduced. In welfare economics, Pareto's criterion had changed status with respect to original pure economics and has become a minimal desired norm. It will be Maurice Allais' role to reintroduce it inside a very Paretian-like "pure economics."

c. Pure Economics Again: The First Contribution of Maurice Allais

Until *A la Recherche D'une Discipline Économique. L'économie Pure* (1943) by Maurice Allais, no one had used the criterion in its Paretian epistemological sense. As a comparison, the important book of Lionel Robbins (1947 [1932]), *An*

Essay on the Nature and Significance of Economic Science, also claimed that economics is a science of means, and a positive discipline, but does not use Pareto's criterion inside this analysis, despite using many other Paretian characteristics (ordinal utility for example). Even Samuelson – whose *Foundations of Economic Analysis* (1971 [1947]) carried the same project of being a manual for a new economic science – mentioned the Paretian criterion solely in the eighth chapter on "welfare economics," which proves that by the end of the Second World War, the criterion had had no echo outside the specific field of welfare economics.

Allais is thus the first to integrate Pareto's criterion inside positive economics. He considered Pareto as his intellectual master, and it is certainly the main influence that shaped Allais' first economic contribution, his 1943 *A la Recherche D'une Discipline Économique. L'économie Pure.* This book has then been published for the second time in 1952, under the title *Traité D'économie Pure.* Pareto's influence on Allais' *Traité* can be grasped by looking at some simple elements such as the title of the book, very similar to Pareto's *Manuel D'économie Politique* (1909), or at the dedication made by Allais to his "masters": Walras, Pareto, Fisher, and Divisia. Allais also writes that the structure of the *Traité* has been elaborated based on the mathematical appendix of Pareto's *Manuel*, and that it takes over Pareto's project, which Allais considers the most promising basis to shape a new economic science:

> In fact, the Paretian thought is actually booming and all the valuable progresses made these past years have been made under its direct or indirect influence. It represents in my opinion the most solid pillar on which tomorrow's economics will rest. (Allais, 1952 [1943], foreword, p. 38).

Most methodological choices made by Allais are similar to Pareto's. As his master, Allais writes that he accepts only the logico-experimental method for economics (Alcouffe, 2010), and considers that the method for physics and economics can be the same, since social sciences are not different by nature from other logico-experimental sciences (Allais, 1968). Allais also believes in the virtues of successive approximations: "The economic knowledge, like any knowledge, can be acquired only by successive approximations" (Allais, 1945, p. 11). Successive approximations allow combining an abstract and formal theorization of pure economics with more empirical elements:

> It is this search for a synthetic conception of all social and economic phenomena which is both the basis for all my work, and the tight link between my work in theoretical economics and in applied economics. (Allais, 1994, p. 21)

Same as Paretian pure economics, Allaisian pure economics are an abstract representation which serves as a first approximation of real social phenomena (Béraud, 2010) but which has to be consistent with the results of applied economics. This similar position regarding economic methodology can be attributed to another similarity in the understanding of the role of economics, considered by Pareto and Allais as a science of means (Lallement, 2010). Paretian and Allaisian "pure economics" are logico-experimental sciences which produce knowledge regarding the best way to reach given ends. Allais' first contribution to economic theory can therefore be considered Walrasian (in the sense of

Pareto's understanding of Walras' model). His main contribution to this model is the inter-temporal dimension, through the introduction of future goods markets (Béraud, 2011; Grandmont, 1989) and the distinction between differentiated and non-differentiated sectors (competition vs. monopoly). In this respect, Allais' work can be considered pioneering in France and Europe, for most of the French economists of the first half of the 20th century either ignored or rejected the Lausanne theories (Arena, 2000; Zylberberg, 1990).

Besides his overall project and its similarity to Pareto's, Allais has also been the first to introduce the Paretian criterion outside welfare economics, as an attribute of some specific types of general equilibria, analyzed inside pure economics. In the 1940s, Allais' project was to unite Walras, Pareto, and Fisher in a single inter-temporal model of general equilibrium (Béraud, 2014). The project can be considered achieved with the demonstration of the Allaisian "maximum of social return" theorem, which is established through a series of publications in the 1940s and which is the main contribution of Allais' *A la Recherche D'une Discipline Économique. L'économie Pure,* published in 1943 and exposing the maximum of social return theorem (Munier, 2020). The book is followed by a condensed presentation of the theorem in *Economie Pure et Rendement Social*[6] (1945). A further step is made in *Economie et Intérêt* published in 1947, which generalizes the theorem to the multiple generations case (see Allais, 1998 [1947], pp. 162–167, and the third appendix, pp. 756–761 for the mathematical exposition).

Demonstration of the maximum of social return theorem relies both on the Paretian criterion and on the concept of surplus, which Allais takes after Pareto's *Manuel D'économie Politique.*[7] This is why Allais writes: "As indicated in my 1943 book, it is Pareto's analysis which has been the basis of my social return theory" (Allais, 1994, p. 57). Allais refers to the Paretian surplus as "equivalent surplus," but improves it with his own concept of "distributable surplus" (Allais, 1973, 1981, p. 20). Indeed, Paretian surplus was expressed only in first-order condition terms, whereas Allais' distributable surplus is also expressed in terms of second-order conditions (see McLure, 2000, pp. 19, 368–369; Montesano, 1997). This allows including the industries with only one firm, provided that they charge a price equal to marginal cost (Béraud, 2014, pp. 132–133). The theorem is stated as follows:

> In any type of economy, the necessary and sufficient condition so that at a given time, (…) social return be maximum is that there is, at that time, explicitly or implicitly, a price system similar to the one which would exist in an exchange economy characterized by:
>
> 1°Freedom of choice for individuals and perfect competition of firms in the differentiated[8] sector;
>
> 2°Minimization of factory price and sale at marginal cost in the nondifferentiated sector;
>
> 3°An individual distribution of the property of production factors' material income, corresponding to the distribution of various consumable services in the considered economy. (Allais, 1945, pp. 17–18; see also Allais, 1952 [1943], pp. 524–525)

The demonstration of the maximum of social return theorem is also based on the Paretian criterion. Although Allais changed the name of the criterion, from "maximum of ophelimity for the community" to "maximum of social return," he explicitly wrote that it is the same criterion:

> Besides, and following Pareto, we consider as an optimal state of the economy, for given demography and capital, any state where it is impossible to increase an individual's economic satisfaction without lowering some other individual's satisfaction. Such a state will be called a maximum of social return. (Allais, 1952 [1943], p. 524)

Diemer (2011, p. 1) also considers that "The maximization of social return refers to what is usually called the Pareto optimum, which is a situation in which it is impossible to expand the satisfaction of a given individual without diminishing that of other individuals." As pointed by Arena (2000), the maximum of social return is rather an inter-temporal version of the Paretian maximum of ophelimity. Same also as Pareto, Allais considers that reaching the maximum of social return is the fundamental problem of economics: "To conclude, the quest for social return maximization is certainly the fundamental question of pure economics" (Allais, 1952 [1943], p. 679).

In his *Cours D'économie Générale*, Allais relates the history of the "maximum of social return" (Allais, 1959, pp. 165–166), which he begins with Smith's idea of invisible hand and the works of Marshall, Mill, and Colson. The second decisive step is Pareto's, Allais tells his students in French Ecole des Mines:

> Pareto has been the first to expose the problem of economic administration on a truly scientific level. He has given for the first time a precise and rigorous definition of the administration optimum which can be considered a final conquest of science. (Allais, 1959, p. 166)

Allais considers that his own contribution regarding the criterion is a better demonstration. According to him, Pareto's greatest merit is of having been the first to try a rigorous demonstration of coincidence between competitive equilibrium and maximum of ophelimity. But in Allais' view, Pareto failed:

> The demonstration given by Pareto in his Manual is both incomplete and partially incorrect. It confuses medium and marginal cost, does not distinguish between differentiated and nondifferentiated sector, does not take into consideration time and therefore interest, does not provide the second order conditions and does not give the exact validity conditions of the theorem. (Allais, 1952 [1943], p. 29)

Those are Allais' personal contributions, as recognized by Georgescu-Roegen:

> The most noteworthy contribution of the *Traité* is undoubtedly the treatment of Pareto's optimum condition of economic welfare. Allais' proof is far more complete than that of Pareto himself or the subsequent adaptations by Barone and Lange. (Georgescu-Roegen, 1956, p. 166)[9]

The second birth of the Paretian criterion is therefore due to Allais, who was the first to use it outside welfare economics. He writes that the search for states of maximum social return does not come under the field of welfare economics and policy but is simply a technical question, of economic administration, independent of value judgments:

> Thus, the search for the maximization of social return is mainly a problem of economic technique, which solution is absolutely **independent** from sociological and political notions that one can have regarding consumption distribution. (Allais, 1945, p. 25)

This change of scope and epistemological status for the criterion might explain as well why Allais called it a "maximum of social return" and no longer an optimum criterion – the more common terminology of the time.

3. THE SECOND MAURICE ALLAIS: SURPLUSES AND PARETO EFFICIENCY

Allais will not stick to this terminology of "maximum of social return," instead, he will be the first to call the Paretian criterion an "efficiency criterion." This change of name appears at the same time when Allais begins to reject the Walrasian model, introducing his own theory of surpluses. This section shows that Allais' surpluses theory stays in line with Pareto and specifically with the Paretian criterion.

a. Beyond Walras: From "Maximum of Social Return" to Efficiency

Retrospectively, Allais has identified two distinct periods in his contributions to economic theory (Allais, 1989, 1994, pp. 44–45), situating the break during winter 1966, when he had abandoned the Walrasian model and had begun reflecting over what was to become his theory of surpluses.[10] The theory is mainly a broadening of the Walrasian model he used to work on,[11] which he calls a *market economy*, in opposition to Walras' *market economy*. Despite breaking with Walras, Allais still considers Pareto as a major source of influence for the elaboration of his new theory. He believes that getting rid of Walrasian general equilibrium allows elaborating a new theory based on Paretian concepts and hunches. The 1981 *Théorie Générale des Surplus* is indeed elaborated upon the Paretian criterion, combined with the notion of surplus introduced by Pareto and Dupuit (Allais, 1973).

Allais describes the economy as a decentralized procedure, where agents try to appropriate surpluses: he uses the notion of surplus that was already present in Pareto's 1909 *Manuel*, under the form of "equivalent surplus," and develops it into a "distributable surplus" (McLure, 2000), which he considers the basis of his new theory (Allais, 1985). The general search for surpluses would then lead to the realization of a final state of "maximum of efficiency," which is characterized by the absence of remaining realizable surplus. The strict Walrasian equilibrium (with a price system guaranteeing that there will be no excess demand nor excess offer on $n-1$ markets) then appears as a specific case of the states of maximum efficiency produced by the global search for surpluses that drives the behavior of the agents (Alcouffe, 2010).

Only the equilibrium conditions differ from Walrasian and neowalrasian models (since they are now defined by the absence of remaining surpluses to appropriate): all of Allais' new developments have had the explicit finality of providing better demonstrations of the fact that an economy organized in markets would lead to the situation previously identified by Pareto as a maximum of ophelimity, to which Allais now refers to as "maximal efficiency":

> The positive and imperishable contribution of Pareto's economic work is to have elaborated a new and fundamental concept, that of "maximum of ophelimity for a society," which is better named now a "situation of maximal efficiency." (Allais, 1981, p. 234)

The maximum of efficiency is still the state that Pareto had previously identified, and it is also the same concept which Allais used to call "maximum of social return":

> My 1967 model of a markets economy is based *on the same definition of a maximum of social return,* that is of maximal efficiency, that my 1943 book: *a state of maximal efficiency can be described as a state where it is impossible to increase the preference indexes of some consumption units without necessarily diminishing that of other's consumption units.* (Allais, 1994, p. 94)

Thus, although Allais has changed the name of the criterion when entering in the second phase of his theoretical productions, the concept recovered by the "maximum of efficiency" has remained the same as Pareto's "maximum of ophelimity," and it has remained the central issue for economics. Allais probably used a different expression than his former "maximum of social return" in order to fit the extension of his theory, but there is definitely a second reason for this change of name, and for the use of the term "efficiency" instead of the more commonly used "optimum."

b. Getting Rid of Welfare Economics

Indeed, the change in terminology can be explained by a second reason, which Allais explicitly formulates in the text presented in Rappallo, Italy (Allais, 1967). At the time, he thought that the term of optimum and the term he had previously used of "maximum of social return" were too prescriptive and contained too many value judgments. Stating again that his criterion fully belongs to pure economics, which is a positive discipline, he emphasizes that the criterion is merely a property of general equilibrium but does not convey any ethical prescription, as it does when it is used inside welfare economic analysis. Even his own former terminology will from now on be considered inappropriate, because of the word "social." The maximum of efficiency is a property of certain economic outcomes, as it was in Pareto's *Manuel,* and it does not carry along any prescriptive message for society in general:

> Since this notion concerns society as a whole, it is a "social" return, and this is why during 20 years (1943–1962) I have called "theory of social return" the theory of maximal efficiency. However, it is doubtless that such a terminology can have an emotional content, because what is suggested by the word "social" can be different from what is suggested by the word "efficiency," and this can only lead to confusions. This is the reason why today, I rather use the expression of "maximum efficiency" than the expression of "maximum of social return." (Allais, 1967, p. 29)

Immediately after, Allais explains that the same problem can be identified with the Anglo-Saxon terminology of "optimum":

> In Anglo-Saxon literature, the theory of maximum efficiency is designated by the expression "theory of optimum allocation of resources." This terminology is even worse than the "social return" I used in my early work, because it suggests that there is one allocation of resources when in fact there is an infinity of situations of maximum efficiency. The emotional content of the term "optimum" suggests that under certain conditions, the allocation of resources can be considered optimum, when there exist no intrinsic optimum on which, from an ethical point of view, various individuals or public authorities can find an unanimous agreement. (Allais, 1967, p. 29)

This understanding of the word "optimum," and its supposed "emotional" content, is probably emphasized by the fact that in 1967 and after, Allais himself uses the word "optimum" in a new sense: to qualify the truly social (or collective) optimum, that is to say the situation collectively preferred – according to the ethical values of the community – between all efficiency maxima. It is a criterion that Pareto had also introduced but outside the scope of pure economics (Pareto, 1916, pp. 1342–1344). Pareto called it "a maximum of utility," meaning a position determined politically by choices that could arbitrate between individual utilities, as opposed to the maximum of ophelimity, which was considered free of ethical considerations, and which did not allow sacrifices of individual utility (Dupuy, 1992). Allais therefore limits the term "optimum" to these ethical considerations and reformulates both Pareto's criteria in his own terminology. Maximum of efficiency belongs to pure economics, whereas the social optimum belongs to politics, and this is why in 1967, Allais writes that these studies regarding the social optimum are out of his current scope: "The examination of this question is out of the scope of the present memoir" (Allais, 1967, p. 34).

This aspect of Allais' theory illustrates even better his pretension to endorse the Paretian positivist project of making of economics a true science, deprived of value judgments. It reinforces the idea according to which Allais desired to take Pareto's criterion outside of the strict scope of welfare economics and used the Paretian criterion in the same way as Pareto himself had done. Even if this was perceivable in his first Walrasian period, it has become more obvious and more explicitly formulated when he has deepened his own theoretical contribution. Later, in the *Théorie Générale des Surplus*, Allais wrote an updated history of the contributions that have dealt with the surpluses' analysis. He began with Walras, included Barone, Dupuit, Marshall, Hotelling, Hicks, Pareto, and concluded with Debreu and Boiteux. His personal comment to these contributions was a regret that most of them have belonged to normative economics and have been carrying political views. Allais wrote that he would rather have elaborated a "scientific theory of surpluses" (Allais, 1981, p. 306):

> Many of these contributions have unfortunately been influenced or inspired by normative views, and a lot of time has been necessary so that the concept of economic efficiency, independently of any view on distribution, could have been elaborated. Here again, Pareto settled the foundations. (Allais, 1981, p. 305)

It has been shown that Allais' role was to integrate Pareto's criterion inside positive pure economics, broadening its scope beyond strict welfare economics. If Allais has made important contributions to the economic theory of the 20th century, his role has not been limited to the rediscovery of Pareto's criterion: he also had a strong influence on some of the main neoclassical theorists and can therefore be considered as one of the links between Swiss 19-century economic theory and the American modern theory.

4. ALLAIS AND THE AMERICAN THEORY OF COMPETITIVE GENERAL EQUILIBRIUM

It has been recently argued that the Cowles Commission – through the work of first Irving Fisher and then Kenneth Arrow and Gérard Debreu – must be considered as the channel through which Walrasian general equilibrium analysis entered North American economics (Dimand, 2021). While many economists – such as Irving Fisher, Robert Triffin, Jacob Marschak, and others (see Dimand, 2021) have played a significant role in channeling the Walrasian version of general equilibrium into the US economics, Allais is also a relevant character in this story. Allais had a twofold influence on the production of American economic theory at the time of "the theory's axiomatization" (Ingrao & Israel, 1990, pp. 158–159), the modern reformulation of general equilibrium theory in rigorous mathematical language. First, his reintroduction of the Paretian criterion as the fundamental questions of "pure economics" (and no longer as a "departure point" for welfare economics) will be found again in Debreu's *Theory of Value,* where he recognizes the influence exerted upon him by his professor Allais. Second, Allais' motivation to rename Pareto's criterion a "maximum of efficiency" to avoid an emotional content carried by the previously used "optimum" and "maximum of social return" will be later shared by Arrow and Hahn. Indeed, in their *Competitive General Analysis* (1971), Arrow and Hahn use the same term Allais did and with similar epistemological motivations.

a. Allais' Influence: The Case of Gérard Debreu

Allais' influence on the developments of the American economic theory, especially the general equilibrium research program, has been acknowledged by many economists (Béraud, 2014; Samuelson, 1983, quoted by Grandmont, 1989). However, the fact that Allais wrote during wartime and in French hasn't helped the diffusion of his ideas.[12] It is not until later that he began gaining reputation inside the Anglo-Saxon world, especially thanks to his famous 1953 article (Allais, 1953) introducing the Allais paradox (Sterdyniak, 2011). Therefore, his early influence got exerted mainly through the students he trained in French École des Mines or in the various seminars he attended or conducted (Béraud, 2010, p. 2), thus largely contributing to the formation of what can be called "the French marginalist school" (Drèze, 1989). One of the first students of Maurice Allais, Marcel Boiteux has often recognized Allais' influence on him. At the same time, Allais was also teaching Gérard Debreu, who was first trained as a mathematician but entered economics because he discovered a new possible application for mathematics when reading Allais' book (Düppe & Weintraub, 2014, p. 58). The story goes that Boiteux and Debreu flipped a coin to decide which one of them would benefit from the 1948 Rockefeller scholarship and travel to the United States and to Sweden (Grandmont, 1989). Debreu won and left and ended up recruited by the *Cowles Commission* in 1950, where he met Arrow.

Allais' influence on Debreu can be noticed through several aspects, and especially by the fact that the French mathematician's work is based on the intertemporal Walrasian model developed by Allais in 1943, as is also the 1954 Arrow–Debreu model (Béraud, 2010, 2014; Düppe & Weintraub, 2014). Debreu also wrote in the preface of the 1952 second edition of Allais' *Traité* that his own search for a proof of the existence of competitive general equilibrium had been launched by his reading of the 1943 *Traité*,[13] which proved stability but not existence of general equilibrium (Grandmont, 1989). More generally, Debreu – like other neomarginalist economists (Arena, 2000) – has mentioned his debt and admiration for Allais several times:

> It was by springtime in 1946 that the impressive elementary book of M. Allais came into my hands, by the greatest chance. My economic reading back then was limited to a few pages, my interest for this part of knowledge had not been stimulated yet ... When I finished reading the book, I was passionate for Economy, for mathematical economics, but perfectly unable to value the contributions of M. Allais and the extent of my own knowledge. (Debreu, mentioned by Allais in the second edition of the *Traité*, and quoted by Diemer, 2006, p. 15)

Even later, in the foreword of his famous *Theory of Value*, Debreu wrote: "My interest for the Lausanne school's theory was aroused when I first met it in Maurice Allais' *Traité*, and a little later in François Divisia's book" (Debreu, 1959, p. IX). Debreu's knowledge of the Lausanne theories comes directly from Maurice Allais; therefore, his familiarity with the Lausanne concepts – such as Pareto efficiency – probably stems from the Allaisian interpretation rather than from a personal reading of Pareto or Walras. And indeed, Debreu has also taken over Allais' interest for the Paretian criterion and has adopted Allais' way of using it, as a simple property of competitive general equilibrium. Debreu's own research began in the 1950s, and his first publication is an article in *Econometrica*, "The Coefficient of Resource Utilization" (1951), in which he wants to measure the loss due to nonoptimal states, associating like Allais did loss and failure to reach Paretian optimality:

> The loss associated with a nonoptimal situation is now a measure of the distance from the actually available complex of resources to the set of optimal complexes. (Debreu, 1951, p. 274)

Drèze (1989, pp. 11–13) considers that this article is a final version of Allais' intuitions and ideas which were exposed only in his long book in French. In 1954, Arrow and Debreu published their famous article where the existence of a competitive general equilibrium was finally demonstrated. In the introduction of this article, Arrow and Debreu justify this research by the fact that:

> It is well known that, under suitable assumptions on the preferences of consumer and the production possibilities of producers, the allocation of resources in a competitive equilibrium is optimal in the sense of Pareto (no redistribution of goods or productive resources can improve the position of one individual without making at least one other individual worse off), and conversely every Pareto-optimal allocation of resources can be realised by a competitive equilibrium. (Arrow & Debreu, 1954, p. 265)

They refer to their own but separate work in 1951. This presentation of their work exposes the importance given to the Paretian criterion. In his *Theory of Value* published in 1959, Debreu dedicates a whole chapter to Pareto's criterion. He uses the criterion in the same way as Pareto and Allais did, since he introduces it in his own pure economics as a property of competitive general equilibrium: he writes that both welfare theorems "explain the role of prices in an economy" (Debreu, 1959, p. 98).

Unlike Allais though, Debreu keeps using the terminology of optimality (rather than that of efficiency), which was more familiar in welfare economics. This is how Debreu introduces the Paretian criterion in the *Theory of Value*:

> An optimum is defined as a realisable state, such as, within the limits imposed by the con-
> sumption sets, the production sets, and the total resources of the economy, it is impossible
> to improve the satisfaction of a consumer's preferences without lowering the satisfaction of
> another. (Debreu, 1959, p. 98)

Indeed, the shift from the word of optimum to that of efficiency in the American modern theory of general equilibrium will not be made by Debreu but only later by Arrow and Hahn. Although no direct link between Allais and Arrow or Hahn can be established, similarity in argumentation regarding the appropriate name of Pareto's criterion is striking.

b. Allais' Indirect Influence: Arrow and Hahn and Pareto Efficiency

From the point of view of general equilibrium theory, there is a direct and obvious continuity between Debreu's *Theory of Value* in 1959 and Arrow and Hahn's contribution in 1971, *Competitive General Equilibrium*. But regarding the specific history of the Paretian criterion, one slight change is to be noticed: if Debreu has used the word "optimum," while inserting it in a project of pure economics, Arrow and Hahn prefer writing about Paretian efficiency when using it inside the same overall project of abstract and formal pure economics as before them Pareto, Allais, and Debreu.

Arrow and Hahn explicitly mention that their theory is the same as Debreu's *Theory of Value* (1959). In the foreword of their book, they write that they expose exactly the same theory as Debreu's but with different proofs and some new questions that Debreu hadn't raised (Arrow & Hahn, 1971). In this respect, it can be said that Allais has influenced the theoretical approach of *Competitive General Analysis*, through the intermediate influence of his former student Gérard Debreu.[14]

Similarity between Allais and Arrow and Hahn regarding the use of the Paretian criterion is also perceptible in the transformation of "Pareto-optimum" in "Pareto-efficiency." Even though no explicit reference is made to Allais, it is striking to notice that the justification of the change in terminology is exactly the same as in Allais. Arrow and Hahn write that it is because they make no mention of welfare economics and because they only use the welfare theorems for their descriptive properties that they prefer calling Pareto's criterion a criterion of efficiency:

> We use the term "Pareto efficient" instead of the more common "Pareto optimal" because the
> latter term conveys more commendation than the concept should bear, since a Pareto efficient
> allocation might assign extremely low utilities to some (indeed, possibly all but one) households
> and thus not be optimal in any sense in which distributional ethics are involved. (Arrow &
> Hahn, 1971, p. 91)

Clearly, Arrow and Hahn consider that the terminology of optimality conveys too much ethics and therefore has to be restricted to the subfield of welfare economics. Having mentioned that their contribution would not deal with developments in welfare economics, they chose a different name to refer to Pareto's criterion in order to fit better the type of economics they wish to make, namely a "descriptive theory of general equilibrium":

> We have refrained also from a development of welfare economics, except for some theorems that also play a role in the descriptive theory of general equilibrium. (Arrow & Hahn, 1971, foreword, p. VI)

It clearly appears that the project they overtake is exactly the same as Pareto's and Allais' of creating pure economics with an ambition of positivity, and this project seems easier or at least more common by the 1970s. Renaming the Paretian optimum in Paretian efficiency is to them – as it was already to Allais – the guarantee that they are simply describing some specific properties of a competitive general equilibrium.[15] This is why it is significant: it reveals what epistemological status they give to a position that can be described as Pareto optimal or Pareto efficient. Like Maurice Allais, Arrow and Hahn have renounced to the word "optimum" because it conveyed too much ethics to fit the production of economics as science; the optimum has to remain the object of welfare economics.

However, the change in name is only a change of scope, since the formal and theoretical content remains exactly the same as Pareto had defined it:

> T.4.4 is the basic efficiency theorem of welfare economics. Any Pareto-efficient allocation can be realised as a sort of competitive equilibrium. (Arrow & Hahn, 1971, p. 94)

> A more extended analysis of the welfare implication of T.4.4 is beyond the scope of this book, which is concerned with the properties of competitive equilibria; T.4.4 has been proved here as a step in demonstrating the existence of equilibrium. (Arrow & Hahn, 1971, p. 95)

Thus, two major common points can be identified between Maurice Allais and Arrow and Hahn's contribution. First, the scope and ambition of economics as "pure economics," understood as an abstract and formal representation of the interdependencies at work in the system is similar.[16] Second, the epistemological motivation for turning Pareto optimality into Pareto efficiency is the same. Although direct acquaintances between these authors are difficult to identify and prove, similarity in argumentation shows that they share the same epistemology and understanding of the role of the Paretian criterion inside general equilibrium theory.

CONCLUSION

The purpose of this chapter has been to highlight some striking similarities between the Lausanne theory (mainly Pareto's theory, for as shown by Bridel (2010) the homogeneity of a so-called Lausanne school is actually a myth), Allais theory, and the theory of general equilibrium elaborated in the United States by Arrow and Debreu. It has been shown that these similarities are not completely casual, since a chronological line of influences between these economists can be drawn, from Pareto to Arrow. But this raises the difficult question of knowing how history is made: under the action of individuals or under global evolutions that shape step by step the elaboration of common knowledge? The purpose here has not been to argue that the history of modern neoclassical economics would not have been the same without M. Maurice Allais himself (see also Finez, 2013, for a similar perspective applied to the reforms in the French railway sector). It has rather been to show that if Allais did have a great influence on the production of modern economics, it is because of his position as a teacher in the French academy and also due to some historical contingencies that have brought to his hands the *Manuel D'économie Politique* of Pareto, that have sent Debreu instead of Boiteux to the United States.

The ultimate purpose of this chapter has been to sketch the history of the key concept of Pareto optimality (or efficiency), in order to understand the progressive elaboration of the modern theory of general equilibrium, which began in Lausanne, and reached its peak in the cold war United States. Indeed, after the publication of *General Competitive Analysis*, it seems that Pareto's views regarding the type of science that economics should be have become more common. The same can be said about his "maximum of ophelimity for the community" criterion, which has integrated the modern version of the theory of general equilibrium, under the name of "Pareto-efficiency." Thus, although the first decades of the 20th century had carried Pareto's criterion toward welfare economics, under the influence of Allais and Debreu, the criterion has progressively gained back its place inside "pure economics," as a positive analysis of economics (Berthonnet & Delclite, 2014), which is illustrated by the shift from the term "optimum" to that of "efficiency" first suggested by Maurice Allais and then by Arrow and Hahn. This shift from optimality to efficiency does not reflect changes inside welfare economics but rather the rediscovery of a Paretian-style "pure economics." Lockwood (2008) writes in the *Pareto-efficiency* Palgrave entrance that the term of optimality has been replaced by efficiency to avoid the implicit desirability that conveyed the idea of optimum, thus arguing in the same sense that Allais and Arrow and Hahn. This transformation probably played a significant role in popularizing the efficiency criterion outside of general equilibrium theory. Indeed, after the 1970s, Pareto-efficiency entered the toolbox of contemporary microeconomics-based "economic reasoning" (Berman, 2022), soon to be used in various branches of economic analysis – such as market design or market failure approach (Berthonnet, 2019) – as well as in public policy design (Berry, 2017). As Davis (2022, p. 92) mentions, nowadays "most mainstream economists regard efficiency as a purely technical tool of analysis."

It has to be mentioned though that Allais' and Arrow and Hahn's introduction of Pareto efficiency inside pure economics is questionable. The criterion being at the junction between normative welfare economics and positive pure economics, the question of knowing whether it carries *in se* value judgments or not, is not closed once and for all. Allais, Arrow, and Hahn were obviously well aware of this, since they suggested changing the name of the criterion, so that it would not appear as an ethical prescription. But a simple change in terminology cannot suppress the problem either. Indeed, as objected by Hicks to conclude a presentation on the desirability of reaching a Pareto-optimal or Pareto-efficient situation:

It is not just the word "welfare" which conveys an aura of approbation. We might substitute the most colourless expression we could find, yet we should not wholly escape the prejudice that more of "whatever it is" is in some sense a "good thing." If it isn't, why do we study it? (Hicks, 1975, pp. 310–311)

NOTES

1. Quotations from Pareto and Allais are my translation, from texts originally in French (except when indicated otherwise).

2. Ophelimity is Pareto's word for utility (considered less scientific).

3. Year 1909 is the date of publication of the French version of the 1906 *Manuel D'économie Politique*, in which the Paretian criterion also appeared; but the French version includes an extended mathematical appendix with the final and complete version of the Paretian criterion (McLure, 2000).

4. But his *Traité de Sociologie Générale* had been translated to English in 1935.

5. Marchionatti (2006) showed that the Paretian influence between 1900 and 1930 was subtle and indirect rather than inexistent. Also, some important fields that have evolved under the Paretian influence can be identified, notably a methodological influence on the Italian tradition in public finance (see Fossati, 2012, 2013).

6. The 1945 book is dedicated to Pareto: "This booklet is dedicated to the memory of V. Pareto, who has been the first to throw the rigorous bases of the theory of social return" (Allais, 1945, p. 3).

7. In his work of the 1940s, Allais relies exclusively on the Paretian approach of surplus. As related by Béraud (2010), Allais wrote in France during wartime and therefore barely knew Marshall, Samuelson, Hicks, and Dupuit. This is why he relied more on the mathematical appendix of Pareto's *Manuel* than on any analyses in terms of surpluses (which he will later do), even if he could have used Hicks and Allen (1934), which he knew (Lenfant, 2005).

8. In Allais's terminology, differentiated sector refers to competitive industries, whereas nondifferentiated sector refers to monopoly.

9. Although Georgescu-Roegen considers that Allais's proof is still wrong.

10. The break begins in the 1967 Rappallo seminar, when Allais criticizes the too restrictive hypothesis of the Walrasian research program (see also Allais' presentation at the Lausanne congress of Francophone economists in 1971). The break with Walras is considered final when the theory is presented at length in a book published in 1981, *La Théorie Générale des Surplus*.

11. Allais criticizes the Walrasian hypothesis, especially the continuity and convexity hypothesis, and demonstrates the two theorems of welfare economics without them (see Allais, 1967, p. 65 and following; Allais, 1981, Part 6, Chapter 5; and Allais, 1994, pp. 49–51); he also rejects the Walrasian virtual behaviour of agents, which implies that equilibrium is realized at once, and the hypothesis of price unicity (see Allais, 1967, pp. 73–76), which he considers too unrealistic (so unrealistic that it is unacceptable; Allais, 1971). See Lesourne (1989) and Alcouffe (2010) for a more detailed analysis of Allaisian Surpluses' theory developed in the 1970s–1980s.

12. Similarly, Allais read mostly in French, and it seems that this is what prevented him from knowing Fisher's full work in mathematical economics (Dimand, 2021).

13. Allais's book has been renamed *Traité D'économie Pure* in its second edition in 1952. Back in 1943, it was called *A la Recherche D'une Discipline Economique. L'économie Pure*.

14. It must be mentioned though that Arrow and Debreu already worked in a similar perspective since the 1950s: both welfare theorems were demonstrated in Debreu (1951) and Arrow (1951), and in his article, Arrow thanks Debreu for his comments.

15. Whereas in Arrow's 1951 paper, he was making a contribution to the subfield of welfare economics, which probably is why he didn't suggest at the time to change the name of Pareto's criterion and kept referring to it as optimality.

16. Although in Pareto and Allais, pure economics had to be complemented with at least applied economics.

REFERENCES

Alcouffe, A. (2010). La théorie des surplus de Maurice Allais et l'histoire de la pensée économique. In A. Diemer, J. Lallement, & B. Munier (Eds.), *Maurice Allais et la science économique* (pp. 49-66). Paris: Clément Juglar.
Allais, M. (1945). *Economie pure et rendement social*. Paris: Dalloz.
Allais, M. (1952 [1943]). *Traité d'économie pure* (2nd ed.). Paris: Imprimerie Nationale.
Allais, M. (1953). Le comportement de l'homme rationnel devant le risque: Critique des postulats et axiomes de l'Ecole américaine. *Econometrica, 21*(4), 503–546.
Allais, M. (1959). *Cours d'économie générale*. Paris: Ecole des Mines de Paris.
Allais, M. (1967). *Les conditions de l'efficacité dans l'économie*. IV seminario internazionale di Rapallo, September 12–14.
Allais, M. (1968). L'économique en tant que science. *Revue D'économie Politique, 1978*(1), 5–30.
Allais, M. (1971). *Presentation*. Lausanne conference in Walras's honor, 1971.
Allais, M. (1973). La théorie générale des surplus et l'apport fondamental de Vilfredo Pareto. *Revue D'économie Politique, 6*(83), 1044–1097. année.
Allais, M. (1981). *La théorie générale des surplus*. Fontaine: Presses Universitaires de Grenoble.
Allais, M. (1985). The concept of surplus and loss and the reformation of the theories of stable general economic equilibrium and maximum efficiency. In M. Baranzini & R. Scazzieri (Eds.), *Foundations of economics: Structures of inquiry and economic theory* (pp. 135–174). Oxford: Blackwell.
Allais, M. (1989). Les lignes directrices de mon œuvre. *L'actualité Économique, 65*(3), 323–345.
Allais, M. (1994). Introduction à la troisième édition. In M. Allais (Ed.), *Traité d'économie pure* (pp. 17–156). Paris: Clément Juglar.
Allais, M. (1998 [1947]). *Economie et intérêt* (2nd ed). Paris: Clément Juglar.
André, Z. (1990). *L'économie mathématique en France 1870–1914*. Paris: Economica.
Arena, R. (2000). Les économistes français en 1950. *Revue Économique, 51*(5), 969–1007.
Arrow, K. (1951). An extension of the basic theorems of classical welfare economics. In J. Neyman (ed.), *Proceedings of the second Berkeley symposium on mathematical statistics and probability* (pp. 507–532). Berkeley, CA: University of California Press.
Arrow, K., & Debreu, G. (1954). Existence of an equilibrium for a competitive economy. *Econometrica, 22*(3), 265–290.
Arrow, K., & Hahn, F. (1971). *General competitive analysis*. San Francisco, CA: Oliver & Boyd.
d'Aspremont, C. (1995). Economie du bien-être et utilitarisme. In L.-A. Gérard-Varet & J.-C. Passeron (Eds.), *Le modèle et l'enquête* (chap. 5, pp. 217–241). Paris: EHESS.
Backhouse, R. E., Baujard A., & Nishizawa, T. (Eds.). (2021). *Welfare theory, public action, and ethical values: revisiting the history of welfare economics*. Cambridge: Cambridge University Press.
Barone, E. (1935 [1908]). The ministry of production in the collectivist state. In F. A. Hayek (Ed.), *Collectivist economic planning* (pp. 245–290). London: George Routledge & Sons, Ltd.
Béraud, A. (2010). *Le traité d'économie pure*, la contribution fondatrice. In A. Diemer, J. Lallement, & B. Munier (Eds.), *Maurice Allais et la science économique* (pp. 1–17). Paris: Clément Juglar.
Béraud, A. (2011). Walras et les ingénieurs-économistes français. Des Éléments d'économie politique pure au Traité d'économie pure. In R. Baranzini, A. Legris, & L. Ragni (Eds.), *Léon Walras et l'équilibre économique général* (pp. 177–200). Paris: Economica.
Béraud, A. (2014). Le développement de la théorie de l'équilibre general. Les apports d'Allais et de Hicks. *Revue Economique, 65*(1), 125–158.
Berman, E. P. (2022). *Thinking like an economist*. Princeton, NJ: Princeton University Press.
Berry, M. (2017). *Morality and power: on ethics, economics and public policy*. Cheltenham: Edward Elgar Publishing.
Berthonnet, I. (2019). Is competition necessarily efficient? An answer through the history of neoclassical theory. *Review of Radical Political Economics, 51*(2), 211–224.

Berthonnet, I., & Delclite, T. (2014). Pareto-optimality or pareto-efficiency: Same concept, different names? An analysis over a century of economic literature. *Research in the History of Economic Thought and Methodology, 32*, 129–145.

Bridel, P. (2010). A propos de l'idée d' "école de Lausanne." *Revue Européenne des Sciences Sociales, 48*, 89–92.

Bridel, P., & Mornati, F. (2009). De l'équilibre général comme "branche de la métaphysique." *Revue Économique, 60*(4), 869–890.

Cot, A., & Lallement, J. (2006). 1859–1959: De Walras à Debreu, un siècle d'équilibre général. *Revue Économique, 57*(3), 377–388.

Davis, J. B. (2022). Economics as a normative discipline: Value disentanglement in an 'objective' economics. In S. Badiei & A. Grivaux (Eds.), *The positive and the normative in economic thought* (pp. 87–107). London: Routledge.

Debreu, G. (1951). The coefficient of resource utilization. *Econometrica, 19*(3), 273–292.

Debreu, G. (1959). *Théorie de la valeur, analyse axiomatique de l'équilibre économique.* Paris: Dunod.

Desreumaux, V. (2008). La justice sociale dans l'économie du bien-être: sortie par la porte et rentrée par la fenêtre? Histoire et analyse de l'émergence du concept d'équité comme absence d'envie. *Economies et Sociétés, 42*(5), 893–930.

Diemer, A. (2006). *Existe-t-il une tradition française de la théorie de l'équilibre général?* Document de travail, Projet CNRS Histoire des Savoirs.

Diemer, A. (2011). Du rendement social dans une économie concurrentielle à la concurrence organisée: Les apports de Maurice Allais. In *Presentation at the foundations, definitions and usages of perfect competition, Paris-Ouest-Nanterre.* (pp. 13–14).

Dimand, R. W. (2021). Léon Walras, Irving Fisher and the Cowles approach to general equilibrium analysis. *Œconomia, 11-2*, 253–280.

Drèze, J. (1989). Maurice Allais and the French marginalist school. *Scandinavian Journal of Economics, 91*(1), 5–16.

Düppe, T., & Weintraub, E. R. (2014). *Finding equilibrium.* Princeton, NJ: Princeton University Press.

Dupuit, J. (1844). De l'utilité des travaux publics. *Annales des Ponts et Chaussées, 2nd Semester*, 332–375.

Dupuy, J.-P. (1992). *Le sacrifice et l'envie.* Paris: Calmann Levy.

Edgeworth, F. (1881). *Mathematical psychics, an essay on the application of mathematics to the moral sciences.* Charleston, SC: BiblioLife.

Finez, J. (2013). Les économistes font-ils l'économie ferroviaire? *Revue Française de Socio-Economie, 11*, 15–34.

Fossati, A. (2012). Pareto's influence on scholars from the Italian tradition in public finance. *Journal of the History of Economic Thought, 34*(1), 43–66.

Fossati, A. (2013). Vilfredo Pareto's influence on the Italian tradition in public finance: A critical assessment of Mauro Fasiani's appraisal. *European Journal of the History of Economic Thought, 20*(3), 466–488.

Georgescu-Roegen, N. (1956). *Traité d'économie pure* by Maurice Allais, review. *The American Economic Review, 46*(1), 163–166.

Georgescu-Roegen, N. (1973). Vilfredo Pareto and his theory of ophelimity. *Presentation at the international Vilfredo Pareto conference,* Roma, Octobre 25–27 (Reprinted in Accademia Nazionale dei Lincei, 1975, Vol. 9, pp. 223–265).

Grandmont J.-M. (1989). Rapport sur les travaux scientifiques de Maurice Allais. *Annales D'économie et de Statistique, 14*, 25–38.

Hands, W. (2012). The positive–normative dichotomy and economics. In U. Mäki (Ed.), *Philosophy of economics* (pp. 219–239). Amsterdam: Elsevier.

Hicks, J. R. (1932). Marginal productivity and the Lausanne school: A reply. *Economica, 37*, 297–300.

Hicks, J. R. (1939). The foundations of welfare economics. *Economic Journal, 49*(196), 696–712.

Hicks, J. R. (1961). Pareto revealed. *Economica, 28*(111), 318–322.

Hicks, J. R. (1975). The scope and status of welfare economics. *Oxford Economic Papers, 27*(3), 307–326.

Hicks, J. R., & Allen, R. (1934). A reconsideration of the theory of value. *Economica, 1*(1), 52–76.

Ingrao, B., & Israel, G. (1990). *The invisible hand* (491 p.). Cambridge, MA: MIT Press.

Kaldor, N. (1939). Welfare propositions of economics and interpersonal comparisons of utility. *Economic Journal, 49*, 549–552.

Kirman, A. (2008). Pareto. In S. N. Durlauf & L. E. Blume (Eds.), *The new Palgrave dictionary of economics*. (pp. 277–290) London: Macmillan.

Lallement, J. (2010). La méthode scientifique en économie selon Maurice Allais. In A. Diemer, J. Lallement, & B. Munier (Eds.), *Maurice Allais et la science économique*. (pp. 23–35) Paris: Clément Juglar.

Lange, O. (1932). The foundations of welfare economics. *Econometrica, 10*(3/4), 215–228.

Lange, O. (1937). *On the economic theory of socialism* (pp. 57–129). Philadelphia, PA: Lippincott.

Lenfant, J.-S. (2005). Psychologie individuelle et stabilité d'un équilibre général concurrentiel dans le Traité d'économie pure de Maurice Allais. *Revue Économique, 456*, 855–888.

Lesourne, J. (1989). La théorie de l'efficacité maximale et la Théorie Générale des surplus de Maurice Allais. In G. de la Rouchefoucauld (Ed.), *Un savant méconnu, portraits d'un autodidacte: Sur l'oeuvre de Maurice Allais, prix nobel de sciences économiques* (pp. 114–129), 2002. Paris: Clément Juglar.

Lockwood, B. (2008). Pareto efficiency. In S. N. Durlauf & L. E. Blume (Eds.), *The new Palgrave dictionary of economics* (2nd ed., pp. 292–295). Basingstoke: Nature Publishing Group.

Marchionatti, R. (1999). The methodological foundations of pure and applied economics in Pareto, an anti-walrasian programme. *Revue Européenne des Sciences Sociales, 37*(116), 277–294.

Marchionatti, R. (2006). At the origin of post-war mainstream of economics: on Pareto's influence on economic theory. *International Review of Economics, 53*(4), 538–559.

Marchionatti, R., & Gambino, E. (1997). Pareto and political economy as a science: Methodological revolution and analytical advances in economic theory in the 1890s. *The Journal of Political Economy, 105*(6), 1322–1348.

Marchionatti, R., & Mornati, F. (2021). Pareto's trattato di sociologia generale: A behaviourist ante litteram approach. *Cambridge Journal of Economics, 45*(2), 353–369.

McLure, M. (2000). The Pareto-Scorza polemic on collective economic welfare. *Australian Economic Papers, 39*(3), 347–371.

Mongin, P. (2006). Value judgments and value neutrality in economics. *Economica, 73*, 257–286.

Montesano, A. (1997). Pareto's analysis of efficiency and its interpretation. *History of Economic Ideas, 3*, 7–18.

Mornati, F. (2013). Pareto optimality in the work of Pareto. *Revue Européenne des Sciences Sociales, 51*(2), 65–82.

Munier, B. (2020). … et le prix Nobel d'économie 1988 fut attribué à Maurice Allais. *Bulletin de la Sabix. Société des Amis de la Bibliothèque et de l'Histoire de l'École polytechnique, 66*, 87–100.

Pareto, V. (1894). Il massimo di utilità dato dalla libera concorrenza. In G. Busino (ed.), *Vilfredo Pareto, Œuvres Complètes, Ecrits d'économie pure* (Vol. 26, pp. 276–294). Genève: Droz.

Pareto, V. (1898). Comment se pose le problème de l'économie pure? In G. Busino (ed.), *Vilfredo Pareto, Œuvres Complètes, Marxisme et économie pure* (coll. "Œuvres Complètes", pp. 102–109). Genève: Droz.

Pareto, V. (1909). *Manuel d'économie politique* (2nd ed.). Paris: Librairie général de droit et de jurisprudence.

Pareto, V. (1916). *Traité de sociologie générale*. Genève: Droz.

Pareto, V. (2014 [1906]). *Manual of political economy, a critical and variorum* (p. 720). Oxford: Oxford University Press.

Picavet, E. (2011). Arguments de choix rationnel et contractualisme: les cas symétriques de Rousseau et de Pareto. *Œconomia, 1*(2), 215–237.

Robbins, L. (1947 [1932]). *Essai sur la nature et la signification de la science économique*. Paris: Editions Politiques, Économiques et Sociales.

Samuelson, P. A. (1971 [1947]). *Les fondements de l'analyse économique*. Paris: Gauthier-Villars.

Schmidt, C. (1999). Le concept d'optimalité parétienne: À l'origine d'un nouveau programme de recherche social. *Revue Européenne des Sciences Sociales, 37*(116), 347–358.

Schumpeter, J. (1949). Vilfredo Pareto (1848–1923). *The Quarterly Journal of Economics, 63*(2),147–173.

Steiner, P. (1995). Vilfredo Pareto et le protectionnisme: L'économie politique appliquée, la sociologie générale et quelques paradoxes. *Revue Économique, 46*(5), 1241–1262.

Sterdyniak, H. (2011). Maurice Allais, itinéraire d'un économiste français. *Revue D'économie Politique*, *121*(2), 119–153.

Walras, L. (1900). *Eléments d'économie politique pure*. Paris: Librairie Générale de Droit et de Jurisprudence.

Weintraub, E. R. (1983). On the existence of a competitive equilibrium: 1930–1954. *Journal of Economic Literature*, *21*(1), 1–39.

CHAPTER 8

FROM REGULATION TO DEREGULATION AND (PERHAPS) BACK: A PECULIAR CONTINUITY IN THE ANALYTICAL FRAMEWORK*

William McColloch and Matías Vernengo

ABSTRACT

The rise of the regulatory state during the Gilded Age was closely associated with the development of institutionalist ideas in American academia. In their analysis of the emergent regulatory environment, institutionalists like John Commons operated with a fundamentally marginalist theory of value and distribution. This engagement is a central explanation for the ultimate ascendancy of neoclassical economics, and the limitations of the regulatory environment that emerged in the Progressive Era. The eventual rise of the Chicago School and its deregulatory ambitions did constitute a rupture, but one achieved without rejecting preceding conceptions of competition and value. The substantial compatibility of the view of markets underlying both the regulatory and

---

*A preliminary version was presented at the Association for Evolutionary Economics sessions at the ASSA Meeting in San Diego, January 6, 2020, and at the Eastern Economic Association Meeting, February 29, 2020. We thank participants' comments, without implicating them. We also thank Thomas Palley, and an anonymous reviewer for comments on a preliminary version.

Research in the History of Economic Thought and Methodology: Including a Symposium on John Kenneth Galbraith: Economic Structures and Policies for the Twenty-First Century
Research in the History of Economic Thought and Methodology, Volume 41C, 131–153
ISSN: 0743-4154/doi:10.1108/S0743-41542024000041C008

*deregulatory periods is stressed, casting doubt about the transformative poten-
tial of the resurgent regulatory impulse in the New Gilded Age.*

Keywords: John Commons; George Stigler; regulatory capture;
deregulation; institutionalist ideas; marginalist theory;
neoclassical economics

1. INTRODUCTION

American institutionalism, perhaps the first truly distinctive and self-conscious
school of economic thought to have emerged in the United States, remains a
much-studied enigma. The evident diversity and eclecticism of the movement, and
its inconsistent definition in the secondary literature, suggests that nearly any gen-
eralization of its character and subsequent influence will be met with challenges.
Our contention is that substantial theoretical continuity exists between one tribu-
tary of this movement, the "Wisconsin Institutionalism" of John Commons and
Richard Ely, and the subsequent deregulatory impulse of the Chicago School. A
focused analysis of this particular strand of American institutionalism provides,
in our view, a more nuanced account of the eventual postwar transformation of
economics in the United States, and of the ascendance of the marginalist theory
of value and distribution. In making such claims, we intend no sweeping critical
analysis of American institutionalism as a whole nor do we mean to diminish
the practical regulatory achievements of the movement. Rather, we suggest that
the eventual deregulatory impulse in American economics emanating from the
Chicago School rested on far less of a theoretical transformation than is commonly suggested.

The genesis of the modern regulatory state in the United States is generally
traced to the Progressive Era. Though the term is often loosely defined, we associate it here with the creation of notionally independent federal bureaucracies
charged with the oversight of delimited aspects of economic activity (DeCanio,
2015; Levi-Faur, 2013). The hallmark regulatory institutions of the Progressive
Era were the Interstate Commerce Commission (ICC) of 1887, the Sherman
Antitrust Act of 1890, and the Federal Trade Commission (FTC) of 1914, and
in the realm of monetary regulation, the Federal Reserve of 1913. Broadly, this
regulatory apparatus was concerned with railroads, the excessive size of trusts,
and the ravages of financial panics, themselves not completely disconnected from
railroad speculation, at least early in the period.

The New Deal Era, running from the 1930s up to the 1960s, opened up and
extended the functions of the regulatory state, with the Securities Exchange
Commission (SEC) of 1934 as the iconic institution of the period. Alongside the
SEC, the sweeping transformations of the Federal Reserve system, and the creation of the National Labor Relations Board (NLRB), both in 1935, are further
representative institutions of the period. Of note, in both the Progressive Era and
in the early stages of the New Deal, institutionalists were a dominant influence,

in contrast with the post-Roosevelt recession period after 1938, when, arguably, Keynesians were ascendant (Sandilands, 2001).

In our present era, calls for a renewed regulatory environment capable of remedying the novel monopolistic forces of the 21st century have become increasingly prominent (Philippon, 2019).[1] We are told that the alleged virtues of free markets – namely, higher growth, more rapid innovation, and reduced inequality – can be reclaimed if only we are willing to protect competition. With these arguments comes fresh attention to the forces that motivated the earlier deregulatory tendency. The practical impact of the Neoliberal Era of deregulation began to be felt in the 1970s, though its intellectual roots developed considerably earlier. Here the literature on the rise of the Chicago School and Neoliberal conceptions of regulatory capture often suggests that there was a marked break with the body of economic theory pervasive in the Progressive and New Deal Eras. One of the suggestions made below is that the economic theory central to the Neoliberal Era of deregulation did not involve a major rethinking of the effects of competition and market power. Instead, the champions of deregulation emphasized the likelihood of regulatory capture and the potentially perverse effects of industry-specific regulation resulting from it.

Admittedly, some authors (e.g., Novak, 2014) acknowledge that the framers of the regulatory state were well aware of the possibility of regulatory capture. Such ideas were indeed part of the textbook presentation of state regulation in the late 19th-century United States. Richard Ely (1893, pp. 292–293) could write that while the regulation of monopolies was certainly just:

> [t]he private interest which will use its resources to secure a vote of land or money or other advantage will do the same thing to ward off a threatened tax or vexatious regulation ... When public clamor at last secures the passage of a law the same corrupting agencies are turned against the officers charged with its execution ... When private interests become monopolistic and powerful they not only do not serve society reasonably, but all efforts to compel them to do so result in corruption of government and in ignominious failure.

Yet the notion that there is subsequently a significant theoretical break with Progressive Era economic theory, and that this new view becomes dominant during the Neoliberal period starting in the 1970s, persists and is rarely challenged.

While proffering an array of explanations for the rupture, Roger Backhouse (2005, p. 355, emphasis added) insists that:

> [b]etween 1970 and 2000 there took place a remarkable and dramatic change in attitudes toward the role of the state in economic activity ... This was much more than a simple change in attitudes toward economic policy: it was a radical shift of worldview, involving a transformation of attitudes across a wide range of the political spectrum *as well as being associated with profound changes in economic theory.*

Such accounts seem to overlook significant evidence for continuity regarding the underlying theoretical in both the regulatory and deregulatory eras. In part, this follows from a lack of attention to what the framers of the original regulatory environment, against which the Neoliberal view rose, really proposed. Regulation was, at times, necessary to curb the excesses of the market arising from monopolistic power or the disadvantaged position of immobile and ill-informed labor.

An implicit notion of market imperfections, disturbing an otherwise efficient and desirable competitive market system, was at the heart of the original regulatory environment.

There is a connection between this interpretation of the potential excesses of the market, the effects of which were evident during the Gilded Age, and the ascendance of marginalism in late 19th-century American political economy. It is true that marginalist methods were not absolutely predominant in the United States until much later, perhaps not until the Keynesian revolution, and emergence of the Neoclassical Synthesis of Keynesianism. But early regulators operated with a limited understanding of theory of value and distribution, grounded first on prominent institutionalist ideas and later on the Neoclassical Synthesis. In both cases, an imperfectionist model was dominant, and one can trace the priority given to marginalist ideas to a host of influential early institutionalist authors, in particular those associated with Wisconsin Institutionalism, and the ideas of John R. Commons and his followers.

It is with respect to these underlying ideas that figures within the Chicago School developed the push for deregulation. As with the institutionalist movement, the Chicago School was far from monolithic in its formative years. Our treatment below gives particular attention to the work of George Stigler and his popularization of the theory of regulatory capture. We suggest that at its core, the deregulatory agenda involved a relatively conventional Marshallian presentation of marginalism. Put simply, the fundamental notion given greater emphasis by the Chicago scholars was that while market imperfections were certainly possible, government failures would be pervasive and considerably worse. In our view, perhaps contrary to conventional interpretations, there is a strange continuity in the subjacent views about how markets operate, particularly among institutionalist authors during the rise of the regulatory state and the Chicago authors that provided intellectual support to the deregulation process. The rest of this chapter is divided into two sections and a conclusion tracing the evolution of the regulatory environment and the evidence for this strange continuity in economic thinking.

2. INSTITUTIONALISM AND THE RISE
OF THE REGULATORY ERA

Our discussion below emphasizes the role of "Wisconsin Institutionalism" and its exploration of the interplay between law and economics as typified by the work of John Commons and Richard Ely. Through its graduates, many of whom found careers in government, Wisconsin-style Institutionalism helped to shape the regulatory environment and social protections of the New Deal Era (Rutherford, 2011, p. 222). Seeing Commons' role in America as analogous to that of the Webbs in England, Kenneth Boulding (1957, p. 7) claimed that "through his students Commons was the intellectual origin of the New Deal, of labor legislation, of social security, of the whole movement in this country towards a welfare state."[2] Undoubtedly, Boulding overstates the case. Wisconsin Institutionalism was not, of course, the exclusive force guiding the growth of the regulatory state, nor is it possible to capture a fully representative image of institutionalism in the work of Ely and Commons alone. Their work was nevertheless a decisive aspect of the theoretical framework that molded the regulatory state, motivating our engagement with their ideas.

Political economy in the Progressive Era, and the place of institutionalism within it, continues to prove a confounding and contentious object of study. While it is commonly acknowledged that the period gave rise to one of the profession's most durable institutions, the American Economic Association, and witnessed the founding of the first indigenous PhD programs, along with a widespread restructuring of the economics curriculum imposed on undergraduate students, the character of the *theoretical* transformations experienced remains unresolved. Walton Hamilton's (1919) plea for the primacy of institutional economics highlighted its relevance to the "modern problem of control," while also suggesting that it should serve as a unifying current, drawing together the insights an extraordinarily diverse array of authors including marginalists, and Austrians. Subsequent characterizations have been less unitarian in spirit. Anne Mayhew (1987, p. 980) is definitive, contending that the joint founders of institutionalism were Thorstein Veblen and John Commons, and that their work was "drastically different" from that of earlier traditions, including the German historical school. In presenting what he deems a more balanced account of the development of institutionalism, Yuval Yonay (1998, p. 52) identifies Veblen, Commons, and Wesley Mitchell as the "canonized fathers of institutionalism." For Yonay,

> institutionalism continued a radical trend in American economics, one which was already quite powerful in the 1880s ... Its enduring mark in economics is evident in the welfare legislation in the United States and the measurement techniques and economic forecast procedures common in our days. (pp. 75–76).

Yonay further emphasizes that many of the institutionalists working in the first third of the 20th century did not necessarily see themselves as a school apart from the mainstream.

Malcolm Rutherford (2009, p. 310) suggests that "the history of Institutionalism can be traced back to the work of German influenced economists of the 1880s and 90s," with the movement assuming mainstream influence only in the interwar years. While acknowledging the methodological diversity within the triumvirate of Veblen, Commons, and Mitchell, Rutherford (2011) is insistent that institutionalism *not* be defined as a species of dissent from neoclassical economics.[3] In this view, the characteristic features of early institutionalism were a commitment to empirical realism and an emphasis on the need to reform existing social institutions. Thomas Leonard (2015) labels the work of Commons and Ely as "left Progressivism," the natural successor of which was interwar institutionalism. With some acknowledgment that the line of demarcation is often blurred, Leonard maintains that this work should be distinguished from the "right Progressivism" exemplified by John Bates Clark, and the embrace of marginalist methods. Bruce Kaufman's (2017) self-labeled revisionist account argues that Veblen's work is not easily integrated within the institutionalist canon. Drawing from the later reflections of Mitchell, John Maurice Clark, and particularly Commons, Kaufman instead contends that Richard Ely's new economics of the 1880s, along with the earlier contributions of the German historical school, were key manifestations of an ongoing institutionally attentive current in economic thought.

All would, however, acknowledge the relevance of the transformation of American political economy that coincided with the Progressive Era. A host of new academic institutions – the products of the Morrill Act's land grants, and of the endowments of private fortunes – sprung into being during the closing four decades of the 19th century. While the nascent graduate programs of these institutions were soon to begin turning out their own cadres of newly minted PhDs, considerable control over the character of graduate education in political economy was seized by scholars who had turned to Germany for their own graduate education. Germany had for some time regularly drawn American students interested in furthering their education in chemistry or medicine, but it was only after 1870 that American students in the social sciences began to swell these ranks (Herbst, 1965, pp. 8–9). Those newly minted PhDs that subsequently found positions "back home," such as J.B. Clark and Ely, were eager to elevate and burnish their scientific credentials as objective researchers. For some, this search for status and security necessitated trumpeting the novelty and the superiority of a loosely defined new approach to political economy. One of the basic suggestions made below is that the attention paid to the alleged "openness" and methodological pluralism of the new economics has had the effect of obscuring the magnitude of this generation's *theoretical* departure from classical political economy.

The brand of political economy that American students encountered in Germany exercised a lasting impact. As Ely's student, Sidney Sherwood (1897, p. 8) put it, during the first century of the republic, "the mind of the American economist, touched only by the practical reason of England and the speculative logic of France, was virgin yet from the intellectual ferment of German thought." Having arrived in Germany in June 1877, supported by a three-year fellowship from Columbia University, Ely was initially intent upon studying philosophy. During his first year of study at Halle, he found himself more attracted to the lectures in political economy of Johannes Conrad, and on the advice of friends moved to the University of Heidelberg for his second academic year, where he came to study under Karl Knies. Ely completed his doctoral degree in two academic years and occupied a third as both tourist and student. Though in his autobiography Ely would famously refer to Knies as his "master," he also attended the lectures of Ernst Engel, and Adolf Wagner during his German sojourn (Ely, 1938, pp. 39–51).

Together with Wilhelm Roscher, and Bruno Hildebrand, Knies is usually thought of as one of the founding figures of the "older" German historical school (GHS). Disagreements over the novel theoretical features of this older GHS and the sustained impact that Ely's German education may have exercised on his later thought appear as the first stumbling block for modern interpreters. Geoffrey Hodgson (2001, p. 138) argues that Ely and his fellow German-educated allies Henry Carter Adams and J.B. Clark shaped a "strong doctrinal theme in the early years of the AEA" that was both receptive to social democracy and the welfare state, "combined with a hostility to deductive and general theorizing."[4] In his view, these scholars were attentive to the grave dangers of trans-historical theory and wary of any and all inviolable laws in economics. While this cohort was not wholly successful in cultivating a distinct school of thought, Hodgson treats their awareness of the problem of "historical specificity" of theory as laudable.

Dimitris Milonakis and Ben Fine (2009) go a step further in suggesting a far more direct linkage between the GHS and American institutionalism. Assuming an inclusive definition of institutionalism as a movement that flourished between the 1880s and the outbreak of the Second World War, they contend that

> there is no doubt that if [the historical school] spawned a successor, it is to be found not in Europe but in America. For at the same time that historical economics was losing ground in Europe, inductivism and empiricism were winning a new lease of life across the Atlantic in the form of American institutionalism. (p. 158)

In this view, if historicism was alive and well in the hands of such diverse authors as Veblen, Mitchell, and Commons, then Ely and his German-educated cohort were the essential transmission mechanism. Though they recognize that the GHS was not wholly antagonistic toward theory, Milonakis and Fine see the rise of marginalism as, at least, a partial defeat for the school.

The notion that the older GHS, or their prominent American students, categorically rejected formal theorizing cannot be sustained. Instead, in both cases, there was a clear willingness to embrace new marginalist methods. Such a recognition is not new, though it warrants emphasis. Erich Streissler and Karl Milford (1993, p. 57) note that while German authors were often careful to present any array of different views in contrast to one another, "Roscher used both marginal utility and above all marginal productivity pricing and a host of other subjective value notions as a matter of course." Streissler (2001, p. 322) further contends that the defining innovations of neoclassical theory, namely the concepts of demand based upon marginal utility and a marginal productivity theory of distribution, were commonplace elements of German economics by the middle of the 19th century. John Chipman (2005) holds that Knies, Roscher, and Hildebrand all adopted and attempted to extend a marginalist theory of value drawn from the work of Karl Heinrich Rau. Kosmos Papadopoulos and Bradley Bateman (2011) are more skeptical of attributing a full-fledged marginalist theory of value to Knies but accept that his work embraced theory and served as a precursor for Carl Menger's value theory. It is not so curious then for Joseph Dorfman (1955, p. 28) to have noted that in Progressive Era American economics "[f]or a while there occurred an overwhelming emphasis on the doctrine of marginal utility as the key to all economic analysis. Interestingly, the German-trained contingent was the first to welcome Jevons' theory as a part of the new economics."

Ely's early essay on "The Past and the Present of Political Economy" (1884) was an outcome of lectures of the history of political economy that Ely had delivered during his second academic year at Johns Hopkins.[5] It therefore offers something of an early snapshot of his understanding of the discipline's history upon his return from Germany. Ely suggests that because the older deductive school had the merit of having focused attention on the production and distribution of wealth as a special object of study, its universal advocacy for laissez faire meant that it "failed first as a guide in industrial life" (p. 23).

In his view, the GHS objected to the "method and the sufficiency of its assumptions or major premises – that is to say, its very foundations" of the English deductive school (Ely, 1884, p. 43). In place of the axiomatic premises of the older school "[a]ll a priori doctrines or assumptions are cast aside by this school; or rather the final acceptance is postponed until external observation has proved them correct" (Ely, 1884, p. 47). Importantly, even at this early stage, Ely does not depict the new school as dismissive of formal theory in general. Instead, Ely suggests that an attentive study of history might confirm existing principles or furnish new ones. The other major advance of the new school consisted in its embrace of an active role for political economy in informing policy. The new school understood the discipline of political economy as both theoretical *and* *practical* and thus welcomed the search for laws and policies that would best promote human welfare. Though economists had an obligation to advocate for the common man, fulfilling this obligation would require the continued development of specialized knowledge.

Much of Ely's subsequent work, though certainly eclectic in character, is replete with increasingly sophisticated presentations of marginalist methods that served as a theoretical core. From its first edition, his *Outlines of Economics* (1893), a textbook presentation that through subsequent editions became extraordinarily popular, helped to advance marginalist methods within the United States. In reviewing the value theory of the classical economists, Ely comes to insist that it is untenable, and that "[i]f man desires a thing it has value, no matter whether it cost anything or not, and if he does not desire it has no value, no matter how much it cost" (p. 123). While Ely's own subsequent description of the theory of marginal utility is not particularly adept, his support for the theory is clear, and he suggests that that the third volume of Böhm-Bawerk's *Positive Theory of Capital* "is the best existing statement of the theory of value" (p. 126). Similarly, in his outline of the theory of distribution Ely sees Böhm-Bawerk's approach as the most "satisfactory." From this, Ely maintains that "the portion of produced goods falling to the share of the different factors of production is determined in the first instance by law independent of human contrivance" (p. 169), with laws and institutions being capable of modifying this "natural" distribution.

Despite failing to complete a PhD at Johns Hopkins, John Commons' graduate education there shaped the subsequent course of his career. Upon arrival in Baltimore, Commons (1963, pp. 42–44) recalled that "I resolved to abandon all the theories of political economy which I had ever picked up, and to start, as John Locke would say, with a blank sheet of paper" and was soon "flaming with enthusiasm over this 'new' economics." As a student, Commons aided Ely in preparing his *Introduction to Political Economy* (1889) and owed his eventual appointment at the University of Wisconsin in 1904 to Ely's support. In his *Distribution of Wealth* (1893), the first systematic work of Commons' early career, the unique character of the new economics was on display. The book foregrounds a marginalist approach to the theory of value with Commons insisting that "Value is the doorway to a theory of Distribution" (p. 2). In competitive conditions, the prices of commodities are driven to their costs of production, and capital receives its legitimate reward justified by the "sacrifice or abstinence of savers of capital, measured by the intensity of pleasures which they forego, the risk they assume, and the length of time they have to wait" (p. 18). The existence of monopoly power, whether artificial or natural, altered distribution as the monopolist enjoyed the power to restrict their output relative to demand and thereby "keep up the marginal utility and the price of the article at some point above its cost of production" (p. 102).[6] Such monopoly power could be counter-balanced by labor unions that served to restrict the supply of labor (p. 177) or by taxes on land values or inheritance (p. 237). His fundamental suggestion was that "[t]he so-called conflict between capital and labor is at bottom a conflict between capital and labor on the one hand, and the owners of opportunities on the other" (p. 249). The continued dynamism of capitalism therefore required more freely competitive conditions that would expand access to such "opportunities" (Gonce, 1996). Dorfman (1965) sees the book as an illustration of the foundations of Commons' economics.[7] Undoubtedly, there was much change in emphasis as Commons' work evolved, but a marginalist analysis of value and distribution remained as the foundational conception of a competitive market economy.

In *Legal Foundations of Capitalism* (1924), Commons gives over much of his effort to tracing the transformation of the jurisprudential understanding of property. The older material conception, a holdover from the use-value orientation of feudalism, treats property solely as the physical and tangible possessions of individuals. Over time, the courts come to define property as a spectrum of tangible and intangible assets including firms' accumulated goodwill, the value of which is governed by the streams of income they are expected to yield in the future. The specific exchange value of factors and assets in contemporary capitalism corresponds to the relative bargaining power[8] of an array of going concerns, alongside the laws and norms that govern them. In the absence of such forces

> economic theory has worked out a mechanistic proportioning of factors according to supply and demand ... Producers, led on by an "invisible hand," are shifting towards the limiting factors whose value is high, and away from the complementary factors whose values are low, thus proportioning the factors by equalizing the incomes of individuals towards a "normal" or "natural" or harmonious standard of wages, interest or profits for each class. (1924, p. 323).

Commons holds that these natural laws have not, however, been allowed to operate without the interference of a multitude of labor and business interests exercising differing degrees of bargaining power.[9]

Commons' analysis of what he terms "reasonable value" is elusive in that it does not propose a singular objective standard of value. Value is never anything but a reflection of the conditions of relative scarcity prevailing at the moment. The judgments of the courts regarding reasonable value are attempts to reapportion bargaining power and move toward a new distribution deemed to be in the public's interest. In that context, "[a] reasonable system of prices can be judged to be such only as it conforms in some way to the psychological or ultimate goal of welfare and the physical or intermediate goal of production of wealth" (1924, p. 382). The appropriate balance between the interests of capital and labor, or likewise between producers and consumers, is not taken by Commons to be self-evident. Still Commons would later argue in his *Institutional Economics* that pursuit of efficiency ought to serve as a guide in judgments of reasonable value. He concludes that

> the gains from increasing efficiency in all industries shall go as much as possible, in the first instance, to producers and not to buyers; that the producers shall make their gains as efficient producers and not as mere sellers by higher prices received from buyers. (1934, p. 804)

The proper role of political economy

> is to uncover that limiting factor and to point out, if possible, the extent, degree and point in time at which it should be modified or counteracted, in order to control all of the other factors for the further purpose deemed important. (1924, p. 378)

A similar characterization appears more recently in Leonard (2015, p. 56), even though he suggests that the vision of the regulatory state restoring the efficiency of markets should be mostly attributed to what he refers to as right progressives like J.B. Clark.[10] Left progressives were, in his view, more skeptical about the bigness of trusts, but he admits that the views of right and left progressives tended to converge (2015, p. 71). Leonard (2015, p. 58) argues that, for Mitchell, scientific management guaranteed the efficient functioning of the new giant corporations, and that inefficiency resulted from the functioning of markets. In that sense, antitrust regulation guaranteed the restoration of efficiency, precluding collusion among corporations.

In practice, the early regulation of cartels was intended to prevent further concentration and to protect peripheral firms within an industry from being taken over by central firms. The jurisprudence, as per the decisions of the Supreme Court of the United States (SCOTUS), implied that corporations were entitled to "reasonable return on the fair value of the property being used for the convenience of the public" (see McCraw, 1984, p. 59).[11] The preoccupation with bigness, and concentration, did not necessarily mean being against higher prices. The question of prices was seen essentially as something that was determined by efficiency, with the theories of value and scientific management of the time being relevant in this context. For example, Thomas McCraw (1984, p. 92) notes how Brandeis opposed higher prices for railroads on a specific brief to the ICC on the basis of their inefficient use of resources. Despite such examples, McCraw (1984, p. 115) notes that "government antitrust actions usually opposed not huge integrated firms, but loose associations of small companies."

Most regulatory intervention involved "advanced advice" to firms. During the Progressive Era, many regulators had seen advance advice as a way of preserving the trusts without breaking them apart. The FTC tried to provide negotiated advance advice to corporations while trying to avoid the conventional adversarial procedure typical of the American jurisprudence (McCraw, 1984, p. 130). During the New Deal period, there was a reduced emphasis on the need to break apart the center firms, the large corporations that came to dominate almost every branch of the economy of the United States, and that dominated the Gilded Age economy.[12]

During the New Deal, deflationary pressures led to legislation concerned with allowing corporations to sustain higher prices. The fear of bigness and cartelization was trumped by the fear of deflation. For many regulators, the Depression itself was the result of the oligopolistic competitive structure and of persistent overproduction.[13] In the New Deal period, the most important legislation concerned monetary and financial markets which were seen at the center of the economic crisis. The regulatory solution implied the need for rigorous disclosure rules of information for corporations, and the elimination of all sorts of conflicts of interest, to preclude the information problems and perverse incentives that had led to market failure.[14]

It is important to note that while during the New Deal policies that were pro-union were passed, enforcement was lax. As noted by Richard Hurd (1976, p. 40):

> Working class gains during the Great Depression cannot be credited to New Deal policies. Unions prospered to be sure ... Although the New Deal contributed only marginally to the unionization of the working class, it did help shape the movement which evolved. It furthered the expansion of unions which worked within the economic system, thus helping to avert the possibility that a new, more radical, movement would form which proposed an alternative to capitalism. Once the crisis was over the state adopted a more obviously pro-capital approach, a clear indication that the New Deal labor policy offered short-term concessions only in the interest of the long-term health of capitalism. Organized labor was thus accommodated within the broader regulatory structure in much the way that Commons had expected and hoped for.[15] The New Deal labor regulations depended, it is worth remembering, on a political coalition that upheld Jim Crow and the power structure in the South, limiting its transformation of labor relations to a great degree.[16]

Seen in total, the regulation that emerged with the fourth branch of government was principally concerned with advance advice and providing the right incentives for economic agents and with protecting workers by making their claims work within the system. In other words, the regulatory environment of the Progressive and New Deal Eras seemed to suggest that market failures were pervasive and that regulation was needed to reduce their impact on consumer welfare or on perceived economic efficiency, and that collaboration between labor and capital was possible and desirable, again in the name of efficiency. It was based on a conception of market failures that was fully compatible with marginalist views of the economy. These views became truly dominant at the end of the period, with the victory of the Neoclassical Synthesis version of the Keynesian revolution in the United States.

3. THE MISINTERPRETATION OF THE DEREGULATION AGENDA

The administrative state that resulted from the Progressive and New Deal Eras was built on the foundations of a mix of institutionalist[17] and Neoclassical Synthesis Keynesian ideas about how markets formed and behaved, and the notion was that unregulated markets regularly fail to achieve socially desirable results. That consensus was challenged by a set of scholars that coalesced at Chicago, often seen as the pioneers of the modern field of law and economics. Emphasizing that an awareness of the interplay between law and economic life is at least as old as political economy itself, Steven Medema (1998) takes Ronald Coase's "The

Problem of Social Cost" as uniquely formative for the new law and economics promulgated from Chicago. In this view, Coase's contribution originated in his close study of the broadcasting industry and was a call to critically evaluate the various institutional remedies that might be adopted in the face of externalities and non-negligible transaction costs. The law and economics tradition that subsequently developed at Chicago largely discarded this aspect of Coase's work, with the article instead serving as the stimulus to apply neoclassical microeconomic tools to the analysis of agents' behavior in the legal realm and beyond.

While the origins and substance of the law and economics movement at Chicago are not contained within the work of any single figure or concept, we take George Stigler and the theory of regulatory capture as our principal illustration.[18] William Novak (2014), among others, puts Stigler and the notion of regulatory capture at the center of the rise of Chicago and of the intellectual movement that provided a theoretical foundation for the Deregulation Era.[19] Likewise, Sam Peltzman (1993, p. 824) credits Stigler's formalization of regulatory capture with a "catalytic role in shifting the professional center of gravity toward skepticism about the social utility of regulation" and with a marked shift in the subsequent course of empirical research. Edward Nik-Khah (2011) contends that while Stigler fell well short of Milton Friedman's influence as a teacher, he was the "empire builder" of Chicago-style economics, attracting and channeling private funding to promote skepticism of the state's ability to effectively control economic life. Stigler's work gave rise to two interrelated literatures, econometric analyses of the price effects of existing regulation, and the theoretical suggestion that small, well-organized groups of producers, rather than the diffuse public, were more likely to capture and shape regulatory institutions in their interest.[20] The fundamental notion was that government intervention was not required even in the presence of market failures, since government failures were likely to be even worse. The presence of market failures was not necessarily denied, but there was an underlying view that markets might be useful to deal with government failures.[21] Chicago-style arguments framed the regulatory impulse born in the Progressive Era as an historical aberration. Novak (2014, p. 33) adds that "[t]he capture thesis turns on a metanarrative of exposing the short-term historical error in the interest of righting the wrong – returning policymaking to fundamental economic principles and restoring some kind of purer and lost original, natural, and classical order." That is, a certain degree of economic heterodoxy was necessary for the regulatory impulse in American history. Further, he suggests that the original regulators, as well as the authors that provided the theoretical background that influenced them, namely Commons and Ely, were fully aware of the possibility of capture by corporate interests. McCraw (1984, p. 187) argues the same, in that early regulators were conscious of the threat of regulatory capture but believed that the threat could be overcome.

In this view, the rise of the Chicago School restored the primacy of the notion of market efficiency and countered the heterodox tendencies of the institutionalist and Keynesian inspired regulators of previous eras. In fact, many progressive New Dealers had moved in the direction of seeing the regulatory agencies as dominated by industry and ineffective in protecting consumers.[22]What we wish to stress is the substantial compatibility of the view of markets underlying both the regulatory and deregulatory periods. Stigler (1957, p. 10) himself suggests that the "complete formulation" of the modern concept of perfect competition was realized "not first, but most influentially, by John Bates Clark." Stigler goes on to propose that "[o]ne method by which we might seek to adapt the definition [of perfect competition] to a historically evolving economy is to replace the equalization of rates of return by expected rates of return" (1957, p. 15). Such an approach is not wholly satisfactory, however, as the process of capitalist development is not smooth, and occurs in "fits and starts." Consequently, the concept of competition should be adapted

> to insist only upon the absence of barriers to entry and exit from an industry in the long-run normal period ... Then we may still expect that some sort of expected return will tend to be equalized under conditions of reasonably steady change. (1957, p. 16)

The notion of free entry was central to the concept of competition adopted by both "true" classical political economy (e.g., Smith, Ricardo, Marx) and for the original marginalist views (e.g., Jevons, Marshall, Menger, and Walras) on the concept of perfect competition. Its centrality was abandoned in the intertemporal General Equilibrium approach developed in this period. Stigler upheld the importance of free entry, as did the Chicago School in general, as he was resistant to adopting the new intertemporal approach to the theory of value, remaining firmly grounded on Marshallian analysis (Roncaglia, 2019, pp. 129–133). But at the same time, Stigler defended a view of competition that went beyond free entry and emphasized the lack of power of individual firms in the market, something that was alien to classical political economy authors.[23] Competition provided a level playing field, where all agents were equally powerless. Thus, in this power free system, a state intervention would likely tilt the field.[24]

Stigler (1965) charged political economy up to his own era as negligent, having failed to scientifically examine the role of the state in economic affairs. Specifically, he emphasized the near absence of empirical studies on the effects of alternative policies, particularly the relative merits of varying forms of relation as against free competition. In the supposed century of laissez faire, "[t]he main school of economic individualism had not produced even a respectable modicum of evidence that the state was incompetent to deal with detailed economic problems of any or all sort" (1965, p. 7). For Stigler, this failure applied even to those Progressive Era economists who sustained an engagement with questions of economic policy, namely Commons and J.B. Clark (1965, p. 11). They lacked a robust theory of government failure. The Chicago revolt against the regulatory state, led by Stigler, was not then conceived as reshaping the theory of value, competition, or oligopoly, which had cumulatively been given sufficient formal statement. It was instead primarily a charge that the regulatory state had failed in practice to efficiently achieve its purported aims. *Some, but not all,* of the limitations of the regulatory environment against which the prophets of deregulation rebelled resulted from the underlying theoretical problems of both institutionalist and Neoclassical Synthesis Keynesians regarding the theory of value and distribution. It is important to note that many institutionalists believed that there was continuity between classical political economy or the surplus approach and marginalism. In fact, Veblen's term neoclassical economics was coined to suggest that very continuity.

Commons (1934, p. 56) clearly believed that neoclassical economics was a synthesis of classical political economy and marginalism. He contended that

> these opposing energies of labor and want, magnified into "elasticities" of supply and demand, could be physically correlated by the materialistic metaphor of an automatic tendency towards equilibrium of commodities in exchange against each other, analogous to the atoms of water in the ocean, but personified as "seeking their level" at Ricardo's "margin of cultivation" or Menger's "marginal utility." This equilibrium was accomplished by the "neo-classicists," led by Alfred Marshall (1890)

Undoubtedly, Commons wanted to go beyond this consensus,[25] though he failed to break with marginalist supply and demand notions. As Biddle and Samuels (1998, p. 41) suggest, Commons "was quite explicit that he considered institutional economics to be a supplement to, rather than a replacement for, neoclassical price theory." Commons' (1934, p. 57) alternative theory of "reasonable value" hinged on the crucial concept of transactions, a "unit of activity common to law, economics, and ethics."[26] Like marginalist theory, the central emphasis is therefore on exchange, rather than on the process of production.[27] This suggests similarities between Commons and the New Institutionalist analysis of Douglas North and, perhaps more directly of Oliver Williamson, which is based on Coase's transaction costs, and far from a break with marginalism.[28]

Commons seemed to believe that his originality depended on the analysis of what he referred to as rationing transactions dealing with issues that involved transactions over time, where credit and expectations of future profitability assumed a determinant role. This, one might speculate, could be related to the rise of consumer credit in the 1920s, and the accompanying expansion of mass consumption and consumer society on a scale not seen before. Commons argued (1934, p. 117) that for "the transactional theorists [like himself], the ultimate unit is an economic activity, in the disposition of ownership of future material things and the creation of debt." In the discussion of rationing transactions, Commons (1934, p. 68) distinguished between the former and what he termed managerial and bargaining transactions. As an illustration of the distinction, he understood that

> [a] judicial decision of an economic dispute is a rationing of a certain quantity of the national wealth, or equivalent purchasing power, to one person by taking it forcibly from another person. In these cases, there is no bargaining, for that would be bribery, and no managing which is left to subordinate executives. Here is simply that which is sometimes named "policy-shaping," sometimes named "justice," but which, when reduced to economic quantities, is the rationing of wealth or purchasing power, not by parties deemed equal, but by an authority superior to them in law ... Bargaining transactions transfer ownership of wealth by voluntary agreement between legal equals. Managerial transactions create wealth by commands of legal superiors. Rationing transactions apportion the burdens and benefits of wealth creation by the dictation of legal superiors.

What Commons seems to add, at least from his own perspective, is a concern with time and expectations, which was missing in classical political economy and the early marginalist authors.[29] Yet, it is hard to see in this contribution a rupture with marginalist theory. The analysis of dynamic situations with expectations was, of course, being developed by marginalist authors of the time, like the Swedish School and John Hicks. Though Bradley Bateman (2011, p. 115) has argued that the "eclectic" use of marginalist methods by early institutionalist figures "was not the same thing as Neoclassicism," his contention ultimately rests on the idea that a distinctive American neoclassicism critical of institutionalism is only identifiable following the First World War. The foregoing discussion of Commons' continued embrace of an evolving set of marginalist methods would seem to belie this claim, a difficulty that Bateman sidesteps by explicitly excluding Ely and Commons from the institutionalist camp.

It is also not possible to suggest that the SCOTUS' deliberations, that according to Commons were at the center of his own view of reasonable value, were built upon the old classical political economy or surplus approach notion of competition. In a series of papers, Nicola Giocoli has attempted to characterize the economic theory adopted by SCOTUS in matters of rate regulation as consistent with classical political economy. Giocoli (2017a, p. 33) argues that SCOTUS operated from 1898 to 1944 with an understanding of the theory of value that "did not stem from an appreciation of marginalist theory but rather ... continued allegiance to classical political economy." In Giocoli's (2018, p. 452) view, the Court judged that

> [c]ompetitive market returns, and only such, represented the morally justified profits that even privileged businesses like railroads and utilities were entitled to gain ... Courts should just establish by factual analysis what the competitive return on the present market value of a given enterprise would be and compare it with that implied by the regulated rates.

While this seems an entirely reasonable characterization of the Court's deliberative process, the suggestion that this constituted a classical approach to the question of value is hard to defend.[30] Classical political economists did not understand the specific rate of profit obtainable in competitive conditions as a morally justified ideal. The classical uniform rate of profit was the outcome of competition, of free entry, and often the notion of market prices tending toward their natural level was described using an analogy to Newtonian mechanics. Only once distributive conflict, which reflected the vested interests of landowners and the comparatively weak bargaining power of labor relative to capital, and technical conditions had been analyzed could the objective costs of production be determined. The cost of production around which competitive equilibrium or natural prices would gravitate was thus grounded in the commodity's social-historical cost of production and reflected objective and impersonal forces.

In fact, during the formative years of the regulatory state, the classical theory of value and distribution was submerged and forgotten. This theory only began to be rediscovered by the mid-1920 as a result of the critique of Marshallian economics developed by Piero Sraffa. It is true that Sraffa's (1926) initial critique led to the development of imperfect competition, within the marginalist framework, but Sraffa himself did not pursue that route. Rather than developing the notion of competition along neoclassical lines, Sraffa in his subsequent work held that the advancement of understanding required the recovery of the classical conception of value and distribution. In that framework, equilibrium prices are not about scarcity but about the material conditions for the reproduction of the system. Stigler and most of the scholars behind the dismantling of the regulatory state were well aware of Sraffa's critique of Marshallian economics and of his work on the reconstruction of classical political economy. In fact, Stigler wrote a review of Sraffa's edition of Ricardo's works, full of praise, but that avoids engaging in any substantial way with the analytical framework proposed by Sraffa (Kurz, 2018).

The regulatory environment that arose, characterized by the reasonable value doctrine, was one that readily accepted that markets might fail to provide efficient outcomes, but this possibility arose on the basis of market imperfections. It further suggested that the relative scarcity of factors of production could be manipulated by the bargaining positions of capital and labor. Legislation only tried to mitigate these imperfections and imbalances of bargaining power, protecting consumers, and creating more favorable conditions for the cooperation between capital and labor. Commons' depiction of this regulatory environment, given in his transactions approach to the determination of reasonable value, is one that accepts the essence of the marginalist approach to value and distribution, albeit with an acceptance that market imperfections are endemic. One can therefore identify significant theoretical *continuity* between the regulatory and deregulatory eras. The critiques subsequently offered by the heralds of free markets and deregulation were skeptical about the prevalence of market imperfections and doubted whether regulatory interventions would be successful given the possibility of regulatory capture. These critiques did not, however, try to undermine the core theoretical framework upon which the original regulatory environment was built.

The new regulatory impulse, if we can talk about one now,[31] also does not depart from conventional views on value and distribution. Instead, it seems to once more involve a reversal concerning the relative importance of market and government failures. The possibility of regulatory mis-steps continues to be acknowledged, though this risk pales in comparison to that of continued inaction against growing market power. Philippon (2019, p. 4) tells us that:

> regulators make policy decisions under a great deal of uncertainty ... We must be able to let the government make some mistakes. Sometimes it will be too lenient. Sometimes too tough. It should be right on average, but it is unlikely to be right in every single case. Tolerating well-intentioned mistakes is therefore part of good regulation, provided that there is due process and that there is a mechanism to learn from these mistakes.

Reasonable mistakes from government regulation are to be tolerated since, on the whole, a rebalancing of relative bargaining power would provide for a more efficient allocation of resources.[32]

4. CONCLUSION

The rise of the regulatory state during the Gilded Age was closely associated with the development of institutionalist ideas in American academia. Notwithstanding the differences between institutionalism and later neoclassicism, the basis for the antitrust legislation and the operations of the regulatory agencies established in this and subsequent periods was the marginalist theory of value and distribution. As illustrated throughout the work of John Commons, this engagement with marginalism was not superficial nor was it an affectation that served as professional bona fides. Rather the marginalist framework consistently supplied Commons with his baseline conception of the competitive market system. His accompanying observations of the Court's judgments, and discussion of the juridical conditioning of agents' relative bargaining power supplement this baseline model without fundamentally reshaping it. For Commons, the legal system is both a producer of and potential remedy for market imperfections. The fact that some key institutionalist authors were involved in developing and complementing the precepts of emergent marginalist theory is a central explanation for the ultimate ascendancy of neoclassical economics and the attendant market failure view of the initial regulatory state in the Progressive and New Deal Eras, on par with the role of the Neoclassical Synthesis Keynesians in the latter period.

The rise of the Chicago School did constitute a rupture with these earlier eras, one achieved without rejecting prevalent conceptions of competition and value. The rupture lies instead in the Chicago School's effort to minimize the practical manifestations of market failure and to magnify the problems associated with government failure and capture, which were known to previous generations of economists and regulators. Capture theory becomes relevant, not because it provides a critique of market failures or an alternate approach to the theory of value, but because it suggests that government failures are even worse. The idea that markets were instruments for the efficient allocation of scarce resources, or that the distributional outcomes achieved in competitive conditions could be regarded as efficient, was not being disputed in any of these transitions. This theoretical continuity and compatibility is all but acknowledged by Alfred Kahn (1970, p. vii), the preeminent prophet of deregulation according to McCraw (1984), who argued in his classic textbook on *The Economics of Regulation* that his work was "an attempt to join neoclassical theory with 'institutional economics.'"

It is beyond the scope of this chapter to elaborate a regulatory framework compatible with the classical political economists' notion of competition, but it would be clearly more concerned with precluding barriers to entry and dealing with asymmetric power of social classes in the productive arena. In that sense, it is important to emphasize that the classical notion of competition, in contrast with the marginalist notion of perfect competition, does not imply absence of power, or that the economic agents are small. Classical competition was compatible with a market dominated by large corporations, with significant power. Regulation that curbs that power exercised by capital in bargaining with labor, or that limits the ability of firms to build barriers to entry against potential competitors, would be more in line with classical ideas. It would be less concerned, hence, with consumer welfare and with cooperation between capital and labor. The aim of regulation would not be to bring back an ideal of perfect competition, in which, in the absence of power, markets efficiently allocate resources but to tame the power that exists and prevails in competitive systems.

Finally, the continuity in the understanding of value theory and the role of markets casts doubts about the resurgent regulatory impulse in the present New Gilded Age, one that is simply concerned with imperfections and consumer rights. We must add that we also do not suggest that all the problems with the regulatory environment can be explicitly connected to the ideas of economists. There are social and institutional factors beyond economic ideas that played an important role, in spite of Keynes' view that ideas and not vested interests are more relevant for policy outcomes. But the ebbs and flows of regulation and deregulation, and possibly reregulation, reflect particular views on the relevance of market versus government failures and are firmly established under marginalist views of the functioning of market economies.

NOTES

1. The intellectuals behind the new regulatory impulse often suggest a connection with the older Progressive Era tradition and refer to its policy agenda as Neo-Brandeisian, Justice Louis Brandeis being one of the key champions of antitrust legislation (Wu, 2018, pp. 127–139). See also Glick (2018) for a critique of the Chicago School and the concept of consumer welfare.

2. For example, Elizabeth Brandeis, daughter of Justice Brandeis, together with her husband, Paul Rausenbush, and Harold Groves, all students of Commons were central in unemployment compensation laws (Rutherford, 2006, p. 172). On the Wisconsin School, see also Henderson (1988).

3. Michael Bernstein (2001) argues that Veblen and Mitchell did in fact attack neoclassical theory but essentially for "its excessive use of abstraction" (p. 45). In particular, Veblen critique rested on the marginalists "presumption of rationality that ignored the social and cultural factors that modulated behavior" (Bernstein, 2001).

4. Almost as an afterthought, Hodgson mentions that J.B. Clark attributed his own work on marginalist theory to the guidance of Karl Knies, his former teacher.

5. During his year spent as a student at Johns Hopkins, Veblen attended Ely's lectures. Dorfman (1934, p. 40) notes that "the lectures made Veblen doubt that Ely had read the works he was discussing, and in exploring the library he found a German encyclopedia that contained almost the exact same material that Ely had been offering."

6. Commons (1893, p. 59) holds that "[t]he place of law in Political Economy is a subject which has received from English economists no attention at all commensurate with its far-reaching importance ... [They] have taken the laws of private property for granted, assuming that they are fixed and immutable ... But such laws are changeable – they differ for different people and places, and they have profound influence upon the production and distribution of wealth." Thus, in one form or another, the perpetuation of monopoly power relied upon the law's structure and enforcement.

7. In a letter to Ely written at the time, Commons outlined some of his plans for subsequent work, noting that "I am planning my work to center around the legal aspects of sociology, expanding the doctrines in my *Distribution of Wealth*" (Dorfman, 1965, p. xiv). Commons' preface to *Legal Foundations of Capitalism* echoes much the same point, somewhat generously contending that the work "commenced thirty-five years ago at Johns Hopkins University under my stimulating teacher, Richard T. Ely" (1924, p. v).

8. In Commons' account (1924, pp. 20–21), "[b]argaining power is the willful restriction of supply in proportion to demand in order to maintain or enlarge the value of business assets."

9. As Fiorito and Vatiero (2011) have shown, Commons' analysis of the interplay between socially constructed legal rights and economic outcomes built upon the work of Wesley Hohfeld. The challenge before the courts was to *redistribute* coercive power to best suit public purposes.

10. On Clark's views on regulation, see Fiorito (2013). He suggests that Clark's "academic and popular writings on the so-called 'trust problem' significantly invigorated the discussion of unfair competition that followed the 1911 dissolutions of the Standard Oil and American Tobacco" (Fioritom 2013, p. 140).

11. Commons argues, for example, that: "The public utility law was designed to ascertain and maintain *reasonable values* and reasonable practices by the local public utility corporations" (1934, p. 2, emphasis added). He is explicit about how the theory of Reasonable Value was created by the SCOTUS in its 1890 decision (1934, p. 649).

12. James Landis, central regulator of the New Deal Era, believed that to minimize the possibility of capture, the regulations had to implicitly provide the correct incentives for those involved to have a self-interest in obeying the law. McCraw (1984, p. 195) highlights "the fundamental SEC strategy of manipulating private incentives to serve public ends."

13. These views about the causes of the Great Depression were only superseded by Keynesian views after the Roosevelt recession of 1938. See Sandilands (2001).

14. It seems reasonable to assume that this view of market failure arose in the period from the mid-19th century, from transition authors like John Stuart Mill, and marginalist authors like Henry Sidgwick, Alfred Marshall, and the latter's pupil Arthur Cecil Pigou. For a discussion, see Medema (2007).

15. Commons et al. (1918, pp. 15–16) distinguished between "class conscious" and "wage conscious" unionism, with the latter accepting the basic parameters of the existing capitalist order. A class conscious, revolutionary unionism was symptomatic of "the unripe philosophy of upstart unionism, or the pessimistic philosophy of defeated unionism." Commons (1963, p. 97) would later suggest that relative to his more radical friends, it was always his trade-union philosophy that had marked him as conservative. In a tidy summation, he noted that "[i]t is not revolutions and strikes that we want, but collective bargaining on something like an organized equilibrium of equality."

16. Commons' support for unions and minimum wage legislation was connected to the idea that the ethnicities and races that were in his view "ambitious," meaning willing to work for less, ended up reducing the real wage, by increasing labor supply. Restrictions on immigration, unions, and minimum wages would counter those tendencies and make higher wages the norm. In his words:

> [t]here is but one immediate and practical remedy – the organization of labor to regulate competition. The method of organization is to do in concert through self-sacrifice what the non-industrial races do individually for self-indulgence; namely, refuse to work. Where the one loafs the other strikes. While the necessities of the workers set the minimum below which wages cannot fall, and their physical endurance sets the maximum hours beyond which they cannot work, the labor-union, by means of the strike or the threat to strike, sets a higher minimum of wages and a lower maximum of hours, which leaves room for ambition. (Commons, 1907, p. 149)

17. Rutherford (2015, p. 78) while noting that institutionalists did not use the term market failure, they believed "market failure to be ... endemic."

18. In his contributions to law and economics, Richard Posner (1976, p. x) regularly acknowledged Stigler's considerable influence on his own thought. Coase (1982, p. 24) similarly held that Stigler played "a major part" in convincing "most economists" of the pernicious results of government regulation.

19. The Coase Theorem, as interpreted by many, reinforced the idea that only secure property rights were required for efficient market solutions. Hayek's notion that complexity implies that control remains out of reach, also played a role. In addition, even though dismissed by Chicago and affiliates, the Arrow-Debreu model, also developed during this period, provided an authoritative argument for the preeminence of markets. In other words, the postwar period saw a flourishing of views that reinstated the importance of free markets, and significant amount of money was poured by conservative groups to fund these ideas, as noted by Phillips-Fein (2009).

20. Stigler (1971, p. 17) notes, however, that the idea of capture was common in the literature, commenting that "[s]o many economists, for example, have denounced the ICC for its pro-railroad policies that this has become a cliché of the literature."

21. Stigler (1971) argues that consumer choice between buying an airplane or train ticket is considerably more efficient than government regulation of the transportation industry as a social mechanism to allocate resources. For him: "[T]he condition

of simultaneity imposes a major burden upon the political decision process. It makes voting on specific issues prohibitively expensive: it is a significant cost even to engage in the transaction of buying a plane ticket when I wish to travel; it would be stupendously expensive to me to engage in the physically similar transaction of voting (i.e., patronizing a polling place) whenever a number of my fellow citizens desired to register their views on railroads versus airplanes" (p. 10). Essentially, government failures tend to occur as a result of higher transactions costs associated with government regulation than with consumer choice. Essentially, the state's failure as a regulator occurs as a result of the higher transaction costs involved associated with government regulation when compared to unregulated consumer choice.

22. Landis would be a central New Dealer that moved in that direction. Progressives like Ralph Nader, and his crusade for consumer rights and Senator Ted Kennedy's hearings on the aviation industry that precede the deregulation of the sector are also examples of the trend toward deregulation among those skeptical of market forces (McCraw, 1984).

23. Heinz Kurz (2018, p. 3) argues that:
Stigler throughout his academic career stuck firmly to methodological individualism and advocated the market form of perfect competition as approximating near enough real world conditions. With perfect competition, no economic agent has any power whatsoever. Market results do not reflect any distortions caused by economic power or control and may therefore be seen to be "just." Stigler defended this position also with regard to the literature on monopolistic competition, championed by Edward Chamberlin and Joan Robinson, and thus denied a significant and lasting influence of monopolies on income distribution.

Moreover, the marginalist conception presumed full utilization of resources in equilibrium, including labor, something that was not true in classical analysis.

24. Stigler (1987, p. 948) argued that "the classical authors felt no need for a precise definition because they viewed monopoly as highly exceptional." A concept of competition was undoubtedly central for classical authors, since it was the force that allowed market prices to gravitate toward natural ones (Eatwell, 1987). Stigler, however, remarks that "the groundwork for the development of the concept of *perfect* competition was laid by Augustin Cournot" (1987, emphasis added). The implication is that he adopted the marginalist concept of competition and discarded the notion of free entry based on classical political economy.

25. Commons (1934, p. 696) also says that "[t]he analytic economists of the classical school (Smith, Ricardo) took scarcity for granted, and it was the hedonic school (especially the Austrian school) and the 'neo-classical' school, especially Marshall, who analyzed and perfected its formula." Clearly, while aware of the distinction between classical and neo-classical authors, Commons thought that they had some type of complementarity, which seems to be based on the objective and subjective aspects of value. In this he followed, not just Marshall himself, and later John Maynard Keynes, but also Veblen.

26. In his own words, "the ultimate unit of activity, which correlates law, economics, and ethics, must contain in itself the three principles of conflict, dependence, and order. This unit is a Transaction. A transaction, with its participants, is the smallest unit of institutional economics" (1934, p. 58)

27. Also, he suggests (1934, p. 118) that historically the unit of analysis had changed with "[t]he commodity economists, of the objective and subjective schools, the former making the usefulness of the commodity (use-value, objective), the latter making the feelings dependent upon the commodity (diminishing-utility, subjective) their ultimate unit of investigation; and the transactional economists who make the various kinds of transactions their units of investigation."

28. In the same vein, Uni (2017, p. 17) argues that "Commons believed that the center of power in bargaining transactions lay in the ability of suppliers to withhold supply based on property rights." There are many similarities here between Commons and the work of Oliver Williamson in particular the importance of sovereignty as the power to settle disputes between transactors (see Dugger, 1996).

29. In this context, he adds, it is:

the factor of time and especially futurity and expectation ... This factor always implies the expected consequences which will follow from present transactions, whereas the analytic method has no time nor futurity – it is pure static relation, without activity and expectation ... Scarcity becomes the present opportunity, competition, and bargaining power in which the abilities of the individuals are exercised (1996, p. 697).

30. It is also possible that Giocoli's interpretation of the classical nature of the SCOTUS decisions is based on his peculiar definition of classical political economy. Indeed, it is instructive that one of Giocoli's (2017b, pp. 182–184) regular citations on the classical conception of competition is Stigler (1957). Giocoli (2017a, p. 40) seamlessly includes Stuart Mill, clearly a transitional author, a representative of classical economics. Subsequently (2017b, p. 185), he seems to suggest that Nassau Senior, clearly a vulgar economist who departed from classical views on profits, was a follower of Smith and adopted his views on competition.

31. It seems reasonable to suggest that reregulation has been seen in more positive light, in particular after the 2008 crisis, even if it might be premature to talk about a new regulatory era. If that is possible, then the Consumer Financial Protection Bureau (CFPB), established in 2010, could be seen as a symbol of this new period. The CFPB's champion and architect, Elizabeth Warren, is equally emblematic. Hailing the virtues of prudently constructed regulation "as the basic framework that permits commerce to flourish," Warren (2018, p. 3) emphasizes that "regulations level the playing field for everyone competing for [consumers'] business." Warren thus understands the basic functions of regulation as the insurance or restoration of competition that once established can be expected to deliver beneficent results.

32. In terms of the labor market, for example, Philippon (2019, p. 23) argues that: "competition increases economic freedom. In a competitive labor market, workers have the freedom to quit and find a better job. When employers compete, they offer more options to workers: different jobs, different hours, and different benefits. Labor market competition is the best defense against employers abusing and bullying their employees." In other words, regulation that reestablishes competition would allow for markets to provide the efficient allocation of resources and remuneration according to productivity.

REFERENCES

Backhouse, R. E. (2005). The rise of free market economics: Economists and the role of the state since 1970. *History of Political Economy*, *37*(5), 355–392.

Bateman, B. W. (2011). German influences in the making of American economics, 1885–1935. In H. Kurz, T. Nishizawa, & K. Tribe (Eds.), *The dissemination of economic ideas* (pp. 108–124). Cheltenham: Edward Elgar.

Bernstein, M. A. (2001). *A perilous progress: Economists and public purpose in twentieth century America*. Princeton, NJ: Princeton University Press.

Biddle, J. E., & Samuels, W. J. (1998). John R. Commons and the compatibility of neoclassical and institutional economics. In R. Holt & S. Pressman (Eds.), *Economics and its discontents* (pp. 40–55). Cheltenham: Edward Elgar.

Boulding, K. E. (1957). A new look at institutional economics. *The American Economic Review*, *47*(2), 1–12.

Chipman, J. S. (2005). Contributions of the older German schools to the development of utility theory. In C. Scheer (Ed.), *Studien zur Entwicklung der ökonomischen Theorie XX: Die Ältere Historische Schule: Wirtschaftstheoretische Beiträge und wirtschaftspolitische Vorstellungen* (pp. 157–259). Berlin: Duncker & Humblot.

Coase, R. H. (1982). George J. Stigler: An appreciation. *Regulation*, *6*(6), 21–24.

Commons, J. R. (1893). *The distribution of wealth*. New York, NY: Macmillan.

Commons, J. R. (1907). *Races and immigrants in America*. New York, NY: Macmillan.

Commons, J. R. (1924). *Legal foundations of capitalism*. Clifton, NJ: Augustus M. Kelley.

Commons, J. R. (1934). *Institutional economics*. New York, NY: The Macmillan.

Commons, J. R. (1963). *Myself: The autobiography of John R. Commons*. Madison, WI: University of Wisconsin Press.

Commons, J. R., Saposs, D. J., Sumner, H. L., Mittelman, E. B., Hoagland, H. E., Andrews, J. B., & Perlman, S. (1918). *History of labour in the United States, Vol. I*. New York, NY: Macmillan.

DeCanio, S. (2015). *Democracy and the origins of the American regulatory state*. New Haven, CT: Yale University Press.

Dorfman, J. (1934). *Thorstein Veblen and his America*. New York, NY: The Viking Press.

Dorfman, J. (1955). The role of the German historical school in American economic thought. *The American Economic Review, 42*(2), 17–28.

Dorfman, J. (1965). The foundation of Commons' economics. In J. Commons (Ed.), *The distribution of wealth*. New York, NY: Augustus M. Kelley.

Eatwell, J. (1987). Classical competition. In *The new Palgrave dictionary of economics* (3rd ed., Vol. 1, pp. 537–540). London: Palgrave-Macmillan.

Ely, R. T. (1884). *The past and present of political economy*. Baltimore, MD: Johns Hopkins.

Ely, R. T. (1889). *An Introduction to political economy*. New York, NY: Chautauqua Press.

Ely, R. T. (1893). *Outlines of economics*. Meadville, PA: Flood and Vincent.

Ely, R. T. (1938), *Ground under our feet: An autobiography*. New York, NY: The Macmillan Company.

Fiorito, L. (2013). When economics faces the economy: John Bates Clark and the 1914 antitrust legislation. *Review of Political Economy, 25*(1), 139–163.

Fiorito, L., & Vatiero, M. (2011). Beyond legal relations: Wesley Newcomb Hohfeld's influence on American institutionalism. *Journal of Economic Issues, 45*(1), 199–222.

Giocoli, N. (2017a). The (rail)road to *Lochner*: Reproduction cost and the gilded age controversy over rate regulation. *History of Political Economy, 49*(1), 31–58.

Giocoli, N. (2017b). Free from what? Competition, regulation and antitrust in American economics 1870-1914. In L. Fanti (Ed.), *Oligopoly, institutions and firms' performance* (pp. 173–222). Pisa: Pisa University Press.

Giocoli, N. (2018). 'Value is not a fact': Reproduction cost and the transition from classical to neoclassical regulation in gilded age America. *Journal of the History of Economic Thought, 40*(4), 445–470.

Glick, M. (2018). The unsound theory behind the consumer (and total) welfare goal in antitrust. *The Antitrust Bulletin, 63*(4), 455–493.

Gonce, R. A. (1996). The social gospel, Ely, and Commons's initial stage of thought. *Journal of Economic Issues, 30*(3), 641–665.

Hamilton, W. H. (1919). The institutional approach to economic theory. *The American Economic Review, 9*(1), 309–318.

Henderson, J. P. (1988). Political economy and the service of the state: The University of Wisconsin. In W. J. Barber (Ed.), *Breaking the academic mould: Economists and American higher learning in the nineteenth century* (pp. 318–339). Middletown, CT: Wesleyan University Press.

Herbst, J. (1965). *The German historical school in American scholarship*. Ithaca, NY: Cornell University Press.

Hodgson, G. M. (2001). *How economics forgot history*. London: Routledge.

Hurd, R. W. (1976). New deal labor policy and the containment of radical union activity. *Review of Radical Political Economics, 8*(3), 32–43.

Kahn, A. E. (1970). *The economics of regulation: Principles and institutions*. New York, NY: John Wiley and Sons.

Kaufmann, B. (2017). The origins and theoretical foundation of original institutional economics reconsidered. *Journal of the History of Economic Thought, 39*(3), 293–322.

Kurz, H. (2018). *Stigler on Ricardo*. Rome, Italy: Centro Sraffa Working Paper No. 27.

Leonard, T. C. (2015). Progressive era origins of the regulatory state and the economist as expert. *History of Political Economy, 47*(Annual Suppl.), 49–76.

Levi-Faur, D. (2013). The Odyssey of the regulatory state. *Law & Policy, 35*(1–2), 29–50.

Mayhew, A. (1987). The beginnings of institutionalism. *Journal of Economic Issues, 21*(3), 971–98.

McCraw, T. K. (1984). *Prophets of regulation*. Cambridge: The Belknap Press.

Medema, S. G. (1998). Wandering the road from pluralism to Posner: The transformation of law and economics in the twentieth century. In M. S. Morgan & M. Rutherford (Eds.), *From interwar pluralism to postwar neoclassicism* (pp. 202–227). Durham, NH: Duke University Press.

Medema, S. G. (2007). The hesitant hand: Mill, Sidgwick, and the evolution of the theory of market failure. *History of Political Economy, 39*(3), 331–358.

Milonakis, D., & Fine, B. (2009). *From political economy to economics*. London: Routledge.

Nik-Khah, E. (2011). George Stigler, the graduate school of business, and the pillars of the Chicago School. In R. Van Horn, P. Mirowski, & T. A. Stapleford (Eds.), *Building Chicago economics* (pp. 116–150). Cambridge: Cambridge University Press.

Novak, W. J. (2014). A revisionist history of regulatory capture. In D. Carpenter & D. A. Moss (Eds.), *Preventing regulatory capture: Special interest influence and how to limit it*. Cambridge: Cambridge University Press.

Papadopoulos, K., & Bateman, B. W. (2011). Karl Knies and the prehistory of neoclassical economics: Understanding the importance of *Die Nationalökonomische Lehre vom Werth* (1855). *Journal of the History of Economic Thought, 33*(1), 19–35.

Peltzman, S. (1993). George Stigler's contribution to the economic analysis of regulation. *Journal of Political Economy, 101*(5), 818–832.

Philippon, T. (2019). *The great reversal: How America gave up on free markets*. Cambridge: Belknap Press.

Phillips-Fein, K. (2009). *Invisible hands: The making of the conservative movement*. New York, NY: Norton.

Posner, R. A. (1976). *Antitrust law: An economic perspective*. Chicago, IL: The University of Chicago Press.

Roncaglia, A. (2019). *The age of fragmentation: A history of contemporary economic thought*. Cambridge: Cambridge University Press.

Rutherford, M. (2006). Wisconsin institutionalism: John R. Commons and his students. *Labor History, 47*(2), 161–188.

Rutherford, M. (2009). Towards a history of American institutional economics. *Journal of Economics Issues, 43*(2), 308–318.

Rutherford, M. (2011). *The institutionalist movement in American economics, 1918–1947*. Cambridge: Cambridge University Press.

Rutherford, M. (2015). Institutionalism and the social control of businesses. *History of Political Economy, 47*(Suppl. 1), 77–98.

Sandilands, R. (2001). The new deal and 'Domesticated Keynesianism' in America. In M. Keaney (Ed.), *Economist with a public purpose: Essays in honor of John K Galbraith* (pp. 55–100). New York, NY: Routledge.

Sherwood, S. (1897). *Tendencies in American economic thought*. Baltimore, MD: Johns Hopkins.

Sraffa, P. (1926). The laws of returns under competitive conditions. *Economic Journal, 36*(144), 535–550.

Stigler, G. J. (1957). Perfect competition, historically contemplated. *Journal of Political Economy, 65*(1), 1–17.

Stigler, G. J. (1965). The economist and the state. *The American Economic Review, 55*(1/2), 1–18.

Stigler, G. J. (1971). The theory of economic regulation. *The Bell Journal of Economics and Management Science, 2*(1), 3–21.

Stigler, G. J. (1987). Competition. In *The new Palgrave dictionary of economics* (3rd ed., Vol 1, pp. 531–535). London: Palgrave-Macmillan.

Streissler, E. (2001). Rau, Hermann and Roscher: Contributions of German economics around the middle of the nineteenth century. *The European Journal of the History of Economic Thought, 8*(3), 311–331.

Streissler, E., & Milford, K. (1993–1994). Theoretical and methodological positions of German economics in the middle of the nineteenth century. *History of Economic Ideas, 1/2*(3/1), 43–79.

Uni, H. (2017). Scope of John R. Commons's criticism of the classical theory of value: Progress and limitations in the 1927 manuscript. In H. Uni (Ed.), *Contemporary meanings of John R. Commons's institutional economics: An analysis using a newly discovered manuscript*. Berlin: Springer.

Warren, E. (2018). Remarks at the coalition for sensible safeguards symposium, Washington, DC. Retrieved from https://www.warren.senate.gov/imo/media/doc/2018-6-5%20Warren%20 Regulations%20Speech.pdf

Wu, T. (2018). *The curse of bigness: Antitrust in the new gilded age*. New York, NY: Columbia Global Reports.

Yonay, Y. P. (1998). *The struggle over the soul of economics: Institutionalist and neoclassical economists in America between the wars*. Princeton, NJ: Princeton University Press.

Printed and bound by CPI Group (UK) Ltd, Croydon, CR0 4YY

23/05/2024

14505908-0004